Martha Finley

Signing The Contract

And What It Cost

Martha Finley

Signing The Contract
And What It Cost

ISBN/EAN: 9783742812414

Manufactured in Europe, USA, Canada, Australia, Japa

Cover: Foto ©ninafisch / pixelio.de

Manufactured and distributed by brebook publishing software (www.brebook.com)

Martha Finley

Signing The Contract

COPYRIGHT, 1879,
BY
DODD, MEAD & COMPANY.

SIGNING THE CONTRACT.

CHAPTER I.

A WANDERER.

"Lost! lost! lost!"

THE sun had set amid angry clouds; deep shadows already filled the recesses of the forest through which the iron horse went thundering on its way, while an icy wind, bringing with it frequent dashes of rain and sleet, swept through the leafless branches of the trees, tossing them wildly against a dull leaden sky.

A lady, gazing out into the gathering gloom, started with a sudden exclamation of surprise and dismay. Her husband leaned hastily past her to see what had called it forth; then, with a smile at his own folly in forgetting that at the rate of speed with which they were moving the object, whatever it might be, was already out of sight, settled himself back again, bending a look of mild inquiry upon her agitated countenance.

She shivered, and drawing her shawl more closely about her, put her lips to his ear, that she might be heard above the noise of the train.

"It was a face, John—a woman's face upturned to the sky, wan, distressed, wretched, with great sorrowful eyes. It just gleamed out upon me for an instant as we swept by, and was gone. Poor thing! poor thing! she must be in sore trouble."

He shook his head with a smile of conscious superiority of wisdom.

"Don't let your imagination run away with you, my dear, or waste your sympathy upon a wandering gypsy, who would not exchange places with you if she could."

The train was slackening its speed, and they could now converse with ease.

"She is no ordinary tramp," was the quick, earnest reply. "And if ever bitter, hopeless grief and despair were written on a human face, they were on hers. I wish we could go back and find her."

"Quite impossible, Dolly; so let us talk of something more agreeable."

"We change cars soon, don't we?" she asked.

"Worse than that; we get out at the next station and wait there two mortal hours for another train."

"Clearfield Station!" shouted the conductor, throwing open the car door.

An acre or two of ground had been cleared of trees, though many of the stumps were still standing; there was no appearance of a town; only a depot and a few shanties scattered here and there, the whole hemmed in by the forest, except on the two sides where the road had cut its way through.

The train stopped, and John and Dolly—otherwise Mr. and Mrs. Kemper—alighted, and the gentleman hurried his wife out of the rain and sleet into the depot.

A very forlorn place it looked with its rusty stove, filthy floor and windows, and hard, straight-backed wooden chairs and settee, which gave small promise of rest or ease to the delayed and weary traveller.

"What a wretched hole!" said Mrs. Kemper, sending a rueful glance from side to side. "How long did you say we'd have to stay here, John?"

"Two hours, Dolly. Here, take this chair by the fire, and I'll go and see what can be done."

He came back presently, and pointing through the window, "You see that light yonder, Dolly?" he said. "It comes from a shanty some hundred yards away, where they tell me we can at least find cleanliness and a cup of hot tea. There seems a lull in the storm at this moment, too; shall we go and try it?"

"By all means," she answered, rising with alacrity and taking his offered arm. "I presume the walking is bad enough, but my boots are thick."

Picking their way carefully between stumps and pools of water, just visible in the deepening gloom, they reached the place.

It was a long, low building of rudest structure, its walls rough boards nailed on horizontally, leaving large cracks between, with merely a covering of painted canvas upon the outside to keep wind and rain at bay. The gable-end with its one door and window, in which burned the lamp that had guided them, faced the road.

Entering, our travellers found themselves in a small waiting-room, very simply furnished, but invitingly warm, clean, and tidy.

A neatly-dressed young woman greeted them with a pleasant "Good-evening," and throwing open an inner door, asked if they would walk out to supper.

"I should prefer just taking something here," said Mrs. Kemper, shrinking back at the sight of a long table with only a number of rough-looking men about it. "Couldn't you bring me a cup of hot tea and whatever you have to eat?"

"Yes, ma'am, of course;" and the girl vanished to return presently with the tea, a piece of steak, bread, butter, and hot corn-cakes.

Out in the forest a woman was battling with the storm—a woman with a child in her arms. A slight, willowy form was hers, once the perfection of grace in outline and movement, now bent and staggering with weakness; a face whose bright, soft eyes, glowing cheeks, and ruby lips were not long ago the admiration or envy of many, though now wan and pinched with famine and wasting sickness.

It was the same face that Mrs. Kemper had seen from the car window, upturned despairingly to the stormy sky as for a moment the weary wanderer paused and leaned against a tree by the roadside to gather strength and breath for renewed exertion.

Both were well-nigh spent, and hope so nearly dead within her that, but for the babe in her arms, she had lain her down to die there in the lonely wood, with no human creature near to pity or console.

But mother-love was stronger than the love of life: she had taken the thin faded shawl from her own shoulders to wrap it about the little one, and so had kept it comparatively warm and dry, while she herself was drenched to the skin. Her limbs were almost benumbed with cold, and the cutting wind, as it dashed the rain and sleet full in her face, seemed piercing to her very vitals.

Twilight was fast deepening into night ; the way grew dark and slippery ; now her feet sank in the mud, and she struggled out only to slip into a pool of water, or to stumble and fall over a stump or log, or to catch and tear her clothing on some thorny bush.

The pauses for breath grew more frequent, the steps, as she moved forward again, weaker and more tottering, the weary arms could scarce sustain the weight of the child, and she knew not how far distant was the nearest human habitation. She was about to give up in utter despair, when the gleam of a not very distant light seen through the trees inspired her with new hope and energy.

She pressed forward, and presently emerged from the wood and found herself at Clearfield Station, with the light in the window of the shanty inn shining out ruddily not a hundred yards away.

She crept to the door and knocked faintly.

Mr. Kemper, who had just finished his supper, rose and opened it.

"Come in," he said. "This is a public house, and I presume no one will object," he added, catching sight of the ragged, dripping figure.

She stepped in, staggered to the fire and dropped down on the floor beside it.

"Drunk !" he muttered, with a gesture of disgust.

"No, no, John ! she is ill—starving perhaps !—poor thing ! poor thing !" cried his keener-sighted wife, springing forward, barely in time to catch the sleeping babe as the weary arms relaxed their hold and the wanderer sank back against the wall in a state of semi-insensibility, her eyes closed and not a trace of color on cheek or lip.

"She's dying!" exclaimed Mr. Kemper in a frightened whisper; and rushing to the inner door, "Somebody run for a doctor, quick! here is a woman who seems to be very ill!" he cried hurriedly.

"None to be had within three or four mile," returned a gruff voice from the table. "What ails the woman? and who is she?"

"I don't know; but something must be done."

"Give her a cup of your tea, Irene," said the voice.

"A few drops of brandy from the flask in our luncheon-basket, John," said his wife. "I always take it along in case of sickness, you know."

But the child, a girl of eighteen months, woke with a cry, "Mamma! mamma!" and at the sound the mother's eyes unclosed.

"Give her to me—my little Ethel!" she said faintly.

"You are ill, my good woman, not able to hold her," Mrs. Kemper said, as she reluctantly complied with the request.

"Yes, and I—have eaten nothing to-day—and have walked many miles."

"Poor soul!" exclaimed Irene, the kind-hearted mistress of the shanty, coming in with the tea, "Here, drink this, and I'll bring you some supper. You look more dead than alive, and the rain has soaked you through and through. Dear, dear! you'll catch your death o' cold!"

She raised the wanderer's head as she spoke, and held the cup to her lips.

It was eagerly drained to the last drop, and seemed to revive the poor creature greatly.

Food was brought, and the babe devoured it as if half famished, but the mother ate sparingly. She was evidently very ill, almost dying, thought those about her, and hastened to do all in their power for her relief and comfort.

Plainly she was, as Mrs. Kemper had said, no common tramp : there was lady-like refinement in face, voice, and manner ; her accent was pure, her speech correct and even elegant, as, in answer to kindly inquiries, she gave a brief account of the causes of her present sad condition.

At an early age she had been left an orphan and without any natural protector ; had married some three years ago, and two years later her husband had died, leaving her penniless, in feeble health, and with a babe to support. She had managed for a time to earn a scanty living by needlework, but there was little demand for it where she lived, and wages were very low ; so, taking her child in her arms, she had set out in search of other employment or a better location.

It had proved a long, weary quest, and here she was, in utter destitution and about, she greatly feared, to die, and leave her helpless babe with none to love or care for it.

With the last words a great sob burst from her bosom ; and clasping the little creature close,

"Ah my darling, my little Ethel, if I might but take you with me !" she moaned in anguish.

"Ah now don't take on so," Irene said kindly. "You'll be better to-morrow. Walking all day in the cold, and gettin wet too, it's no wonder you're down-hearted like; but cheer up, you'll get over it and find work, and maybe see as good days as ever you did."

The wanderer thanked her with a grateful look, as she continued silently to caress Ethel; the child, no longer cold and hungry, hanging about her mother's neck, stroking her face lovingly, and prattling in innocent glee.

Mrs. Kemper watched her with delighted, longing eyes, the tears starting to them once and again.

"What a lovely, darling little creature she is!" she whispered to her husband; "just the age our Nellie was." And then she added a few words in a still lower tone.

He nodded acquiescence; and turning to the mother, said that he and his wife would like to adopt the child and bring it up as their own; that they would do so if she would at once give it up entirely to them.

A look of mingled grief and terror came over her face at the bare suggestion. She clutched her treasure in a death-like grasp.

"No, no! how could I? how could I?" she cried, "my baby! my precious baby! my all! no, no, never, never!"

"Take time to consider," he said soothingly. "I am sorry to distress you, but, as you have yourself said, your child will soon need another protector, and it is very unlikely that another will be readily found to do as well by her as we would."

"But wait—wait till I am gone!" she moaned. "She is my all, my all! Oh, 'tis hard to die and leave her! My baby, my baby, your mother's heart will break!" and the tears fell like rain on the wondering little face upturned to hers.

"Don't ky, Ethel's mamma! Ethel love 'oo!" cooed the babe, lifting her dress to wipe away the tears, while with the other arm she clung about her neck, then kissing her wet cheek again and again.

Mrs. Kemper, with great tears of sympathy rolling down her own cheeks, knelt at the wanderer's side, and, taking one thin hand in hers, said:

"I feel for you, my poor, poor friend! I do indeed. I know a mother's heart, for I once had a little one like this, and when death snatched her from me I would gladly have gone down into the grave with her, for she was my only one. That was ten years ago. I have never had another, and it is not likely I ever shall; and now when you feel that you must leave this darling, will you not let me have her to fill the vacant place in my heart—in *our* hearts and home, for my husband will love her dearly too, and be a good father to her?"

"Oh, gladly, when—when I am gone!"

"But we cannot wait; we must go on our journey in another hour. And it will be to you only parting a little sooner; for her good too. You cannot be selfish where your dear child is concerned."

"No, no, God knows I would suffer anything for her. I love her better than my own soul. But I cannot give her up till—I must. Have pity, have pity! she is all I have left—parents, sister, husband, home, all—everything gone but her—my precious

precious baby! Oh, don't, don't ask me to let her go from my arms while I live!" she pleaded in heart-broken accents, and with bitter sobs and tears.

"We would not if it could be helped," sobbed Mrs. Kemper, "but it cannot; and for her sake you will give her to us now?"

Mr. Kemper joined his arguments and entreaties to those of his wife. They engaged to do all in their power for the well-being and happiness of the little one, treating her in every respect as if she were their own offspring, on the one condition that she should be given up entirely to them, never to be claimed by any one—even a near relative, or the mother herself, should she by any possibility survive.

Mr. Kemper had torn a leaf from his note-book, and, with pen and ink furnished by Irene, had drawn up a deed of gift to that effect, which he was urging the mother to sign.

"No, no! I can never, *never* agree to *that!*" she cried in reference to the last stipulation. "Live without my own precious child! never, never!"

"A mere form," he said. "You cannot live many days, my good woman; do you not feel that it is so?"

She but clasped her child closer, while her whole frame shook with the violence of her emotion. She seemed almost ready to expire with the mental anguish superadded to her great physical prostration.

At length the distant rumble of an approaching train was heard.

"There, you have but a moment left for decision," said the gentleman; "that is the train we must take. Will you sacrifice your child's welfare or your own feelings?"

She was now seated beside the table, her child asleep in her arms.

He laid the deed of gift he had made out before her as he spoke, and put a pen between her fingers.

She lifted her eyes to his with a look of wild anguish fit to move a heart of stone.

He simply pointed to the unconscious babe.

She looked at it, seized the pen, hurriedly scrawled a name at the foot of the deed, and fell back fainting.

But the shrill whistle of the locomotive and the thunder of the train close at hand aroused her.

"We must go now; let me take her," Mrs. Kemper was saying in tones tremulous with great compassion. "I will love her dearly, dearly; I will cherish her as the apple of my eye. Let me wrap this warm shawl around her."

"No, Dolly, I'll carry her," Mr. Kemper said, in a tone of half-suppressed delight, as he finished buttoning up his overcoat after safely depositing the note-book, with the deed of gift, in an inner pocket.

But silently the mother put them both aside. There was agony in her wan, emaciated face. She could not speak for the choking in her throat; but she strained the child to her heart, laid her cold white cheek to its warm and rosy face and kissed it passionately again and again.

"We must go," repeated Mrs. Kemper. "Oh, my heart aches for you, but we *must* go!"

"We must indeed, poor thing! there's not a moment to be lost," added Mr. Kemper, taking the child from her with gentle force. "Here, this will supply your needs while you live, I think," putting a roll of notes into her hand.

She dropped them as if a serpent had stung her, and with a wild cry rushed after him, as, hastily wrapping a shawl about the infant, he ran with it toward the train, his wife close behind him.

They had already tarried almost too long ; had scarcely time to gain the platform of the nearest car ere the train swept swiftly on its way.

"My child, my child ! give me back my child !" shrieked the distracted mother, pursuing with outstretched arms, the storm beating pitilessly on her uncovered head, her long, dark hair streaming in the wind.

For a moment she seemed to fly over the ground, love and despair lending her unnatural strength and speed ; the next—as the train was lost to sight in the depths of the forest—she tottered and would have fallen but for the strong arm of a kindly switchman, who, hastily setting down his lantern, sprang forward just in time to save her.

"She's in a dead faint, poor thing !" he muttered to himself. "Here, Bill," to a comrade, "take a holt and help me to carry her into the depot."

"Who is she, Jack ? an' what ails her ?" asked Bill, hurrying up and holding his lantern high, while he peered curiously into the white, unconscious face.

"No time to talk till we git her in out o' the wet," returned Jack gruffly.

They laid her down on the settee.

"She's a human critter and in sore trouble, that's all I know," remarked Jack quietly, drawing his coat-sleeve across his eyes as the two stood gazing upon the pitiful sight.

CHAPTER II.

RESCUED.

"Amid all life's quests,
There seems but worthy one—to do men good."—BAILEY.

A LIGHT covered wagon had just drawn up at the depot door, and out of it quickly stepped an elderly gentleman. Hurrying in with youthful alacrity, he glanced with eager haste from side to side of the dingy apartment. A look of keen disappointment swept over his features, changing instantly to one of grief and terror as his eye fell upon the little group about the settee.

"What—who—who is it? What has happened?" he asked tremulously, turning pale, and laying his hand on a chair-back as if to steady himself; then heaving a sigh of relief as the men stepped aside, giving him a view of the prostrate form, Jack Strong saying:

"It's not Mr. Rolfe, sir, but on'y a poor female woman as has fainted. Mr. Rolfe, he didn't come. Somebody's took her child away from her, I do believe. Leastways she was screamin' for it, and runnin' arter the cars, which of course she couldn't ketch. I reckon she's sick too. Looks mighty bad, anyhow."

"So she does, poor creature!" said the gentleman, approaching. "We must do something at once to bring her to. Water, Jack—quick! I wish Dr. Wright was here."

But at that instant a moan came from the pale lips, and the eyes—large, dark, and lustrous—opened wide. They caught the pitying gaze of the new-comer. Feebly she lifted her arms toward him, then dropped them again, faintly murmuring:

"You have been gone so long, father, and I am ill —dying. Take me home."

"That I will!" he said, obeying a sudden generous impulse, for he was much moved by the appeal. "Jack!"

"Do you know her, sir, Mr. Heywood?" queried the switchman in surprise.

"No more than you do, Jack, but surely she is in sore need of help, and I'm able to give it. In fact, I think it is a plain call of Providence. I've brought the dearborn, thinking to take home Rolfe and his luggage; but he hasn't come, and here it is—the very thing to carry her in."

"But wait a moment; what do you know of her? Is she quite alone?"

"Indeed I don't know nothin' more than—" began the switchman, but was interrupted by the hurried entrance of Irene.

"Is she livin'? where is she?" asked the girl, rushing into their midst breathless with haste and excitement. "Here's some money the gentleman gave her, and she throwed it on the floor; I reckon because she thought 'twas paying her for the child."

"My child! my Ethel!" cried the wanderer, starting up, but only to fall back again, overcome with weakness. "Come to mother, darling, come!"

she murmured, her hand feebly extended, her eyes closed, while she moved her head restlessly from side to side.

"She's out of her mind," whispered the girl.

Mr. Heywood nodded assent; and drawing Irene aside, asked a few rapid questions, in reply to which she imparted all the information she could give in regard to the sufferer.

All he heard but strengthened his resolution to befriend the poor creature, and he at once set about making preparations for removing her to his own house, some three miles distant.

A quantity of clean straw was bestowed in the bottom of the dearborn, a buffalo-robe laid over it, making a not uncomfortable bed. On this the invalid was gently placed, and carefully covered with a second robe.

She made no resistance. She was quite delirious, and knew nothing of what was passing around her.

"Carefully now, Mike," the old gentleman said, taking his seat beside the coachman; "the poor thing's in no state to bear unnecessary jolting."

"Hallo! hold on there a minute; here's a message for you, Mr. Heywood!" cried the telegraph operator, rushing out from his office with a piece of paper in his hand. "From Rolfe, sir; he's all right—missed the train, that's all; will be here to-morrow morning."

"God willing," added the old gentleman reverently, taking the paper with trembling fingers; "and His name be praised that my boy is safe. I'm obliged to you, Dixon."

The storm had increased in violence: the showers

of rain and sleet now fell almost without intermission, and the wind blew with a fury that threatened danger from falling trees as they drove on through the forest, their progress necessarily slow because of the state of the road and the intense darkness.

The raging of the tempest was not favorable to conversation, and few words passed between them, while the woman for the most part slept heavily under the influence of a narcotic, only a moan or a muttered word or two now and then escaping her lips.

Mr. Heywood was one of the early settlers of Iowa. He had invested largely in land on his arrival, and in the course of years had, by its rise in value, become quite wealthy. The log cabin in the wilderness, in which the early years of his married life were passed, and where his children had first seen the light, was now replaced by a large, handsome brick house standing in the midst of well-kept gardens and cultivated fields. "Sweetbrier" Mrs. Heywood had named the place, and it was often pointed out to strangers as one of the finest residences in the county. The Heywoods had not, however, been exempt from trials: four out of six children had passed away from earth. Of the two survivors, the eldest, a son, had emigrated to California several years before this, and was now returning for his first visit to his old home, parents, and sister.

Ada, the daughter, a fair girl of eighteen, was full ten years younger than Rolfe, he being the eldest and she the youngest born.

In the sitting-room at Sweetbrier mother and daughter eagerly awaited the coming of the loved travellers—father and son.

The room was tastefully furnished, a bright wood fire crackled cheerily on the hearth, and an astral lamp on the centre-table shed a soft, mellow light on two happy faces, on books, pictures, lounges, and easy chairs.

In the adjoining room a table was set out with snowy damask, fine French china, and silverware, in readiness for the feast preparing in the kitchen, whither Mrs. Heywood occasionally hied to oversee the labors of her cook.

"How the wind does blow!" she remarked, returning from one of these little excursions. "It's a dreadful night for your father to be out. I wish Rolfe had come yesterday."

"I wish he had," said Ada, running to the window. "How very dark it is! I'm sure they can't see the road, or any tree that may be blown down across it. Mother, I am afraid they've met with some accident, for it's nearly ten o'clock—high time they were here."

"We'll not distress ourselves, dear, with anticipating evil; both we and they are in the Lord's keeping," replied the mother, striving to put away anxious thoughts. "I think Peace and Plenty will be able to find the road; I never knew them to miss it yet, even in nights as dark as this. Come, sit down by the fire, Ada, and read me again the letter you received from your brother the other day; that will help to while away the time till they come."

The girl complied, drawing the letter from her pocket, and seating herself on an ottoman at her mother's feet.

"I wonder," she said, refolding the missive, "that

Rolfe has never married. I pity the somebody that's missing such a good husband."

"Time enough yet," said the mother, smiling; "he is only twenty-eight. There! I hear the rattle of the wheels." Both sprang up and hurried to the outer door, each heart beating high with delighted expectation.

They were just in time to see Mr. Heywood alight from the vehicle, which had already drawn up before the entrance.

"My dear," he said, hurrying up the steps into the portico, "don't be alarmed. I have not brought our boy, but he's safe and well; sent me a telegram to say he'd missed the train, and will be here to-morrow, God willing."

"Well," she said, with a sigh, "it's a sore disappointment, but I'm thankful it's no worse. You've had a hard ride, and—"

"Have brought an unexpected guest with me," he interrupted hastily. "Mary, dear, remembering the Master's words, 'Inasmuch as ye have done it unto one of the least of these, ye have done it unto me,' you'll not object to taking her in, for she may be one of His."

"Who, Joseph?" she asked in a startled tone.

"A poor, forsaken, dying creature, Mary; I've not been able to learn her name." And he hurried to the assistance of Mike, who had fastened his horses and was preparing to lift the woman from the wagon.

Taking each an end of the buffalo-robe on which she lay, they carried her in between them and laid her gently down before the sitting-room fire.

Mrs. Heywood had hastened to order a room and bed made ready, and now, returning with such restoratives as were at hand, knelt by the side of the sufferer to apply them.

"How young! how pretty!" she said in surprise, gazing down at the unconscious face with its broad white brow, cheeks now slightly flushed with fever, sweet mouth, and large, lustrous eyes, which suddenly opened wide upon her, then closed again, while a deep moan escaped the lips and the head moved restlessly from side to side.

"She's very ill, poor dear!" said the old lady. "Ada, my child, don't come near lest her disease should be contagious. We ought to have the doctor here as soon as possible, Joseph."

"I'll go for him," said Mike, starting for the door.

"Hark!" cried Ada, "there's a horse galloping up the drive. Who can it be coming at this hour on such a night?"

Mrs. Heywood rose to her feet, and they all stood for a moment intently listening; then, at a "Hallo!" from a familiar voice,

"Why, it's the doctor himself!" they exclaimed simultaneously, the old gentleman and Ada running out to the hall to greet him.

He had already alighted from his horse, and was coming in.

"All well?" he asked almost breathlessly, not even pausing to say good-evening.

"Yes—no!" returned Mr. Heywood. "This way as quick as you can, doctor; we've a poor creature here who is very sick indeed."

"Ah, that explains it," remarked the physician,

as if thinking aloud, while hastily following his host.

He pronounced his patient in a brain-fever and very ill indeed.

"The poor creature (evidently a lady) must have been half famished for months past, and has hardly strength to cope with the disease," he said, "yet with the blessing of Providence upon skilful treatment and the best of nursing"—with a bow and a smile directed to Mrs. Heywood—"she may possibly recover."

"Poor dear! my heart is strongly drawn to her," said the old lady, twinkling away a tear as she bent over the bed where they had laid the sufferer, and softly smoothed back the hair from the pale forehead, "and she shall not die for lack of anything it is in my power to do for her."

"Singular!" murmured the doctor meditatively. Then glancing from the face of his patient to those of his old friends, "It doesn't seem to have occurred to you to wonder how I came here so opportunely to-night," he remarked.

"Why no, to be sure," said Mr. Heywood. "How was it? We have been so taken up with this poor creature's critical condition as to have no thought for anything else."

"Just so. Well, I was hurrying home from the bedside of a patient some two miles from here; very anxious to get home, too, out of the darkness and storm; when suddenly it was strongly impressed upon my mind that I was needed here and ought to come at once. It was a good half-mile out of my way, as you know; bad road, too, through the thickest of the woods, where the wind was blowing down trees, and one might at any moment fall on and crush me and my horse; but so strong was the impression I speak of that I really could not resist. And there surely was a providence in it," he added reverently, "for by to-morrow morning medical aid would have come too late to give this poor woman even a chance for life."

"I am sure of it," said the old lady; "and in her coming here also. I shall watch with her through the night, doctor."

"And I shall share your vigil," he replied.

The morning sun rose bright and clear, but its cheerful light brought no alleviation of the wanderer's pain. She lay tossing on her couch unconscious of all the solicitude felt for her, all the kindness lavished upon her, now muttering incoherently, now crying out for "her child, her Ethel, her sweet, darling baby."

Immediately after breakfast Mr. Heywood went himself in search of a nurse, and having procured one, and seen her established by the bedside, he and Mike again drove over to the depot at Clearfield, reaching there in time for the morning train. When they returned Rolfe was with them.

CHAPTER III.

ONE FOR LIFE.

"And doth not a meeting like this make amends
For all the long years I've been wand'ring away?"—Anon.

A NOBLE, handsome fellow was Rolfe Heywood, and though the suffering stranger guest was neither forgotten nor neglected, "joy crowned the board" at Sweetbrier upon his return, and the weeks that followed were full of quiet happiness to himself, parents, and sister.

He was succeeding well in the new State of his adoption, and hoped to persuade these dear ones to join him there at some not very distant day.

He took a benevolent interest in the sick woman, and rejoiced with the others when the physician pronounced the crisis of the disease past and the patient in a fair way to recover.

"She's come to her full senses now, and there ain't no doing anything with her," announced the nurse a few days later, looking in at the open door of the room where the family were at breakfast. "Not a morsel of food will she take, not a drop of medicine will she swallow. She just lays there with her eyes shut, and every once in a while I see a big tear a-rollin' down them thin, white cheeks o' hern."

She withdrew with the last words, and while finishing their meal the family held a consultation on the case.

On leaving the table, Mrs. Heywood repaired to the sick-chamber.

The face resting on the snowy pillows was not only wan and emaciated, but wore an expression of deepest melancholy. The eyes were closed, but not in sleep, as Mrs. Heywood at first thought. Stepping softly to the bedside, she stood silently gazing upon her, thinking how sad it was that one so young and fair should be already weary of life.

"My baby, my baby!" came from the pale lips in low, heart-broken accents, and tears trembled on the long silken lashes that lay like dark shadows on the white cheeks.

"My poor, poor child," said the old lady, bending down to press a gentle kiss upon her brow, "do not despair. Try to get well, and who knows but we shall be able to find your treasure and restore her to you."

"Yes, to be sure," said the nurse, putting a spoon to her patient's lips. "Swallow this that the doctor left for you, there's a dear, and then take a little of this beef-tea, and I'll warrant you'll feel a heap better."

"No, no, take it away. Let me die in peace," she sighed, averting her face, and with her wasted hand feebly putting the spoon aside.

"I want to die—I've nothing to live for now." And great tears rolled down the pale sad face. "Ah, me! I gave her to them, and they will never, never give her up! Oh, my darling! my baby! my little Ethel!" she cried, bursting into hysterical weeping.

Endearments, persuasions, caresses, reasoning, exhortation on the duty of doing everything in our power to preserve the life God has given—all were tried by turns, but in vain. She lay there in silent despair, seeming neither to hear nor heed.

Though nearly as much interested in the suffering stranger as were his parents and sister, Rolfe had not ventured into the sick-room, and so had never yet seen her face; nor had he ever heard her voice or learned her name, of which last, indeed, they were all ignorant.

Something was taking him to his own apartments that evening on leaving the tea-table, when he met Mrs. Scott, the nurse, coming down the stairs.

"Do you leave your patient alone?" he asked.

"Never for long. I'm going down to my supper, and I'll speak to Miss Ada to come up and take my place for a bit."

She had left the door of the sick-room ajar. A moan caught Rolfe's ear in passing, then the words, "Oh, my baby, my baby!" He started violently, a strange pallor suddenly overspreading his face. He stood still, intently listening. The words were repeated; and hastily pushing the door open, he stepped to the bedside.

"Ethel, Ethel! Can it be? Oh, Ethel, my light, my life!"

"Rolfe!" she cried, starting up in the bed, with both hands extended, the large, lustrous eyes full of joy and amazement.

He took her in his arms, seating himself on the side of the bed; her head dropped upon his shoulder, and folding her to his heart, "Yes, it is Rolfe," he said. "Oh, Ethel, have I found you again? Are you mine at last?"

"Yes, yes," she faintly whispered. "But they told me you were married to another; then—"

"Never, never, my darling! I have loved you always—you alone. Oh, why did you write so coldly, rejecting my offered heart and hand, and telling me that another had won you?"

There was no answer. The strength excitement had supplied for the moment was gone, and she lay apparently lifeless in his arms.

With a sharp cry of agony he laid her back upon her pillow, and began chafing the cold hands and pressing passionate kisses on the pale lips.

Hearing his cry as she neared the door of the sick-room, Ada hurried in, full of wonder and alarm.

"Rolfe!" she exclaimed in astonishment.

"Ada, make haste! Throw up the window to give her air! Hand me that bottle of ammonia—quick, quick! she's dying! she's dead! Oh, Ethel, my life, my love! have I found you only to lose you again?" he groaned, redoubling his efforts to restore her to consciousness, while Ada, divided between amazement at his presence there and excessive agitation, and her fear that life was really extinct, hastily obeyed his orders.

"Thank God, she yet lives!" he said in tones tremulous with emotion, as at length the eyelids began to quiver and a long, sighing breath came from the white lips.

"Rolfe," they whispered very low and feebly.

"Yes, yes, I am here, my poor little Ethel," he answered, kneeling by her couch and fondly caressing her hair and cheek. "You will live for me, and nothing in life shall ever part us again."

A beautiful smile crept over her face as she opened her eyes for a single instant; then closing them again, she fell asleep with her hand in his.

Ada stood on the farther side of the bed, looking and listening in increasing surprise and wonder.

Mrs. Heywood and the nurse stole in on tiptoe and beheld the scene in no less astonishment and perplexity, but Rolfe motioned them all away, and kept guard over the slumbers of the invalid as one who had a superior and undoubted right.

She slept quietly, awoke refreshed, and refused neither food nor medicine at his hands.

But he would not let her talk.

"Wait, my Ethel, till you are stronger," he said, "and then we will tell each other all. In the mean time we may rest content in the knowledge that we are restored to each other, and no earthly power can part us."

Lips and eyes smiled brightly, and a faint color stole into her cheek, but faded again as she moaned sadly, "My baby, my baby!" the tears stealing down her face.

"We will find her; she shall be restored to you. Nothing is impossible to a determined will," he said with energy.

She believed him, and once more resigned herself to peaceful slumber.

It was now near midnight, yet a bright light burned in the sitting-room. Mr. and Mrs. Heywood and their daughter, too much excited to think of retiring, sat there waiting for they scarce knew what. Reluctantly leaving Ethel to the care of the nurse, Rolfe joined them.

"Yes," he said, in answer to their inquiring looks, "we knew and loved each other years ago in Jefferson, where I first set up business. She was an orphan, and the sweetest creature I ever saw, but very much under the influence of an older sister—a proud, selfish, scheming, domineering woman. She, I have always thought it was, who came between my love and me. I meant to speak before I left, and tried to do so, but she contrived to foil every attempt. Then I wrote, and the answer was, I have little doubt, dictated or forged by her."

"She rejected you?"

Mrs. Heywood's tone was both inquiring and indignant.

"Yes, mother; but don't condemn her unheard," he said, with a smile of filial affection. "That in so doing she did not follow the dictates of her own heart I now know beyond a question."

"I don't want to be uncharitable, or to wound you, Rolfe," returned his mother, flushing slightly, "but that any woman should reject the man she loves and marry another seems to me both weak and wicked."

"Wait, my dear, till you have heard her story," said the old gentleman. "We don't know how she may have been deceived and betrayed."

A few days later Rolfe came to his mother with an explanation which even in her eyes exculpated Ethel.

"Ah, well, poor thing! she's had a hard time of it," said the old lady, wiping away a tear. "And I hope, Rolfe, if she falls into your hands you'll try to make it up to her."

"I shall indeed," he said, with a peculiar and very

happy smile. "Come, mother, come to her room with me. The minister is there, my father and Ada too, and Ethel and I are now to be made one for life."

"Rolfe!" she cried in astonishment.

"Yes, mother; I cannot let her feel herself alone in the wide world any longer, and I must have the right to nurse her back to health. You will not withhold your consent, mother dear?"

"No," she said, with a half-bewildered look as she accepted the support of his offered arm, "not if it is to make you and that poor young thing happy; but it is very sudden."

CHAPTER IV.

A STRANGE REVELATION.

"The web of our life is of a mingled
Yarn, good and all together."—SHAKESPEARE.

FOR a few days the little Ethel was quite inconsolable, crying sadly for "Mamma;" but the new parents were very tender, patient, and affectionate, and the old love gradually faded from the baby memory, till at length it was utterly forgotten in the new. So also was the name her true mother had given her, Mrs. Kemper changing it to Florence, which she liked better.

Anxious that the child should believe herself their own by birth, the Kempers considered it fortunate that it was while journeying to a new home in the West, among strangers, in the little town of Cranley, that they obtained possession of her.

They breathed no hint of the little one's history, and none of their new acquaintances had the least suspicion of the truth, as indeed how should they when to both parents "our little Floy" was evidently as the apple of the eye?

So loved and cared for, and blessed with a sweet, generous, affectionate disposition, hers was a bright, sunny childhood. She was spared even the loneliness of many an only child, finding companion, playmate, and friend in the little son of the nearest neighbor.

The grounds of the Aldens and Kempers adjoined, and immediately upon the arrival of the latter, friendly relations were established between the two families. Mrs. Alden called upon her new neighbors, taking with her her five-year-old Espy, a flaxen-haired, blue-eyed boy, who straightway fell in love with the lustrous, laughing brown orbs and dark curls of baby Floy.

She sat on a cushion by the side of her new mamma, daintily habited in white, a gold chain about her neck, knots of blue ribbon at her shoulders, and a wide sash of the same at her waist. The plump little arms hugged close to her bosom a doll half as large as herself, while the sweet baby voice sang cheerily, " Bye, baby, bye !"

" What's your name ?" asked Espy, regarding her with admiring eyes.

" Florence," answered Mrs. Kemper quickly, " but we call her Floy for short."

" That's a pretty name, and you're a pretty baby," he said, giving her a kiss. " Nex' time I come I'll bring my kitten. She's a nice cat, and I love her ; but I'll just give her to you, if you want her."

" I was never more surprised," remarked Mrs. Alden in an aside to Mrs. Kemper. " He prizes that kitten above all his other possessions."

And thus it ever was from that first moment. Nothing could be, in Espy's esteem, too good, beautiful, or precious to be given to Floy—" his little wife," as he began to call her before she was three years old, challenging a special proprietorship in her with which no other boy was allowed to interfere.

A day seldom passed in which he did not present

some offering at her shrine, though it were no more than a sweet-scented clover-blossom or a brightly-tinted autumn leaf.

They shared each other's joys and sorrows : all her little griefs were confided to him ; to her he recounted all his boyish dreams of future achievement when he should arrive at man's estate.

He was a born artist, and found in Floy his chief inspiration ; for while his parents and older brothers and sisters laughed at and discouraged him, she believed thoroughly in him, and was sure he would some day be a Rubens, a Raphael, a Michael Angelo, or something even greater than any of them or all put together ; and her graceful little figure and winsome face furnished him with a model that he was never weary of copying.

Mr. Alden, hoping that this son would embrace one of the learned professions, determined to give him a liberal education ; and the first great grief either Floy or Espy had known was the parting when the latter went away to school. Yet there was compensation in a steady correspondence, kept up with the knowledge and approval of their parents, and in the joy of the reunion when vacation brought Espy home again.

Cranley could boast of a good school for girls, and Floy did not go from home for her education. At seventeen she was a very pretty, engaging girl, and as Mr. Kemper had prospered, and was known to be in easy circumstances, she had plenty of admirers ; but she remained true to Espy, though theirs was as yet only a tacit engagement.

Floy graduated from school in June of that year

and Mr. Kemper took her and his wife on a summer trip to the East. They spent several weeks at the seashore, visited Philadelphia and New York and other places of interest, then turned homeward.

All had gone well with them, and now within a few miles of Cranley they were speaking of this gladly, thankfully.

"Oh, yes, we've had a delightful time," said Floy, "and yet I am eager to be in our own dear home again. There is no place like home when it is as happy a one as ours."

Mr. Kemper smiled indulgently upon her.

"Quite right, my little girl," he said, "and our Floy makes half its brightness to us. Is not that so, mamma?" addressing his wife.

"It is indeed," she answered, half sighing as the thought suggested itself that, some day, another would have a stronger claim than they upon this darling of her heart.

The whistle blew, the train slackened its speed, then came to a stand-still at a little country station.

"Peaches! apples! pears!"

A boy had come in with a basket of fruit on his arm.

Mr. Kemper bought liberally of him; then selecting a gold half-eagle from the contents of his purse, he dropped it into Floy's hand, saying, "There's a trifle for you. I wonder how long it will be before you spend it."

"A good while, papa, if you keep me in greenbacks enough to supply my wants," she returned gayly, as she deposited it in a dainty portemonnaie. "Thanks for the gift; I'll be sure to think of you when I look at it."

"Better put it in bank along with the rest; there's five hundred dollars there now to your credit."

"Then I can afford to keep this to look at."

The smile died on her lips almost before the words left them.

"Something's wrong with the engine," a voice was saying behind her. "Nobody knows how long we'll have to stop here, and we're not up to time by half an hour. Hark! what's that? Another train coming! we shall be run into!"

Faces paled with sudden fear; men and women started to their feet in wild affright. There was a shrill whistle, answered by another, a rush and roar, then a crash, many voices blending in an awful cry, and Floy knew no more till, waking as from a deep sleep, she felt herself gently lifted, while a strange voice said:

"She's only stunned; not much hurt, I hope. But this other woman is horribly mangled, and the man—well, his pains are over for this life at least."

Instantly restored to perfect consciousness, Floy opened her eyes with a cry, "Mother! father! oh, where are they? Let me go to them!"

The men set her down on a fragment of the wreck, and turned to help those in greater need.

The girl passed her hand over her eyes as if to clear her vision. Oh, was it not all a horrible dream? The heaped-up ruins, the bleeding, mangled forms of the dead and dying, the shrieks, the groans, the cries for help, the running to and fro of those who were trying to give it, the frenzied search for missing loved ones, the wail of anguish over the wounded and the slain!

What was that they were bearing past her? Could that be her mother's voice asking in quivering, agonized tones for husband and child?

She sprang up and ran after the rude litter on which the crushed and bleeding form was borne along toward a farm-house a few rods distant. She caught sight of the face, white with the pallor of death and convulsed with pain. A gleam of joy shot over it as the eyes fell on the face and figure of Floy. "My darling! safe, thank God!" came from the pale, quivering lips.

"Mother, mother!" cried the girl.

"Be comforted, darling; I can bear it; 'twill not be for long," gasped the sufferer.

They carried her into the house and laid her on a bed. Floy knelt by her side, grasping the dear hand in hers, laying it to her cheek, pressing it to her lips, passionately weeping with a grief that seemed to rend her heart asunder.

"Floy, dearest, it is all right. God's will be done. He knows best. He will comfort you."

The quick ear of the girl scarcely caught the low-breathed words, and with the last Mrs. Kemper fainted.

At the same moment a gentleman came hastily in and stepped to the bedside.

Instinctively Floy comprehended his errand, even ere he laid his finger on the pulse or raised the shawl that half concealed the shattered form.

She rose, outwardly calm and collected.

"Can my mother live?" she asked.

"For some hours," he said, looking pityingly into the grief-stricken face of his questioner.

"Where is she hurt?"

"Poor child! how shall I tell you? Her lower limbs are completely crushed, and even amputation would not save her life."

Floy caught at the bedstead for support, a low cry of heart-breaking anguish bursting from her lips. "Oh, mother, mother! And my father!" she gasped, "oh, where is he?"

"The gentleman who occupied the same seat with this lady? Ah, my dear child, he is done with pain."

The girl sank upon her knees again, hiding her face in her hands and trembling in every fibre. So sudden, so terrible were these successive blows that the very earth seemed slipping from beneath her feet.

"Dear Lord, her heart is overwhelmed; lead her to the Rock that is higher than she."

The words were spoken by an old woman in homely attire who was assisting the physician in his efforts to restore Mrs. Kemper to consciousness. The tones were very tender and pitiful, and the aged hand rested lightly for an instant upon the bowed head.

"Oh, could not *one* have been spared to me?" cried Floy in a burst of agony. "Fatherless! motherless! oh, that I too had been taken!"

"Dear child, He will be your Father and your Friend, and life will grow sweet again, and now He knows and feels for all your pain."

A groan of agonizing pain came from the crushed form on the bed.

Floy rose and bent over her, the hot tears falling like rain upon the pallid, death-like face.

"Mother, mother! how can I bear to see you suffer so?"

The white, quivering lips tried to wreathe themselves into a smile, and the anguished eyes looked tenderly into hers.

"Beloved child, it will—soon—be over, and I—shall be at home—indeed."

Her eyes sought the doctor's face. "How long—"

"A very few hours at the most."

"Then leave me alone with my child," she said, speaking in a stronger voice than before.

The physician gave Floy some directions in regard to the administering of restoratives, and he and his assistant withdrew.

Left alone together, hand clasped in hand, mother and daughter gazed tenderly, mournfully into each other's eyes, silent tears trickling down the cheeks of both. Then gathering up all her failing energies for the task, Mrs. Kemper told Floy in a few brief sentences the story of her adoption and all they had heard from her true mother's lips in the little shanty inn at Clearfield Station.

Some things she said which, though they fell almost unheeded upon Floy's ears at the time, afterward, when she had come to care for that unknown mother, were a great comfort. It was pleasant to have learned from the dear dying voice that she who gave her being was unmistakably a lady by birth and breeding, whom even a stranger recognized as gentle and lovable.

"I have never been able to remember without a pang of regret and remorse her agony of grief in parting from you," said Mrs. Kemper. " We have never heard from her, and I think she must have died soon after, for she seemed then in an almost dying condition.

" Oh, then why tell me of her? why, dearest, darling mother, rob me of the belief that I am your own child—your's and father's?" sobbed the heart-broken girl.

The dying eyes looked into hers with yearning tenderness.

" Precious one," she whispered faintly, for her strength was waning, " I would spare you every unneeded pang. But," she went on with frequent pauses for breath, " the knowledge may some day be of use to you. You may find relatives, my poor, lonely darling. You will find the deed of gift among your father's papers ; your mother's name is signed to it. There is a will, my husband told me, leaving everything to you and me, all to be yours at my death ; so, my—"

" Oh, mother, darling mother, what do I care for that now—now when I have lost my father, and you too are going from me !" cried the girl in an agony of grief.

" Nothing now, I know," the mother said with pitying tenderness, " but I am glad my darling will not be left penniless ; it would be hard for you to earn your own bread. And the dear home, Floy, will be yours."

Her eyes closed, but the lips still moved, and Floy, bending over her, caught the broken, faintly murmured words, " Home—many mansions—my Father's house—" Then all was stillness and silence.

"Mother, oh, mother! speak to me once more!" cried the girl, pressing passionate kisses on the pale brow where the dews of death already gathered. "Is it well with you, darling mother? No fear? No doubt, no darkness?"

A beautiful smile played about the dying lips, and again a faint murmur reached the daughter's intently listening ear: "All is peace—peace—the sweetest peace; I know that my Redeemer liveth. Trust Him, trust Him; He will—never—leave you."

A gentle sigh, and Floy knew that she was alone. No wail of sorrow broke the deep hush of that death-chamber, no tears fell from the burning eyes of the solitary mourner. They found her with the still form clasped in her arms, her dead mother's head pillowed upon her bosom, the tearless eyes gazing with mingled love and anguish upon the calm, sweet face on whose unruffled brow Peace had set its signet. The lovely smile yet lingered about the pale lips which to Floy's ear seemed ever whispering, "All is peace, peace, the sweetest peace."

CHAPTER V.

BETROTHED.

"We all do fade as a leaf."—Isaiah 64 : 6
"My Adah! let me call thee mine."—Byron.

"Floy!"

Only a word, yet what a world of love and tender sympathy spoke in the tone and in the touch of the hand that gently caressed her hair.

The girl started and looked up.

"Oh, Espy!"

Her cheek dropped again upon the head resting on her bosom, and now the blessed tears came in a flood.

Espy, just returning from college, had been scarcely an hour at home when the news came flashing over the wires that about five miles away a terrible railroad accident had occurred, in which several prominent citizens of Cranley, among whom were the Kempers, had been killed or wounded.

Nearly frantic with fear for Floy, Espy rushed to the depot, and learning that a special train would be sent immediately to carry aid to the sufferers, hurried home again with the tidings.

Mrs. Alden had already packed a basket with such things as she thought might be needed, tied on her hat, and, with a shawl on her arm, stood in the doorway anxiously looking for her son's return.

He came running, caught up the basket, and, giving her his arm, began to retrace his steps, merely saying in a voice hoarse with emotion, "We must make all haste, mother, or we'll be left."

"Floy?" she cried pantingly, as they almost flew over the ground. "Oh, I don't know!" he gasped, "there are a thousand reports."

It was only on reaching the scene of the disaster that they learned who, of all their friends, had been killed or injured. What a relief to know that Floy was not of the number! But ah, was she unhurt, with that crushed and almost broken heart?

They found her as we have described. They shared her grief, for they had both become strongly attached to those whose sudden, untimely, and terrible death she mourned.

"Thank God for those tears!" sobbed Mrs. Alden. "Dear child, our loss is her gain; and she has gone to be with the husband she loved so well. The Lord was good to both in letting them go together."

"Yes," whispered Floy, laying her precious burden gently down.

Wiping away her tears, she pressed one more long, lingering kiss upon the pale lips, then turned, and giving her hand to Espy, suffered him to lead her from the room.

Truly the girl's heart was overwhelmed. Her adopted father—whom, until within the last hour, she had deemed in very truth her own—was only less dear than his wife, and the double bereavement, so sudden, so terrible, was enough to crush her young spirit to the earth; and yet was there an added depth of anguish in the thought of the strange revelation made to her by that beloved dying voice.

It seemed to rob her of the full right to the poor luxury of grief. Others also were nearer by the ties of blood; yet oh, it could not be that any other loved them with half the strength of devotion that filled her heart, that any could mourn for them as she who for sixteen years had been enshrined in their affections, and lived continually in the sunshine of their love!

She could not bear to tell this sorrow to any earthly creature; not even Espy must know the sad secret. There was only One into whose ear she could pour out *all* her griefs. That she could tell Him all and know that He listened—that in all her afflictions He was afflicted—saved the poor heart from breaking.

Mrs. Kemper had been an only child; Mr. Kemper had outlived his brothers and sisters; so that there were no nearer relatives than nephews and nieces, all of whom resided at a great distance. Word was sent to those whose addresses were known, but they were not waited for, as it was impossible they should arrive in time for the funeral.

The Aldens were very kind, treating Floy quite as if she belonged to them, and relieving her of every care in regard to the necessary arrangements for performing the last offices of love to the departed.

It was the evening of the day on which she had looked for the last time upon the dear faces of the loved and lost. At her own request sympathizing friends had all withdrawn and left her alone, and Espy, coming softly into the parlor unannounced, found her weeping bitterly before Mrs. Kemper's portrait.

"Floy, dearest Floy, my own little wife, would that I could comfort you!" he whispered, taking her in his arms.

"You have been—you are a great comfort to me, Espy," she said, gently releasing herself.

"Then why may I not embrace you, dear Floy? Ah, I understand! it is because there has never been a formal engagement between us. But we know we love and belong to each other. Is it not so? Darling Floy, promise to be my wife."

She answered with a look that made his heart bound.

"You are all I have now, Espy," she sobbed, allowing him to draw her head to a resting-place on his shoulder; "all I have to love or to give love to me."

"I wish you knew how much I love you, Floy, my poor stricken one, and how I long to comfort you!" he whispered, clasping her close with many a tender caress.

"The cloud is very, very black!" she sighed. "Oh, it seems as if my heart will break! The blow has been so sudden, so terrible—I cannot fully realize it yet. I am stunned. I seem to be living in a dream—a horrible dream; a dreadful nightmare is upon me," she moaned. "Oh, Espy, wake me and tell me the dear father and mother, alive and well yesterday, are not now lying in the cold grave!" and she shuddered and hid her face, while choking sobs shook her from head to foot.

"They are not there; they are beyond the stars, in the region of unclouded light, dear Floy," he said.

"Yes, yes, that is true! and oh, thank God that you are left me still!"

No one intruded upon them, and they parted only when it was time for Floy to retire.

Worn out with grief and the fatigue of her journey, she fell asleep the moment her head touched the pillow.

The sun was up when she woke again, birds were singing in the tree close to her window, and the glad voices of children at play on the other side of the street came pleasantly to her ear. Had she escaped from her horrible nightmare?

Alas! for only an instant; it was upon her again. Bitter tears coursed down her cheeks. How lonely and desolate was her lot! but ah, Espy's love was left her still. There was balm for her wounded spirit in that thought.

Then came another—the secret imparted with Mrs. Kemper's dying breath. Had not Espy now a right to know the truth as well as she?

She pondered the question for a moment. She was sure it would make no difference in his love, as why should it indeed? But he should know; she would have no concealments from him who was to be her second self.

And, after all, how little there was to tell! What did she know beyond the bare fact that she was the child of her reputed parents only by adoption?

Ah, the paper, the deed of gift her mother had spoken of—she must find it; it would at least tell her her true name. Oh, what an added grief to think that she had no right to the one she had borne since her earliest recollection! and yet, they having given it to her, had she not a right?

On leaving the breakfast-table, where she had

gone through the form of taking her morning meal, she went directly to the room where Mr. Kemper's books and papers were kept, and began her search, at first with confident expectation, though in trembling, eager haste, then anxiously, and at length in sadness akin to despair. She had examined one receptacle after another, till all had been gone over without coming upon the object of her quest. A leaf torn from a note-book—it must be a small paper, easily overlooked; and with that thought in her mind she began her exploration anew. She had not given it up yet when the servant-girl came to say that Mr. Alden was in the parlor.

Floy repaired thither at once.

It was not Espy, but his father, who came forward as she entered, took her hand in his and led her to a sofa, where he seated himself by her side.

"My dear child," he said, "Espy has told us all, and we are very glad; though of course it is only what we had looked forward to as a settled thing for years past."

His manner was so paternal and affectionate that for a moment Floy was too much overcome for speech, so vividly did it remind her of the father she had lost.

He understood her emotion, and tried to console her with the assurance that she need no longer feel herself orphaned and alone in the world, since he and his wife would henceforth regard her as their own child.

Then he went on to speak of the necessity of a settlement of Mr. Kemper's estate, asking her whether there was a will, and who was appointed executor, adding :

"Your father once expressed a wish that I would undertake that office for him, at the same time telling me that his intention was to make a will dividing his property equally between you and his wife, her half to revert to you or your heirs at her death ; but the subject was not mentioned between us afterward, and I do not know anything more about the matter."

"Mother told me there was a will," said Floy, "and it would give me everything. But I do not know where to find it."

"Doubtless it is somewhere among his private papers," said Mr. Alden ; adding reflectively, "It will be quite a task for you to examine them, and you should have help. I am very busy just now, but Espy is entirely at leisure. Shall he come and help you look them over ?"

The young man came in while his father was speaking, and, on hearing an explanation of the matter, eagerly seconded the offer. Anything to assist Floy, especially if it kept him in her dear society.

"I am ready to begin at once, if it suits your convenience and inclination," he said to her, and she answering that it did, his father left them, and they repaired together to the room where she had been so busy all the morning.

CHAPTER VI.

THE SEARCH.

"'Omission to do what is necessary
Seals a commission to a blank of danger."—SHAKESPEARE.

THERE were papers scattered over the table, and one or two had fallen on the floor.

"You see I had begun the task before your father came," Floy said, with a sad smile; "but before we resume it I have something to say to you," she added with an effort, growing so pale that Espy caught her in his arms, thinking she was about to faint.

"My poor Floy!" he said, "if it is anything painful, don't tell it; there is no need."

"I want you to know it, Espy," she sighed low and tremulously, "but to keep it secret from all others unless—unless it—circumstances should render it necessary that—"

Her head dropped upon his shoulder, and with a burst of hysterical weeping, "Oh, Espy, Espy!" she cried, "I'm more than orphaned; I've lost my identity; I'm not Floy Kemper—not the child of the dear parents I mourn, except—except by adoption!"

He was greatly surprised, but only drew her closer to him, as one made dearer still by her sore distress, her utter loneliness; and as she went on in her low, quivering tones, "I've none now but you; I'm all alone in the wide world—not a relative living, so far as I know," a strange thrill of joy mingled with his sympathetic grief—joy that she was his, his alone to love and cherish to life's end ; that on him only she would lean as her earthly stay and support.

Something of this he whispered in reply, accompanying his words with fond caresses and endearing epithets.

"How good and noble you are, my Espy!" she said. "You still hold me to your heart without waiting to learn who or what I am."

"You are my own little Floy, whom I have loved from her very babyhood," he interrupted, holding her fast as she made a movement as if to release herself from his embrace, "and that is all I care to know."

She lifted her large, lustrous eyes to his with a look of grateful love. "No, no, I will not take advantage of your generous affection," she said, the tears streaming down her cheeks. "Wait till I have told you all—till you know everything. Till then I will not hold you bound by—what passed between us last night."

"I will not accept my freedom"—he began impetuously. But she stopped him with an imperative gesture.

"Hear my story." And in a few rapid sentences she gave him the facts as learned from Mrs. Kemper.

His face brightened as she proceeded.

"What is there in this, Floy, to come between us, or even to raise an objection to our union in the mind of the most captious?" he asked. "You were born in wedlock, your mother was a lady, and presumably your father a gentleman. Besides, there is absolutely no need that any one but our own two selves should ever learn these facts. You are known as the child of Mr. and Mrs. Kemper, and that you are not, concerns us alone."

"Is that so?"

"Certainly; and now let us look for the will."

"The will!" A sudden painful thought had flashed upon her. Espy saw it in her face.

"Well, dearest, what is it?" he asked.

"If we should not find it?"

Her voice was low and husky.

"Then we shall do the best we can without it," he answered cheerily, turning to the table and taking up a roll of papers tied together with a bit of red tape. "Have you looked at this?"

"No—yes, but only with care enough to make sure that the deed of gift was not among them. But the will—if it is not found, does not the law give everything to father's relatives? and will not that make this—this secret of mine public?" she asked, speaking with difficulty, as if the subject were almost too painful for discussion.

Espy started, and dropped the packet upon the floor; but recovering himself, stooped to pick it up, saying with determination:

"But we *will* find it; of course it must be here or somewhere about the house. Cheer up, Floy dear, and let us go to work."

They spent the greater part of three days at their task. Every paper was unfolded, shaken out, examined and re-examined, every nook and corner diligently ransacked, and thorough but unavailing search made for secret drawers, yet neither will nor deed of gift could be found.

At last they were forced to the conclusion that the deed of gift was irrecoverably lost; the will also, if it had ever existed, which seemed very doubtful.

"Ah, what success to-day?" asked the elder Mr. Alden, coming in upon them as they were slowly replacing the papers in the secretary, almost hoping, even against hope, to yet come upon the missing papers.

"None, sir," answered Epsy.

"What! no will? Surely you must have overlooked it. Mrs. Kemper you say, Floy, told you there was one—just such as Mr. Kemper had told me he purposed making—and he could have no motive for concealing it. Let me think; possibly he may have carried it on his person. Have you examined the pockets of—"

"No!" cried Espy, starting up with animation. "Floy—"

"Oh, I cannot!" she groaned, hiding her face.

"No, no, assuredly not; forgive me, darling," he whispered, bending over her; "but may I?"

She gave a silent assent, and he and his father left the room.

In a few moments they returned, Espy carrying a large-sized pocket-book, old and worn, which he placed in Floy's hands, saying, "This is all we found. It is for you to open and examine it."

She did so, her tears dropping over it all the time. It contained a little change and a few papers of no great importance—receipted bills, memoranda, etc.

"It is not here; he never made it," she said

huskily, pushing the book and its contents from her. "Ah, father, father, what has your neglect cost me!"

"Don't be so distressed, child; there is really no occasion," said Mr. Alden soothingly. "I don't know why, as I told Espy yesterday, you and he have taken so much trouble to hunt for the will, as, you being the only child, the law gives all to you in case your father died intestate, as it seems he did."

She lifted her white face, which she had hidden in her hands; she would not see Espy's imploring look.

"No, Mr. Alden, you mistake," she said; "I, lacking the will, am not the heir."

"Nonsense, my dear child! 'Tis you who are mistaken. Why, how could you doubt that you, his only child, inherit Mr. Kemper's property by natural right, unless he chose to will it, or part of it, to some one else?"

She seemed shaken with contending emotions; but controlling herself by a strong effort, and looking with steady, mournful gaze into the eyes of him whom she addressed, "I thought—I believed—oh, I never *doubted* till the hour that I became doubly orphaned—that I was his own child and—and hers!"

She paused for an instant, with her hands tightly clasped over her heart, then went on in lower and more tremulous tones. "But she—my mother—as I must call her still—she told me with her dying breath that—that I was theirs only by adoption."

Mr. Alden, who had been standing, staggered back and dropped into a chair, looking perfectly astounded.

"Who—who are you then?" he gasped at length.

" I—I do not know, except—"

" Never mind, Floy, my own little wife," whispered Espy, throwing a protecting arm about her and making her lean on him.

Then turning to his father, he stated the facts as succinctly as possible.

Mr. Alden listened with a grave and troubled air, and, when his son had finished, sat for some moments in silent cogitation.

"Well," he said at length, "this is a rather bad business ; and yet—perhaps not so bad as it looks. Floy, how many are in this secret—about your birth, I mean ?"

" Our three selves only," she answered.

" Good ! very good !" he said, rubbing his hands with a complacent smile. " Your sex is not famed for ability to keep secrets, but I'll trust you for this one."

She gave him a look of surprised inquiry.

" So long as you are believed to be Mr. Kemper's own child," he went on to explain, " no one will dispute your right to the property, and it's very considerable, Floy—worth taking some pains to secure."

Her dark eyes opened wide upon him in half-incredulous, indignant surprise, but he gave her no opportunity to speak.

" And it is yours of right, for, as we all know, Mr. Kemper intended it for you, and you will only be fulfilling his wishes in retaining possession, which, as the old saying has it," he added, with an unpleasant laugh, " is nine points of the law."

CHAPTER VII.

A WICKED SUGGESTION.

> " All your attempts
> Shall fall on me like brittle shafts on armor
> That break themselves, or like waves against a rock."
> MASSINGER.

UTTER amazement at so base a proposal kept the girl silent for an instant; then releasing herself from Espy's supporting arm, she stood erect before her tempter, her hands tightly clenched, a crimson tide rushing over the face so pale but a moment ago, the great dark eyes flashing with indignant anger, then filling with tears of deeply wounded feeling.

"Ah, I see; you were not serious. You could not believe me capable of such a crime. But it was a cruel jest," she said in a choking voice, and ending with a burst of almost hysterical weeping.

"Crime!" echoed Mr. Alden testily. "Girl, you don't know what you are talking about! How can it be a crime to take the property your father accumulated expressly for you?"

"I beg, sir, that the matter may be allowed to rest for the present," interposed Espy; "we have had a hard day's work, and Floy is not in a condition, either mentally or physically, to attend to business."

"Well, well, just as she pleases; there's no particular hurry, and I'd be the last one to want to distress her," returned Mr. Alden, and taking up his hat he stalked out of the room, evidently not overpleased In fact, his ire was roused not a little by the term Floy had applied to his proposition.

"Crime indeed!" he muttered to himself as he hurried down the garden path. "As if I—I could be thought capable of suggesting a crime!"

He hastened to his wife with his grievance.

"Oh, well, never mind the child; she's only a slip of a girl, and I dare say hardly knows what a crime is," Mrs. Alden answered soothingly. "But really, remembering how they doted on her and petted her, I never was more surprised at anything in my life than to hear that she wasn't their own."

"Nor I, Jane; and if she's going to be such a fool as to publish the thing and give up the property that she knows, and we all know, was intended for her, why—I'll withdraw my consent—"

"Oh, now, Nathan, don't say that!" hastily interrupted his wife, knowing that he was an obstinate man and prided himself on keeping his word. "You might come to wish you hadn't, for she's a nice girl, and we're all fond of her—you as well as the rest of us. There, now, I must go and see about supper," she added, making an excuse to leave him before he had had time to commit himself.

Worn out with grief, excitement, and over-exertion, Floy went to bed that night with a raging headache, and for the next two or three days was able to do little but lie on the sofa.

Espy was with her almost constantly, saving her as much as possible from every annoyance, and comforting her with his sympathy and love.

They were not days of mirth and gladness, but of much heaviness of heart, yet often looked back upon in after years with tender regret, a mournful sweetness lingering about their memory.

As by mutual consent both Floy and Espy avoided the subject of the missing papers and her future action in regard to the property. It frequently obtruded itself upon Floy's thoughts, but she refused to consider it for the time being; it must wait until she had strength for the struggle which she foresaw was before her if she would follow the dictates of an enlightened conscience.

Mr. Alden grew impatient.

"Espy," he said at length, "what is Floy going to do?"

"She has not told me, sir; the subject has not been mentioned between us."

"Then it's high time it was; I hope you'll talk to her about it to-day, and try to convince her of the reasonableness of the course I have recommended."

"I should rather not undertake it, sir. I am not at all sure that hers is not the right view of the matter."

"Come, now, don't be a fool, Espy!" returned his father angrily. "You'd be standing amazingly in your own light, if you mean to marry the girl; it's a fine property, and would give you just the start in life you need. Why, you might give up studying for a profession and devote yourself at once to your beloved art," he added, with an unpleasant laugh.

The young man flushed deeply. "I should despise myself, sir, if I could act from such motives," he said, forcing himself to speak quietly, though the hot blood coursed through his veins.

"Your father doesn't mean that he wants you to marry for money, or to do anything dishonest to get it," interposed Mrs. Alden. "All he asks is that you will persuade Floy not to throw away what we all know was meant for her."

"No, I'll take back that request," said the elder gentleman. "Leave her to me; that's all I ask."

"I shall not try to influence her one way or the other," said Espy. "But, father, be patient with her if she can't see things just as you do. She's almost heart-broken already, poor child!"

This conversation had taken place at the breakfast-table, and immediately on the conclusion of the meal Espy hastened to Floy to learn how she was in health, determined to save her from an encounter with his father until she felt quite equal to it.

He found her free from pain, calm and quiet in manner, though with an expression of deep sadness in her large dark eyes and about the lines of her mobile mouth. She was strangely changed from the careless, light-hearted creature of a week ago. Sorrow and bereavement had done the work of years, and the child of yesterday had become a self-poised, self-reliant woman.

She had spent some hours that morning in earnest thought, asking wisdom and strength from Him who has declared Himself in a peculiar sense the "Father of the fatherless," and in searching His Word for direction; and now her mind was fully made up.

Espy told her of his father's intended call, and asked if she would see him, adding, "Don't hesitate to decline, Floy. You can guess his errand."

"Yes," she said, sighing slightly, "and I cannot follow his wishes, because it would be doing violence to my conscience. But I will hear all he has to say. Ah," she added, tears filling her eyes, "it is hard to be compelled to do what vexes and angers those you love and would fain please rather than yourself! Espy, will you turn against me?"

"Never, never, my poor child! I will stand by you through everything."

The door opened, and the elder Mr. Alden came in.

"Ah, good-morning, my dear child," he said, taking Floy's hand. "Glad to see you about again! should have been here before, but Espy insisted that you were better let alone."

"Thank you," she said. "Please be seated."

He was not long in introducing the real object of his visit, but approached the subject with mcre caution than before. He spoke of Mr. Kemper's great fondness for her and his fatherly pride in her, and the determination he had been frequently heard to express, that if he could prevent it his darling should never know what it was to want for the comforts and even luxuries of life.

"Yes," murmured Floy, the tears stealing down her pale cheeks, "father loved me very dearly, and was always tenderly careful of me."

"And can you believe that he would want the property he accumulated to be enjoyed by some one else, and you left to struggle with poverty?" asked Mr. Alden.

"No; oh no, no!"

"Ah!" There was a world of meaning in the slight exclamation. It said, "So you are coming to your senses at last! you see now that I was right, and I'm delighted that such is the case."

"Do not mistake me, Mr. Alden," said the girl, sighing. "I am certain father would have preferred to leave me well provided for, but he may have finally concluded that it would be more just to leave his property to those who were related to him by ties of blood."

Emotion stopped her utterance; she had not yet learned to think and speak calmly of the fact that there was no natural tie between herself and those who had been as the dearest of parents to her.

"Nonsense!" was the angry exclamation that rose to Mr. Alden's lips; but checking himself, he said in a tone of mild expostulation, "I am sure, my dear child, you need not trouble yourself with any such fears. He made every cent of his money, and certainly had a perfect right to leave it as he pleased. And there is not the least doubt in my mind that you would be following out his wishes in retaining possession of it. Indeed I think it would be very wrong as well as foolish to do otherwise."

"Why wrong?"

"Because it would be disposing of his property as he would not have wished it to be disposed of."

"Ah, Mr. Alden, suppose you were his next of kin, would you not see this matter differently?"

"Well—possibly our own interests are very apt to blind us to the rights of others."

Floy smiled faintly, thinking how nearly akin to a man's own interest was that of his son.

"Yes," she said, "that is human nature; we are naturally selfish, I as well as others; so much so that if I knew the property was lawfully mine I should never think of giving it away."

"Then don't."

"Ah, it is not mine to give or to keep, but must go to the rightful heirs."

Mr. Alden bit his lips with vexation, rose and paced the room for some moments; then, having recovered control of himself, came and sat down by Floy.

"I know you want to do right," he said pleasantly, "and I have only to convince you that the course I wish you to take is right to induce you to take it."

"I cannot tell you how gladly I should do so," she answered.

At this moment Espy, who had taken no part in the conversation, though a deeply interested listener, was, much to his discontent, summoned away by a message from his mother.

Mr. Alden did most of the talking for the next hour, going over the old arguments again and again, but bringing forward little that was new except that Mr. and Mrs. Kemper, in adopting her as their own child, had given her all the rights of a child, and therefore, will or no will, she was the proper heir.

"Is that according to the law of the land?" she asked, a gleam of hope shining in her eyes.

He evaded the question. "Human laws are very faulty; we need not always be bound by them."

"No, not when they come in collision with the higher law of God; but that is not the case in this instance."

After a moment's thought and stroking of his

beard, he began on another tack, speaking of Espy and his plans, and dwelling at considerable length upon the great advantage it would be to the young man if his wife had sufficient means to give him a start in life.

Floy heard him to the end in unbroken silence, her hands tightly clasped in her lap, a look of pain more than once crossing her features, while the color came and went on her cheek.

He seemed to have finished, but she neither moved nor spoke.

"Well," he said, rising and taking up his hat from the table where he had placed it on entering, "I'll leave you to think it all over. Good-morning!"

"Stay!" she said, suddenly rising and standing before him, her hands still clasped, a look of anguish in her eyes as she lifted them to his, her voice tremulous with emotion, not from any faltering of purpose. "I need no further time for deliberation. I have thought and prayed over this matter, and my duty has been made very clear to me. Right and justice must be done, at whatever cost to me or to—"

The last word was lost in a bitter, choking sob.

Mr. Alden turned abruptly on his heel and left the house.

CHAPTER VIII.

MRS. ALDEN AN ABETTOR.

"A settled virtue
Makes itself a judge: and satisfied within,
Smiles at that common enemy, the world."—DRYDEN.

"WHAT is it, Nathan?"

Mrs. Alden had come upon her husband pacing the front porch of their dwelling with angry strides.

"That girl!" he said between his shut teeth. "I wash my hands of her and her affairs, and Espy shall never marry her with my consent, mark that, Jane!" and he brought down his clenched fist with emphasis upon the open palm of the other hand.

His wife looked disturbed, but after a moment's thought said cheerfully, "She'll come round yet, Nathan, and you don't mean that to stand if she does?"

"No, of course not; but she isn't going to come round; she hasn't the sense to understand and appreciate an argument, and has somehow got her head full of Quixotic notions. I suppose she thinks she'll make a grand heroine of herself by giving up everything to Kemper's relations, and that they'll generously hand back a share of it, or maybe the whole; but she'll find out when it's too late that she's made a wonderful mistake."

Mrs. Alden had her own opinion regarding Floy's

sense, but was far too wise to contradict her husband.

"I haven't lived with him forty years for nothing," she sometimes said. "I've found out that the only way to manage him is to seem to give in to all his notions. So I never cross him, and I generally contrive in the end to have things pretty much as I want them."

Seeing she made no reply to his remark, Mr. Alden went on to give her a detailed account of his interview with Floy, winding up with, "There, now, what do you think of that?"

"Poor young thing!" sighed his wife, "it's really dreadful to think what she's gone through in the last two weeks, and perhaps she couldn't quite put her mind on what you were saying so as to take it all in. Give her a little time; she may come around yet to your way of thinking. I must go and see about dinner now."

"Yes," he answered absently. "Suppose you go over after dinner; coaxing will move a woman sometimes when argument won't."

"I'll try," she said as she hurried away. It was what she had intended, though she had not thought it best to say so.

Mr. Alden's departure had left Floy alone, for Espy had not yet returned. Sinking down upon the sofa, she wept convulsively for some minutes. Presently she grew calmer, and, wiping away her tears, rose and went to her father's writing-desk.

Seating herself before it, she selected a sheet of note-paper, took up a pen, and was in the act of dipping it in the ink, when Susan, the maid of all work, put her head in at the door, saying, "Mr. Crosby's in the parlor, Miss Floy, asking to see you."

"Thank you very much for coming," Floy said when she had shaken hands with her visitor. "I was just about to write a note asking you to call."

"I shall be glad if I can be of service to you," he said. "I should have called sooner, but returned only last night from a pleasure-trip, the first I have taken in years. Now what can I do for you?"

Mr. Crosby, the first lawyer in the place, had been Mr. Kemper's legal adviser.

At first Floy seemed unable to speak. She rose, and motioning Mr. Crosby to follow her, led the way to the room she had just left. They were closeted together there for an hour, in which Mr. Crosby learned the whole story of Mrs. Kemper's death-bed revelations, and the unsuccessful search for the deed of gift and the will.

"I am extremely sorry to hear all this," he said "I was pretty certain there was no will, because Mr. Kemper had spoken to me about drawing one up for him, telling me that he intended leaving the bulk of his property to his wife and daughter, but not going sufficiently into particulars to enable me to write out the instrument without further instructions. These he delayed giving me from time to time, being always so much occupied with his business. If you were, as I always believed till now, his own child, the omission would make little or no difference; but as it is, it leaves you quite unprovided for. If I had known the truth I should have urged him strongly to attend to the matter without delay. It's a bad business, a very bad business for you,

Miss Floy! I feel for you from the bottom of my heart, and I would do anything in the world I could to help you."

"I believe it, Mr. Crosby," she said with emotion, "and if you will undertake—"

"To communicate with the heirs at law? Certainly; and I shall try to induce them to allow your claim to a share in the property you have so generously resigned to them—"

"Not generously, Mr. Crosby," she interrupted, "only justly."

"Ah, well, if you will have it so; but Miss Floy, you might have kept the secret revealed by your mother locked up in your own breast, and retained the property without the least danger of interference from any one. Did you know that?"

She gave a silent assent.

"And even leaving the inheritance of the estate out of the question, you would have been glad to keep the secret?"

"Yes; oh, yes!" she said, covering her face with her hands, while the tears trickled between her fingers.

He looked at her with undisguised admiration.

"You are a noble girl!" he exclaimed; and rising, paced the floor to and fro.

"Oh!" he cried, "the mischief that simple neglect will do! It has been the ruin of thousands, and through it men have, in multitudes of instances, frustrated their own most cherished plans and purposes. Mr. Kemper schemed and toiled to provide for the old age of himself and wife, and that he might have wealth to bestow upon you, the darling of his heart;

and now, through his own omission, it will pass to others, one or two of whom, I happen to know, are spendthrifts, who will probably speedily waste their shares in riotous living. It's a thousand pities! If we could but bring proof of your formal adoption, making you his legal heir—"

"There is none," she sighed, "and perhaps they are very needy—those heirs—and may do better with this than you expect, Mr. Crosby. We will not blame poor dear father. How ungrateful it would be in me to do so after all that he and mother did for me—after all the love and care they bestowed on me for so many years! I had not the slightest claim on them, yet they clothed, fed, educated me—made my childhood and youth so bright and happy. Oh, never did poor little waif fall into hands so kind and tender!"

"Your sentiments do you honor, Miss Floy," said Mr. Crosby, "and now I will return to my office and attend to this matter at once. I shall write the heirs, letting them know how entirely they are indebted to you for this accession of property, and urge upon them the justice of allowing you a share in it."

He shook hands with her, said a few encouraging, hopeful words, and departed.

"Glad he's gone at last," said Susan, putting her head in at the door again. "Thought he never would go, and your dinner is drying up over the fire till 'tain't hardly fit to eat. Come, Miss Floy, I'll have it on the table by the time you can get out to the dining-room."

Floy brought little appetite to her meal, and ate mechanically, scarcely knowing what the viands were.

She had just risen from the table when Mrs. Alden came in. Floy flushed slightly on seeing her. She knew that Mr. Alden had gone away very angry, and was doubtful how far his wife would be in sympathy with him.

But the greeting of the latter was kind and motherly as usual.

"I'm so glad the poor head is better again," she said, kissing the girl affectionately. " You must forgive me for calling Espy away this morning. I had to get him to drive out to the country for butter and eggs, for there were none to be had in town, and I'd nobody else to send. He hasn't got back yet, or you may be sure he'd have been in again."

Talking on, with hardly a pause for a reply, Mrs. Alden gradually approached the subject of the morning's conversation between her husband and Floy.

"I honor you for your intentions, my dear," she said. "I know they are altogether good and right, but you're very young and inexperienced, and I think have a morbid conscientiousness that blinds you to your own interests, and, if you'll allow me to say it, to Espy's too, because if you're going to be man and wife you can't have separate interests."

"Dear Mrs. Alden," said Floy, with a patient sigh, "you cannot surely think it is ever right to do evil that good may come, or that ill-gotten wealth will be of real benefit to its possessor?"

"No, child, certainly not," she answered with some annoyance, "but those questions don't apply in this case. You needn't be afraid that anything my husband does or advises could be wrong, because he's too good a man."

It probably did not occur to the loyal wife that she was reversing the Bible test—judging of the fruit by the tree, instead of the tree by its fruit.

"I do not think he would do or advise anything that he thought wrong," returned Floy gently; "but you know each of us must act according to his or her own conscience, and mine absolutely refuses to see this matter as Mr. Alden does."

"Well, I mostly let him judge for me," said Mrs. Alden. "I find it's the only way to have peace, and I can't live in a constant broil; not that he's particularly ill-natured, but he naturally thinks he ought to be master in his own house. Another thing, Floy: if he once sets his foot down there's no getting him to lift it again, and he vows that if you persist in giving up this property Espy shall never marry you with his consent. So, you see, if you can't be persuaded there'll be endless trouble for us all."

Floy's cheek crimsoned and her eye flashed, while the pretty head was thrown haughtily back as she drew herself up with an air of wounded pride.

"It was your son who sought me, Mrs. Alden, not I him; nor shall I ever thrust myself into a family where I am not wanted and should be made an element of discord."

Mrs. Alden was thoroughly dismayed.

"My dear child," she hastened to say, "I did not mean to hurt your feelings, and I can't bear the thought of losing you. But Espy will never give you up; he'd break with his father and all of us first, and—"

"He can't marry me against my will," interrupted Floy; "so pray dismiss all anxiety on that score. I would no more rob you and Mr. Alden of your son than—than I would steal the inheritance of the heirs at law of this property."

"Oh, Floy, Floy, to make you break with Espy is the very last thing I intended; don't do it; he'd never forgive me; but oh! if I only could persuade you to keep this secret of your birth and—"

"It is already too late," answered the girl in a low, quiet tone, "the deed is done."

CHAPTER IX.

WHAT ESPY SAID ABOUT IT.

> "Dost thou deem
> It such an easy task from the fond breast
> To root affection out?"—SOUTHEY.

"WHAT shall I do? what *shall* I do?" Mrs. Alden asked herself again and again as, in great perturbation of spirit, she awaited Espy's return. "How angry and distressed he'll be, poor boy!"

She was at a loss to determine whether it would be best to break the news to him herself, or to let him hear it first from Floy or his father.

But circumstances decided for her. As she sat at the window watching the lengthening shadows as the sun drew near his setting, and saying to herself that Espy was very late—it was nearly tea-time, and she almost began to fear that he had met with some accident—she heard the gate swing, and turning her head saw him coming up the gravel walk that led from it to the house.

He moved with rapid strides, and there was an angry flush on his cheek, an indignant light in his eye, which told her at once that he had already been made aware of the unfortunate turn affairs had taken.

In a moment more he stood before her with folded arms, firmly-set mouth, and stern eyes.

"Espy, my son! Oh, I am so sorry!"

"Yes, mother," he said, "my father and I have had a quarrel; he called me into his office as I passed, and ordered me to give up all thoughts of Floy—my little Floy that I've loved from my very infancy!"

"And what did you say, Espy?" she asked tremulously, feeling as if the very unreasonableness and tyranny of the command must have of itself almost deprived him of the power of speech.

"Say, mother? that he might as well ask me to shoot myself through the heart, and that I'd never give her up; I'd die first."

"But—but, Espy, what—what if she gives you up?" gasped his mother, fairly frightened by his vehemence.

He staggered back as if struck by a heavy blow, while a deathly pallor overspread his face for an instant.

"But she will not!" he said hoarsely; "she has pledged herself to me, and she'll never prove false to her word."

"But she is very proud, Espy—too proud, I think, to come into a family where she's not wanted; and she's a good girl, and will see that it's your duty to obey your father."

He dropped into a chair, and for a moment seemed lost in thought; then with a sigh, "My father may have a right to control me even in this while I am a minor; but, as you know, mother, in six months I shall have reached my majority, and then I'll be my own master, and shall consider that in a matter which will affect my happiness so much more nearly than his, and probably for my whole life, I have a right to follow my own wishes. Besides, there is Floy's happiness to be taken into account. She says she loves me; we've pledged ourselves to each other, my father consenting to it at the time—and could he ask me to play so base a part as to forsake the dear girl merely because she has become poor and friendless? I think even he would despise me if I could be guilty of such meanness; and most assuredly I should despise myself!"

He had risen to his feet with the last sentence, and now, as he stood erect before her, with kindling eye and glowing cheek, he looked so noble and manly that his mother's heart swelled with pride in her son.

"No, you'll never do anything mean or dishonorable, Espy," she said, smiling up at him.

Then growing suddenly grave, and an anxious, troubled look stealing over her face at the recollection of her husband's anger, which she knew must have waxed hot at his son's resistance to his demand: "But there'll be no peace between your father and you if you go against his will; so if Floy chooses to break the engagement herself, you needn't feel called upon to try to hold her to it."

"Mother," he said, "you are keeping something back; tell me all. You have spoken to her—told her what father says?"

His eyes were gazing steadily into hers, and there was a mingling of grief and suppressed wrath that made her fear to answer him. She hesitated, then said hastily:

"You'd better go to her. She can tell you what she likes."

He turned without a word, caught up his hat, and went.

CHAPTER X.

FLOY'S RESOLVE.

"A beam of comfort, like the moon through clouds,
Gilds the black horror, and directs my way."

PRIDE—her woman's pride—had sustained Floy in the late interview with Mrs. Alden, and enabled her to resign Espy with apparent indifference; but when his mother had gone, leaving her alone, a sudden sense of utter desolation came over the girl, and hastening to her own room she locked her door, and throwing herself on the bed, buried her face in its pillows, while bitter, bursting sobs shook her whole frame.

"Was ever sorrow like unto my sorrow?" was the cry of the poor aching heart. "Have I not seen the grave close over my more than parents, earthly possessions swept away, and now resigned my love—all, all that was left me!"

The storm of grief was violent but brief. She seemed to hear again the prayer offered for her by the aged saint standing at her side in that other hour when heart and flesh were failing, and with passionate earnestness went up the cry, "Lord, my heart is overwhelmed; lead me to the Rock that is higher than I!"

Ah, all was not lost! Himself He had left her still, and with the thought she grew strong to do and endure.

She was endowed by nature with vigor of body and mind, and much firmness and decision of character. Her sobs were stilled, her tears ceased to flow, while with determined resolve she forced her thoughts to leave the past and busy themselves with plans for the future.

A new hope, a new desire had been gradually growing in her mind for the past few days. Her mother—her own mother, who had so loved her in her infancy—was there not a possibility that diligent, persevering search might be rewarded by success in finding her?

Perhaps she was still poor and ill—feeble in health—and if so, oh, how gladly would her daughter toil to supply her needs! how lavish filial love and tenderness upon her—the poor weary one who had hungered for them so long!

How she was to earn a support for herself alone Floy did not know, but hope was strong within her young breast, and she felt that with such an incentive to exertion she could not fail.

"Yes, she does live, and I shall find her—my poor, sorely-tried, precious mother!" she caught herself saying half aloud.

There was a gentle rap on her door at that moment, and a sweet-toned voice asked, "Shall I come in, Miss Floy? If you would rather see me at another time, dear, I'll go away and come again."

Floy sprang to the door and opened it, admitting a little, plainly-dressed woman with a sweet face framed in with silvery hair. A pair of mild blue eyes looked pityingly into the tear-stained, sorrowful face of the young mourner, and hastily depositing upon a chair a large package which she carried, the little woman held out her arms.

Floy threw herself into them, hid her face on the kindly bosom, and burst into a fit of passionate weeping.

Her friend soothed her with silent caresses till she grew calmer, then spoke a few tender, sympathizing words.

"You feel for me, dear Auntie Wells," sobbed Floy, "and yet you do not know nearly all that has come upon me. I have one Friend who does; but oh! our hearts crave human sympathy, and counsel too, when we are young and inexperienced."

"Tell me all, dear child, if you will; I have no great store of worldly wisdom, only such as years can give, but I have seen many more of them than you, and my sympathy you shall certainly have."

"I think you must have just the kind of wisdom I want, because you have gone through just such a lonely, struggling life as seems to be before me," Floy said, calming herself and wiping away her tears.

"A lonely, struggling life for you, child!" Miss Wells exclaimed in an incredulous tone as she passed her hand caressingly over the pretty head resting on her shoulder. "Struggling! with the fortune your father has left you? lonely! with Espy still yours? How can it be?"

"The fortune is not mine, and Espy!—I have— have given him up!"

The first words were spoken low and hurriedly, and the last came from the white lips in a sharp cry of agony.

Utter astonishment dominated for the moment every other feeling in Miss Wells's breast; then infinite pity and tenderness took its place, and gathering the girl to her heart, she wept over her as her own mother might, asking no questions, feeling no curiosity, every other emotion lost in the boundless compassion which would have done or suffered almost everything to restore its object to happiness.

Hannah Wells, now far on the shady side of fifty, a woman with a large, loving heart, had found few upon whom to lavish the wealth of her affection, and upon Floy she had poured it out without stint.

For many years she had maintained herself by her needle, first as seamstress, then as dressmaker; and employed by Mrs. Kemper in both capacities ever since the coming of the latter to Cranley, had often made her home in that house for weeks and months together, always treated with the kindly consideration accorded to a welcome guest or one of the family; for, spite of her poverty, Miss Wells was unmistakably a lady.

She was a woman, too, of excellent common-sense, sterling integrity, and deep piety, evinced by a life of blameless purity, a thoroughly consistent walk and conversation.

She was now enjoying a moderate degree of prosperity, having a little home of her own and something laid by for a rainy day.

She kept a number of apprentices now, who usually carried home the finished work, but loving Floy so dearly, she had herself brought home the poor child's mourning.

The love and caresses of this old and tried friend

were as balm to the sorely-wounded heart. Floy presently grew calmer, and poured out her whole story, including her half-formed plans for the future, seeking advice in regard to the latter.

Miss Wells entered into them with deep interest, highly approving Floy's course in regard to the property, and of her resolve first to search for her long-lost mother, then to seek employment by which to earn a living for herself and for her mother if found.

"Don't be afraid to try it, dear," Hannah said; "try it with determination to let no difficulty conquer you, yet trusting in the Lord, and you will succeed. It is better to trust in the Lord than to put confidence in man. Yes, dear, I've tried it, and proved it in my own experience. Like you I was left an orphan early in life, and without means. I had relations who gave me a home, enough to eat, and decent clothes, and didn't seem to grudge it either ; but I saw that they had plenty of other uses for their money, and I couldn't bear to have them do without anything in order to provide for me ; so I resolved to strike out bravely for myself, trusting only in the Lord, and from that day to this He's taken care of me : and its so sweet, *so* sweet to take everything as a gift right from His dear hand."

CHAPTER XI.

LOVE AND PRIDE.

> "Had we never loved so kindly,
> Had we never loved so blindly,
> Never met or never parted,
> We had ne'er been broken-hearted. —BURNS.

As the dressmaker left, Espy came in and went direct to the parlor, where Floy sat in an attitude of deep dejection, her elbow on the arm of the sofa, her cheek resting on her hand.

He sprang to her side, and, as she started and half rose from her seat, caught both hands in his.

"Floy, Floy, what have they been doing? What have they been saying to you? Never mind it, darling, nothing shall ever come between us."

The eyes that met his were full of anguish; the lips moved, but no sound came from them.

He threw his arms about her as if to shield her from harm. "Floy, dear, don't mind it. I can't bear to see you look so. Isn't my love enough to make you happy? Ah, if you only knew *how* I love you, dearest!"

"But—oh, Espy, I've given you up! I've no right now to your love!"

"Given me up! Do you not love me, Floy?" His voice grew hoarse with emotion.

"You are all I've left—all."

He bent his ear to catch the low-breathed words,

His heart gave a joyous bound, and he drew her closer to him ; but she struggled to release herself.

"Espy, you are free. I have given you up."

"I will not accept my freedom, nor give you yours, my own little wife—I may call you that, because we are pledged to each other, and it's almost the same : we belong to each other quite as much as if we were already married."

She shook her head with sad determination. "Your father refuses his consent, and—I—I cannot go into a family that is not willing to receive me."

"My father had no right to withdraw the consent already given !" he exclaimed hotly.

"That was given to your union with the rich Miss Kemper, not with a poor and nameless waif," she returned, with a bitter smile.

"Ah ! but I pledged myself to neither the wealth nor the name, but to the dear girl who has not changed unless to grow dearer and lovelier still."

"But I think children are bound to respect the wishes, and certainly the commands, of their parents."

"I'm not a child !" he cried, with a mixture of anger and pride. "I shall be my own master in a few months ; then I shall not consider his consent absolutely necessary, and in the mean time I shall not break my engagement to you."

"No, Espy, but I release you."

"I will not be released !" he cried, with increasing anger, "nor will I release you !"

"You will surely not be so ungenerous as to hold me to it against my will ?" she said coldly, averting her face and moving farther from him.

A sudden suspicion flashed upon him, a pang of jealous rage stabbed him to the heart, and he grew white and rigid.

"You love another; you have played me false, and are glad of an excuse to get rid of me!" he said in cutting tones.

She made no reply, but drew herself up proudly, yet kept her face turned from him.

"Farewell, then, false girl; you are free!" he cried, rushing madly from the room.

Floy looked after him, with a dreary smile more pitiful than tears.

"Oh, Espy, Espy! must we part like this?" she sighed inwardly, putting her hand to her head.

"Miss Floy, are you sick? got a headache?" queried Susan, coming in. "What can I do for ye?"

"Nothing, thank you, Susan; I'll be better soon."

"Try a cup o' tea; it'll do ye good. I heard Mr. Espy go 'way, and I thought I'd just come and tell you that supper's ready."

Something in Susan's tones jarred upon Floy's sensitive nerves, and, with a sort of dull comprehension that the girl's rising suspicions must be lulled to rest, she rose, went to the table, and forced herself to drink a cup of tea and swallow a few mouthfuls of food.

The blow dealt her by Espy's parting words began to lose its stunning effects, and to be succeeded by a feverish impulse to fly from him and from these scenes of former happiness, of present sorrow and loss. She left the table with the sudden resolve that she would set out that very night on her intended journey in search of her long-lost mother.

Fortunately Mr. Crosby, thinking of some new question to ask, called at the door just as she was passing through the hall on her way upstairs.

"Have you any idea where to go, Miss Floy?" he asked, when she had told him of her intention to depart immediately.

"Yes," she said, "I remember having heard what route father and mother took in coming out West, and she told me the name of the station where they met my own mother and obtained possession of me; I mean to go directly there and make inquiries."

"You will find things greatly changed since then," he remarked, meditatively stroking his beard. "Let me see: how many years?"

"Nearly sixteen."

"Ah, yes! and these Western places grow so fast! The lonely little station may have become a city, and you are very young and—comely," he added, with a look of kindly concern. "My child, I hardly like to see you start on this expedition alone, and yet I have no authority to forbid it. Do you think you can take care of yourself?"

"No, sir, I cannot," she answered, low and tremulously, "but the Father of the fatherless will not leave me alone, and I am not afraid."

A train going in the desired direction passed through Cranley at midnight; it was the one Floy must take. Mr. Crosby engaged to procure a ticket for her, and to see her and her luggage safely on board.

Also he advised her of the best mode of procedure on arriving at Clearfield, exacting a promise that she would write to him, giving an account of the progress made, and seeking further counsel if needed, while on his part he engaged to keep her informed of his movements in regard to the settlement of the estate.

"And now," he said, rising to go, " is there not some lady friend whom I can call upon to come and assist you in your packing or other necessary preparations for this sudden flitting ?'

"Oh, yes, thank you ! Miss Wells ! I know she would come ; and if you please, Mr. Crosby, will you tell her it would be the very greatest comfort to me ?"

" I will, with pleasure, and I will be here in time to take you to the train."

CHAPTER XII.

"LOST ! LOST ! LOST !"

Espy did not go home on leaving Floy; he was in no mood for meeting his father, against whom fierce anger was swelling in his breast. The lad's ire was not easily roused, but when once kindled it was apt to blaze with fury until it had burnt itself out.

At this moment he felt like one whose hand was against every man, and every man's hand against him; for had not Floy even, his own darling Floy, cast him off and given her love to some one else? Oh, the very thought was intolerable pain! he had loved her so long and so dearly, and never better than now; and yet he was angry with her, more angry than words could express; angry with himself, too, that he could not cast her out of his heart.

Full of these violent and contending emotions, he hurried onward and still onward, heedless whither his steps were tending, taking no note of time or space or of the gathering darkness, till suddenly he felt his strength failing, and in utter weariness cast himself down on the grass by the roadside.

He glanced about him. Where was he? He could not tell; but miles away from Cranley, for there were no familiar landmarks.

"Lost!" he said aloud, with a bitter laugh, "actually lost here in my own neighborhood; a good joke truly. Well, I'll find myself fast enough by daylight. And what matter if I didn't, now that Floy has given me up?" And he dropped his head into his hands with a groan.

The sound of approaching wheels aroused him.

"Why, hallo! can that be you, Alden?" cried a familiar voice.

"Yes," Espy said, getting up and going to the side of the gig. "How are you, Bob?"

The two had been schoolmates, and Robert Holt, whose home was near at hand, soon persuaded Espy to accompany him thither to spend the night.

Ill-used as Espy considered himself, and unhappy as he certainly was, he found, when presently seated before a well-spread board, in company with a lively party of young people, that he was able to partake of the tempting viands with a good deal of appetite. Coffee, muffins, and fried chicken did much to relieve his fatigue and raise his spirits, and the evening passed quite agreeably, enlivened by conversation and music.

It was late when at last the young people separated for the night, Holt taking Espy with him to his own room.

"Hark! there's the twelve o'clock train; I'd no idea it was so late," said Holt as he closed the door and set down the lamp.

Espy stepped hastily to the window, just in time to see the train sweep by with its gleaming lights, the outline of each car barely visible in the darkness. Why did it make him think of Floy? He had no suspicion that it was bearing her away from him; yet so it was.

Thoughts of her in all her grief and desolation disturbed his rest. He woke often, and when he slept it was to dream of her in sore distress, and turning her large, lustrous eyes upon him sadly, beseechingly, and anon stretching out her arms as if imploring him to come to her relief.

Morning found him full of remorse for the harsh words he had spoken to her, and so eager to make amends that he could not be persuaded to remain for breakfast, but, leaving his adieus to the ladies with Robert, set off for Cranley before the sun was up.

He reached the town in season for the early home breakfast; but feeling that he could not wait another moment to make his peace with Floy, turned in at her gate first.

Glancing up at the house, it struck him as strange that every door and blind was tightly closed.

He had never known Floy to lie so late when in health, and a pang shot through his heart at the thought that she must be ill.

He rang the bell gently, fearing to disturb her; then, as no one came to answer it, a little louder.

Still no answer, not a sound within the dwelling; he could hear his own heart beat as he stood waiting and listening for coming footsteps that came not.

He grew frightened; he must gain admittance, must learn what was wrong. Once more he seized the bell-pull, jerked it violently several times, till he could distinctly hear its clang reverberating through the silent hall.

Still no response.

He hurried round to the side door, knocked loudly there, then on to the kitchen.

Sti.l no sign of life.

He made a circuit of the house, glancing up and down in careful scrutiny of each door and window, till perfectly sure that every one was closely shut.

"What can it mean?" he asked himself half aloud, turning deathly pale and trembling like an aspen leaf.

"Oh, Floy, Floy, I would give my right hand never to have spoken those cruel words! inhuman wretch that I was!"

Waiting a moment to recover himself, he then hastened home. His father had eaten his breakfast and gone to his office; his mother still lingered over the table.

"Oh, Espy," she said as he came in, "I'm glad to see you. I've been keeping the coffee hot; beefsteak too; and Rachel shall bake some fresh cakes. Come and sit down. How dreadfully pale you look! You've had too long a walk on an empty stomach."

He seemed scarcely to hear her; but leaning his back against the wall as if for support, "Mother," he said hoarsely, "what has become of her? Where is she?"

"Who?" she asked in surprise.

He simply pointed through the window in the direction of the next house.

She looked out. "Well, I declare! they're not up yet! I never knew them to lie abed till this hour before."

"They're not there; nobody's there unless—" he gasped and shuddered, a new and terrible thought striking him.

"Unless what?"

"Burglars—murderers—such things have been; we—we must break open the door or window—"

His mother's face suddenly reflected the paleness and agitation of his.

But Mr. Alden came hurrying in. "The house next door is all shut up!" he exclaimed pantingly. "Oh, Espy, so there you are! Come, come, don't look so terribly frightened! I met Crosby, and he tells me Floy has left town—went off in the midnight train, nobody knows where, after, like a fool, telling him the whole story I so wanted her, for her own good, to keep to herself. And he's to have the settling of everything; so there, we're done with her!"

His son's countenance had undergone several changes while he was speaking—terror, despair, relief, indignation, swept over it by turns.

"Done with her!" he repeated, drawing himself up to his full height and gazing at his father with flashing eyes; "done with her! No, sir, not *I*, if I can ever find her again and persuade her to be friends with me once more!"

CHAPTER XIII.

FLOY'S QUEST.

"Hope, of all passions, most befriends us here ;
Passions of prouder name befriend us less."—YOUNG.

VERY lonely and desolate felt poor Floy as the train sped onward, bearing her every moment farther away from childhood's home and friends out into the wide, wide, unknown world.

What sad, unforeseen changes the past few days had wrought in her young life! What a little while since she had been moving thus swiftly toward her home, instead of away from it, and under loving, protecting care ; whereas now she was utterly alone so far as earthly companionship was concerned !

Alone and screened from human eyes behind the closely-drawn curtains of her berth, she poured out her tears and prayers to her one ever-living, ever-present Friend.

"Do not fear, my poor dear child! do not fear to trust Him!" Miss Wells had said in parting. "He will help you and raise up friends for you wherever you go."

The words dwelt in the girl's mind with soothing, comforting power. She tried to cast her care on Him, and presently her fears (for she could not forget the dreadful accident of her last journey), her griefs, her losses and perplexities, were forgotten in sleep.

It was late in the afternoon of the next day that she reached Clearfield, no longer a little country station in the depths of a forest, but a flourishing town numbering several thousands of inhabitants.

She had several times heard a description of the place from both Mr. and Mrs. Kemper, but without any allusion to the episode which had fixed it so firmly in their memories. She glanced eagerly about on stepping from the cars, but failed to recognize a single feature of the scene. The shanty inn had long since disappeared; the old dingy depot had been replaced by a new and larger one, affording much better accommodation to the travelling public; and dwelling-houses, fields, and gardens now occupied the space then covered by the wild growth of the forest.

Floy had inquired of the last conductor on the train the name of the best hotel in the town, and an omnibus speedily carried her thither.

She asked for a room, and while waiting stepped into the public parlor and, completely overcome with fatigue, dropped into an easy chair, laid her head back, and closed her eyes.

A kind voice spoke close at her side, the speaker, a motherly old lady glancing pityingly at the pale, sad face and deep mourning dress.

"You are ill, my poor child, and seem to be quite alone. What can I do for you?"

Floy opened her eyes languidly.

"Nothing, thank you; I think I am not ill, only very weary. They will show me to a room presently, and then I can lie down and rest."

"A cup of hot tea, Nelson," said the old lady,

turning to a servant who had just entered, " and have a room—the one next to mine—made ready immediately for this young lady."

This old lady, as Floy soon learned, was the mother of Mr. Bond, the proprietor of the hotel. She proved a most kind and helpful friend to our heroine, listening with great sympathy and interest to the sad story which the young girl, won by her motherly manner, presently told her without reserve, except in the matter of the loss of the will and the troubles growing out of it; then assisting her with advice and needed co-operation in her self-appointed task.

There were two weekly papers published in the town. In the next issue of each of these an advertisement was inserted, giving a brief statement of the facts, with an offer of reward for any certain information in regard to the missing woman or any of those who had seen her and heard her story. At the same time private inquiries were set on foot, and the search prosecuted in every way with the utmost activity and perseverance.

CHAPTER XIV.

A RIFT IN THE CLOUD.

"And then that hope, that fairy hope,
 Oh ! she awaked such happy dreams,
And gave my soul such tempting scope,
 For all its dearest, fondest schemes !"—MOORE.

FOR more than a month Floy tarried at Clearfield, diligently pursuing her investigations, yet without gaining the faintest clue to the fate of her whom she so ardently desired to find.

The proprietors of the shanty inn had removed farther west years ago, but to what particular point none could tell ; the two switchmen had gone into the army early in the civil war and were probably among the slain, and the telegraph operator, it was conjectured, had met the same fate.

Floy of course knew nothing of the Heywoods ; but they too had left the vicinity so long ago that no one who heard of her through the advertisements or otherwise thought of connecting them with the object of her search.

At length she was forced to give it up in despair. She had spent a good deal in advertising, and her means were nearly exhausted. The heirs, as Mr. Crosby had duly informed her, had refused to allow her any share in Mr. Kemper's estate, and five hundred dollars which he had deposited in a bank in her name was all her inheritance.

She must now do something for her own support. Her education qualified her for teaching, but finding no opening for that, while one presented itself for the learning of dress-making, for which she possessed both taste and talent, she decided to avail herself of it.

Her plan was to go to Chicago and apprentice herself to one of the most fashionable mantua-makers there.

Miss Wells would have been rejoiced to take Floy under her wing, but the girl felt an unconquerable repugnance to beginning her new career in Cranley, the scene of her former prosperity, and where she could not hope to avoid occasionally meeting with the Aldens.

In fact, her sensitive dread of such encounters led to the resolve not to return thither at all, but to go directly to the city and begin the new life at once, such a place as she desired having been already secured for her through some of her Clearfield friends.

She had formed a strong attachment for Mrs. Bond, which was fully reciprocated. They could not part without pain, yet cheered each other with the hope of meeting again at no very distant day, as Floy thought of returning to Clearfield to set up business on her own account when once she should be prepared for that.

"Don't despair, dear child; brighter days will come; something tells me you will find your mother yet," the old lady said in bidding her good-by.

As the train sped on its way through the busy streets of the town, over the prairies dotted here and there with neat farm-houses, and anon plunged into forests gay with the rich coloring of the Frost King's pencil, Floy set herself resolutely to put aside thoughts of her losses, disappointments, anxieties, and perplexities, and to fix them upon the blessings that were still left her.

Gay and light-hearted she could not be, but hope kindled anew within her as she thought on Mrs. Bond's last words. Ah, she would not despair! her long-lost mother, and Espy too, would yet be restored.

His words had deeply wounded her, but surely the love which had been given her from their very infancy could not be so suddenly withdrawn.

"We are moving very slowly; something must be wrong. Don't you think so, miss?" queried a woman in the next seat, turning suddenly around upon Floy.

The words startled our heroine from her reverie, sending a sharp pang of grief and terror through her heart as they vividly recalled the horrors of the accident which had wrought her such woe. She had been hardly conscious of the fact, but certainly the train had gradually slackened speed for the last ten minutes or more; and now it stood still.

"What is wrong? why do we stop here where there is no station?" she asked of the conductor, who was passing the car window.

"Don't be alarmed," he said; "the boiler has sprung a leak, and we'll have to stand here a while till they can get another engine sent down from Clearfield."

"Dear, dear!" fretted a thoughtless girl, "we shall be behind time all along the route now, miss our connections, and have no end of trouble."

But Floy's heart swelled with gratitude that things were no worse.

They had two long hours of waiting ere the train was again in motion, for the spot where it had halted was several miles from the nearest town, to which a messenger must be sent on foot to telegraph back to Clearfield for another engine ; and when at last that arrived it had to propel the cars from behind, and the progress made was much slower than by the ordinary mode.

Many of the passengers ventured to relieve the tedium of the detention by strolling about the prairie in the near vicinity of their train, and for the greater part of the time the car in which Floy sat was nearly deserted.

Her attention was presently attracted by the fretting of a little child.

"Mother, I'm hungry ; gi' me a cake."

"Now do be quiet, Sammy ; you know I hain't none for you," returned the parent, "so what's the use o' teasin'? I'd give it to you in a minute if I had it."

By Mrs. Bond's thoughtful kindness Floy had been supplied with a bountiful lunch. She was very glad of that now, and opening her basket, she invited mother and child to partake with her.

"Thank you, miss," said the former, a decent-looking countrywoman. "Sammy'll be very glad of a bit of bread if you've got it to spare. I'd have brought a lunch along, but expected to be at my sister's afore this, and it didn't seem worth while."

"I have abundance for all three of us," returned Floy, with a winning smile, displaying her stores ;

"so do let me have the pleasure of sharing with you."

"Yes, come, mother," said Sammy, tugging at her skirts.

Thus urged, the woman accepted the invitation.

"Are you from Clearfield, miss?" she asked.

"I have been there for the past month or more. Is it there you live?"

"A little ways out o' the town, on t'other side. I've been in that neighborhood nigh on to fifteen year now. Clearfield wasn't much of a town when father moved out there, but it's growed powerful fast these few years back."

Floy's heart gave a sudden bound, and she turned an eager, questioning glance upon the speaker. "I suppose you knew—everybody knew—every one else in the place when it was so small?"

"Why yes, of course we did, an' mother she kep' a boardin'-house an' boarded the railroad hands. She was always for helping father along, and that's the way I do by my Sammy. He's named for his pap, you know," nodding toward her boy and smiling proudly on him.

"Yes, sirree! and I'm a-goin' to be as big a man as him some day!" cried the young hopeful, swallowing down one mouthful with great gusto and hastily cramming in another.

Floy pressed her hand to her side in the vain effort to still the loud beating of her heart.

"Did—did you ever hear any of those men—speak of a sort of shanty inn that stood not very far from the old depot?"

"Oh my, yes! and I've see it many a time; 'twas

there better'n a year, I should say, after we come to the place. And I've heard Jack Strong (he was one o' the switchmen on the road, and boarded with us a long spell after those folks pulled down their shanty and moved off)—I've heard him tell a pitiful kind of a story about a poor woman that come there one night clear beat out travellin' through the storm (for 'twas an awful wild night, Jack said, so he did, a-rainin' and hailin', and the wind blowin' so it blowed down lots o' big trees in the woods). Well, as I was a-sayin,' the woman she'd been footing it all day, and with a child in her arms too ; and Jack he told how some other folks that were there, a man and his wife, coaxed her to give the little girl to them, tellin' her she'd got to die directly, and she'd better provide for it while she could ; and how she give it to 'em and then ran screamin' after the cars, 'My child, my child ! give me back my child !' till she dropped down like dead, and would have fell flat in the mud and water in the middle of the road if Jack hadn't a-caught her in his arms."

Floy's hands were clasped in her lap, cold beads of perspiration stood on her brow, her breath came pantingly, and her dilated eyes were fixed on the face of the narrator, who, however, was too busy brushing the crumbs off Sammy's Sunday jacket to observe the look, but went on garrulously :

"Jack he carried her into the depot and laid her down on the settee ; and while they were tryin' to bring her to, an old gentleman (I disremember his name now) come in his covered wagon fur to git his son as was expected home from 'way off somewheres, but wasn't there (he didn't come till next day, Jack said), and the old gentleman he took the poor thing home with him.

"There, now, Sammy, hold still till I tie this hankercher round your neck. Them clo'es won't be fit to be seen if you keep on droppin' greasy crumbs over 'em."

Floy was making a desperate effort to be calm.

"Where did he take her?" she asked, half concealing her agitated face behind the folds of her veil.

"Out to the old gentleman's place; a splendid place they said it was. I can't say just how fur off in the woods, where he'd cleared acres and acres of land. Jack never see her after she was took out there, but he said she didn't die after all, but got married to the young feller that I told you was comin' home on a visit to the old folks (I think they'd know'd each other afore she was married the first time, and kind a got separated somehow), and when she got about again he took her back with him, and I guess the old folks follered 'em after a bit."

"Where, oh! where?" asked Floy imploringly.

The woman started and turned an earnest, inquiring gaze upon her.

"I beg pardon, but was they anything to you, miss?"

"I was the baby! and I'm looking for my mother. Oh, can you tell me where to find her?"

"That must a been a long while ago; you're a heap bigger'n me, and I ain't no baby," remarked Sammy, disposing of the last mouthful of his lunch and wiping his hands on his mother's handkerchief.

"Well, I never!" ejaculated the latter in wide-eyed astonishment. "And you was the baby! well now! Oh, do tell me! was those folks good to you?"

"As kind, as tender and loving as my own mother could possibly have been," answered Floy, with emotion. "But oh, tell me where I shall find her!"

"Indeed, I wish I knowed! but I never did know whether 'twas to Californy or Oregon or some other o' them fur-off places that they went."

"And the man who told you the story?"

"Jack Strong? he went off years and years ago. They say he went to the war and got killed, and I guess it's true."

CHAPTER XV.

ALONE

"Though at times my spirit fails me,
And the bitter tear-drops fall,
Though my lot is hard and lonely,
Yet I hope—I hope through all."—Mrs. Norton.

THE shrill whistle of a locomotive coming from the direction of Clearfield sent the strolling passengers hurrying back to the train. Pouring into the cars, they settled themselves in their seats with relieved faces and exchange of congratulations that this tedious detention had at last come to an end.

Floy, who had borne it with resignation from the first, was now more deeply thankful for it than words can express. There came over her such a rush of glad hopes and expectations as to leave no room at the moment for the recollection that she had as yet not the slightest clue to her mother's whereabouts. Even her sad bereavements and the cruel misunderstanding with Espy were for a short space half forgotten in the glad anticipation of again experiencing the blessedness of the possession of a mother's love.

She was leaning her head back against the side of the car, her face concealed by her veil.

"Miss," said Sammy's mother, gently touching her on the shoulder, "excuse me for waking you, but we're just 'most at my stoppin'-off place, and I didn't like to go without sayin' good-by to you."

"No, that was right; I was not asleep," said Floy, putting aside her veil and offering her hand, tears springing to her eyes, while a beautiful smile played about her lips. "I can never thank you enough for what you have told me to-day."

"La sakes! 'tain't nothin' to thank me for," returned the kind-hearted creature, grasping the soft little hand warmly in hers hardened by honest toil; "you're as welcome as can be, and Sammy and me's a thousand times obliged for the good dinner you give us. Well, I hope you'll find your mother, miss, and when you do won't you let me know? Just drop a line to Mrs. Sam Dobbs, Clearfield, and I'll be sure to git it."

"Wildbrier!" shouted the conductor at the door, and Mrs. Dobbs hurried from the car.

The morning's detention, causing more than one failure in making connections, brought several vexatious delays—long hours of tedious waiting in depots in the loneliness of a crowd, and with few appliances for comfort.

But Floy felt no temptation to fret or murmur; all this was so infinitesimal a price to pay for what she had gained.

When the train reached Chicago it was five o'clock in the morning, and still dark.

No one to meet Floy, and she so utterly strange to the city that she knew not which way to turn to find the street and number given her as the address of Mrs. Sharp, whose apprentice she was to be.

No express agent had come on the train to attend to the delivery of baggage; not a hack nor an omnibus was in waiting.

She was looking this way and that in search of one, when a young man of rough exterior but kindly, honest face, as she could see by the light of a lamp near by, stepped up with the question :

"Any baggage, miss?"

"Yes ; can you tell me where to find an omnibus or hack?"

"No, miss, there's none here ; they come to meet the regular trains, but this un's out o' time— about three hours behind."

"Then what am I to do?" she asked in perplexity.

"Well, miss, I'll take your trunk wherever it's to go, and if you like you can just go along in the express wagon. 'Tain't as suitable for you as a nice carriage, to be sure, but it'll carry you safe and comfortable. Where's the place?"

Floy gave him the number and street, and, accepting his offer with thanks as the best she could do under the circumstances, mounted to her elevated perch on the front seat, the young man giving her the assistance of his hand.

She saw her trunk placed behind her in the wagon, and presently found herself being driven rapidly through the almost deserted streets, for the city was but just beginning to rouse from its slumbers.

The morning air was chilly, blowing fresh and keen from the lake ; the girl's mood silent and sad, for, alas ! no glad welcome, no loving caress, nor even a familiar face would greet her in the new abode (she could not call it home) to which she was hastening.

But her gallant charioteer, who had, perchance, never before had so sweet a face by his side, did his best to entertain and amuse her, pointing out the district swept by the great fire, relating incidents connected with it, and calling her attention to the fine buildings which had already sprung up in the places of those destroyed.

Arrived at her destination, he leaped nimbly from his perch, gave the door-bell a vigorous pull, and assisted her to alight.

There was a sound of quick pattering steps, the forcing back of a bolt, the turning of a key; the door was hastily jerked open, and Floy just caught a glimpse of a narrow hall with its oil-cloth-covered floor, an unkempt head and dirty face in the foreground, and all was darkness.

"There, the wind's blowed the candle out! Miss Hetty, Miss Hetty, come right here! quick!" screamed the owner of the head. Then to Floy, "Who are you? and what d'ye want so awful early? We don't never 'spect no customers this time in the morning."

But before Floy could speak another person appeared upon the scene—a girl not many years older than herself, neat and trim in dress, and with a bright, intelligent, cheery, though homely face.

She came from the farther end of the hall, carrying a lighted lamp, and, holding it high over her head, peered into the darkness beyond.

"What *are* you making such a racket about, Patsy Devine? You'll wake everybody in the house and our Sharp Thorne will give you a prick." Then catching sight of Floy just stepping aside out of the way of the expressman, who was bringing in the trunk, "Oh! how d'ye do?" she said. "I suppose its—"

"Miss Kemper—"

"Ah, yes, the young lady Aunt Prue—Mrs. Sharp—was expecting. It's all right."

The expressman set down the trunk, received his pay, and departed.

Miss Hetty secured the door after him, and turning to Floy, said:

"Breakfast's about ready to set on the table, so it won't be worth while for you to climb the stairs till afterwards."

"I am hardly fit to—"

"Oh, I'll provide you with means for removing the coal-dust from face and hands," interrupted Hetty briskly, leading the way into the dining-room and across it to a closet, where she turned the water into a stationary washstand, and taking a clean towel and piece of soap from a drawer, laid them down beside it.

"There, just take off your things and give them to me."

"Thank you, but—my hair?" said Floy, "I never sat down to breakfast in my life without first using a comb and brush."

"Oh, just smooth it a little on top, and it'll do well enough for this once; we're all women and girls together; not a man in the house except Mr. Sharp, and he never comes to our early breakfast."

The shadow of a smile flitted over the face of the new-comer.

"No," laughed Hetty, divining her thought, "I would not be a slattern if all the men were at the bottom of the sea. Don't judge of me by Patsy, I beg of you," she added, with an odd grimace; "dirt and she have so strong an affinity for each other that there's no keeping them apart." And taking Floy's hat and shawl, she hurried away. She was back again by the time our heroine had finished her hasty toilet.

Floy's story had not preceded her. She had not felt willing that it should, and even Mrs. Sharp knew little more than that she was a young girl of good family who wished to learn dress-making and millinery.

But the deep mourning told of recent bereavement, and something in the patient sadness of the face went to Hetty's warm heart. With a sudden impulse she threw her arms about Floy and kissed her.

"You poor thing, so far away from home and all you love!" she said, "it must seem terribly hard."

Floy's lip trembled and her eyes filled. She could only return the embrace in silence; her heart was too full for speech.

"Hetty!" said a voice from the dining-room, "Hetty, isn't it time to ring the bell?"

"In a minute, mother, as soon as I can dish up the meat and potatoes," answered the girl, stepping out and drawing Floy with her. "Mother, this is Miss Kemper, the young lady that was expected to come from the West, you know."

Mrs. Goodenough, as Floy afterward learned to call her, was a heavy-featured, gray-haired, sallow woman, as dull, absent-minded, and slow as Hetty was bright and quick.

"Ah, yes; how d'ye do? But I didn't know there was a train came in so early," she said, shaking hands with Floy. "Ring that bell quick, Patsy!" as a step was heard in the hall, slipshod but hasty and impatient.

Mrs. Goodenough waddled into the kitchen (she was stout in figure and clumsy in gait). Patsy seized the bell, and Hetty came hurrying in with a dish of baked potatoes just as the door opened and another woman, alert in movement and sharp of feature, with a keen black eye, hair in crimping-pins, and a tall, wiry figure arrayed in a calico wrapper, clean and fresh but evidently thrown on in haste, came bustling in.

"Sarah, it's getting late, and you know how the work's hurrying us—six or eight dresses to be made this week, and—ah?" in a tone of inquiry as her eye fell upon Floy standing silently there.

Patsy's bell was clanging in the hall.

"Miss Kemper, Aunt Prue!" shouted Hetty. "Breakfast's ready now, and it isn't quite six yet."

Floy received a hasty nod, the black eyes scanning her from head to foot; then dashing into the hall, Mrs. Sharp seized Patsy with one hand, the bell with the other.

"That's enough! will you never learn when to stop? How do you suppose Mr. Sharp can sleep through all this din? Come, girls, make haste!" and she turned into the dining-room again, followed by four apprentices, to whom the last words were addressed as they came flying down the stairs.

In a trice all had gathered about the table, Mrs. Goodenough pouring out the coffee, Mrs. Sharp helping to the meat, and the others passing the bread, butter, and potatoes; then all fell to work as if their lives depended upon finishing the meal in the shortest possible space of time—all but the new-comer, who bent reverently over her plate for a moment ere she took up her knife and fork.

She had been assigned a place at Mrs. Goodenough's right hand. Hetty, who sat opposite, looked approval, but Mrs. Sharp's comment was an impatient gesture, which, however, Floy did not see.

"We expected you last night," Mrs. Sharp said presently.

Floy explained about the detention.

"Ah! and you're tired out most likely? won't be fit to work to-day, I s'pose?"

"I am willing to try," was the quiet answer.

"She ought to have a nap first," said Hetty impulsively.

"Yes, she looks tired," remarked Mrs. Goodenough slowly; "and what is it Shakespeare says?"

She dropped knife and fork, and with eyes fixed upon vacancy seemed to be vainly striving to recall some apt quotation which had half suggested itself, then slipped away before she could quite secure it.

"Pshaw, Sarah!" exclaimed her sister impatiently, pushing back plate and chair and jumping up in haste, "I'm the first done, as usual. Girls, don't be all day over your breakfast. Wash your hands and come right into the work-room as soon as you're done; there's no time to waste. Miss Kemper, take a nap if you need it. I'm not hard on my employees, even though my customers do drive me almost to distraction."

She left the room without waiting for a reply, and

the four apprentices followed almost immediately in a body. Floy rose too.

"Patsy and I will take your trunk up, Miss Kemper," said Hetty. "It's small, and we can easily carry it."

"But is there not some man I could hire?"

"No, none near that I know of. Just let me have my own way. I'm used to it, ain't I, mother?" laughed Hetty.

"Of course you are, Hetty," returned Mrs. Goodenough absently, sipping her tea. "What is it Shakespeare says?"

CHAPTER XVI.

INITIATED.

"Come then, oh care! oh grief! oh woe!
Oh troubles mighty in your kind!
I have a balm ye ne'er can know—
A hopeful mind."—F. VANE.

Up three flights of stairs the trunk was carried, Floy following close behind, laden with satchel, hat, and shawl.

"There!" cried Hetty pantingly, setting it down in the corner and straightening herself with her hands upon her hips, "I feel relieved; I've had my own way, and that's something I always enjoy," and she wound up with a cheery little laugh.

All Floy's protestations had been good-naturedly overruled, Hetty declaring herself a sort of female Samson, and the trunk very small and light.

"You are very kind," said Floy, "but you should have let me hire some one."

"No, no! no telling how long we'd have been kept waiting, or how many customers would have stumbled over or against it, or caught their dresses on it in the mean time. Whew! how close this room is! The girls rush down without waiting to open a window," hastily throwing up one as she spoke. "I'm sorry I've no better or lower accommodations to offer you, Miss Kemper," she went on laughingly. "It's a shame to make you climb so many stairs, but one of the things that can't be helped. That's your bed in the corner there," pointing to a single bed which seemed not to have been occupied. "Do lie down and rest a little; sleep if you can. I must run right away," and she flew downstairs.

Floy glanced about her. A great bare attic room, an old carpet, faded and worn, covering the middle of the floor; furniture scanty—just an old bureau, three chairs, all much hacked and scratched with long, hard usage; several unmade beds, each of which had evidently been occupied by two persons through the past night; and her own little one, which looked neat and inviting with its coarse but clean sheets and cheap white counterpane.

Everything indeed was clean, yet the room was disorderly and without a suggestion of comfort or prettiness in its appointments.

What a contrast to her own cosey, tasteful room in the old home!

She walked to the window and looked out. Day had fully dawned, and the busy hum of the awakening city came to her ear with no unpleasing sound. No velvety lawn, no garden gay with flowers, no nodding trees or softly wooded hills met her view; instead, bare roofs and domes and spires; but beyond these lay the great lake, its waters rippling in the morning breeze. And even as she gazed, far away to the east where sea and sky seemed to meet, a long line of rose color showed itself, deepened rapidly to crimson, brightened into gold; rays of light shot upward, quickly followed by the sun, "rejoicing as a strong man to run a race," and sending his bright beams over the wide expanse of waters till each wavelet's edge was tipped with burnished gold.

Floy leaned against the window-frame, hands clasped and eyes drinking in eagerly all the glory and beauty of the scene, loneliness, bereavement, all earthly ills forgotten for the moment.

"Ah," she sighed half aloud, "if Espy were here! if he could but transfer this to canvas!"

Then all the grief and anguish of their estrangement, all the sorrow and loss that preceded and mingled with it, came rushing back upon her with well-nigh overwhelming force, and her slight, willowy form bent like a reed before the blast.

She sank upon her knees, her head resting upon the window-seat, her hands tightly clasped above an almost breaking heart.

A burst of wild weeping, tears falling like rain, bitter choking sobs following thick and fast upon each other, then a great calm; an effort at first feeble, but growing stronger by degrees, to roll the burden too heavy for her upon One able and willing to bear it, a soothing, comforting remembrance of His promise never to leave nor forsake, and anon the glad thought that she whose love was only second to His might yet be found.

"She may be near, very near me even now," whispered the girl to herself, "in this city, this street, but a few doors away; it may be for that I have been sent here. Oh, what a thought! what joy if we should meet! But would we recognize each other? Mother, oh, mother! should I know your face if I saw it?"

She rose, tottered to the glass over the bureau.

and earnestly scanned her own features. With a half-smile she noted their worn and haggard look. Grief, care, and fatigue seemed to have done the work of years.

"It is well," she said. "I think I know now how she looks—my own poor, weary, heart-broken mother!"

Mrs. Kemper had told Floy that, allowing for difference in age, health, and circumstances, she was in face and form almost the exact counterpart of her own mother, and this was not the first time that the girl had earnestly studied her own face, trying to anticipate the changes to be wrought in it by the wear and tear of the next eighteen or twenty years, that thus she might be ready to know at a glance that other one she so longed to look upon.

She turned from the glass with a long, weary sigh, took off her dusty dress, shook out her abundant tresses, donned a wrapper, crept into the bed that had been pointed out as hers, and when Patsy came up an hour later to tidy the room, was sunk in a slumber so profound that she knew of neither the coming nor going of the child.

She was roused at last by a slight shake and the voice of the little maid.

"Miss, miss, they're a-settin' down to the table; don't ye want some dinner? Miss Hetty she told me to ax ye."

"Thank you!" cried Floy, starting up. "Yes, I'll be down in a moment; I'd no thought of sleeping so long!"

It was the work of a very few minutes to gather up her hair into a massive coil at the back of her head and put on one of her simply-made but becoming mourning dresses. She entered the dining-room with a quaking heart, not knowing what severe looks or reproaches might be meted out to her unpunctuality. Patsy's report had been, however, not quite correct, and she was but a moment behind the others. They were the same party she had met at breakfast, with the addition of a middle-aged, cadaverous-visaged man with a perpetual frown on his brow and a fretful expression about the mouth, who, as she entered, was in the act of carving a leg of mutton. He honored our heroine with a stare which she felt like resenting.

"Miss Kemper, Uncle Thorne," said Hetty.

"Ah, how d'ye do, miss? Will you be helped to a bit of a poor man?"

"Sir?" she said with a bewildered look.

"Ha! ha! ha! don't you know that's what the Scotch call a leg of mutton? I'm sure you'll find it relishing. Just send me your plate by the fair hands of our young Devine. I fear her divinity lies altogether in name, for certainly she's neither heavenly nor spiritual, supernatural nor superhuman in appearance."

"No," remarked Mrs. Goodenough in her slow, absent way as Patsy took the plate, "she's not equivalent to that. What is it Shakespeare says?"

"My classical sister—" began Mr. Sharp, in mock admiration.

"Aunt Prue," asked Hetty hastily, "did Mrs Cox decide whether she would have real lace on her bonnet?"

"Yes, and on the dress too. She's running up a large bill, but she is able to pay it."

"She or her husband?" asked Mr. Sharp with a sneer.

"She has none."

"Fortunate creature!" exclaimed Hetty in an aside.

"She's a rich widow," continued Mrs. Sharp; and from that the talk went on, running altogether upon flowers, laces, and ribbons, hats, bonnets, and dresses, and the latest styles for each.

"What puerilities!" remarked Mr. Sharp at length; "but the average female mind seems capable of dwelling upon nothing but trifles."

"And some male bodies—not a few either—appear to be quite willing to live upon—"

"Hetty, Hetty," interrupted her mother, "don't be personal."

"Humph! let her talk!" he said with sarcasm; "it amuses her and harms no one. It's no fault of hers that she wasn't given an intellect capable of appreciating literary labor."

"Very true," remarked his wife. "How does the work progress, Thorne? I hope this has been a good day for you."

"A woman of sense, knowing how my morning nap was broken in upon by unnecessary noises, and how very unsuitable was the breakfast served up to me afterward, would not ask such a question," he answered loftily.

"Come, girls," said his wife, rising hastily, "I think we are all done, and there's not a minute to be lost."

Floy rose with the others and accompanied them to the work-room.

"What can you do, Miss Kemper?" asked Mrs. Sharp.

"I think I may say I have been thoroughly drilled in plain sewing both by hand and with the machine," Floy answered modestly; "and for the last year I have fitted and made my common dresses, and generally assisted with the better ones."

"You may begin with this," said Mrs. Sharp, handing her a dress-skirt of cheap material.

"That sounds very well, but we shall see what we shall see," was what Floy read in her countenance. "And she shall see," was the girl's mental resolve.

"She's a treasure—this new arrival—if she only keeps on as she's begun," Mrs. Sharp said, with a triumphant smile, talking to Hetty that night after the apprentices and journey-women had retired: "as handy and neat a sewer as ever you saw, both by hand and on the machine, and turns off nearly twice as much work as any one of the others."

"That's splendid, Aunt Prue," returned Hetty, "but we must be careful not to work a willing horse to death."

"Of course, Hetty; did I ever do that?"

An odd little smile played about the girl's lips, but she only said:

"We've taken in a good many orders to-day; sold off most of our stock of ready-made hats too, and—there! it's striking eleven, and I have two hats to trim before I go to bed."

"You're worth your weight in gold, Hetty, and

it's a fine thing you need so little sleep," remarked her aunt. "But I think Sarah should relieve you of the oversight of Patsy and the meals more than she does."

"Mother's not well," said Hetty shortly.

"Oh, she's hipped; it's more that than anything else," laughed Mrs. Sharp. "Good-night," and she left the room.

"Hipped! of course she is! Everybody is that complains of anything, except that Sharp Thorne of hers," muttered Hetty, adjusting flowers, feathers, and loops of ribbon with deft and rapid fingers. "And of course I wouldn't enjoy being in bed now, or lying an hour later in the morning! Well, thank Heaven, I haven't a man to support, and don't need one to support me," she added cheerily.

CHAPTER XVII.

HETTY TO THE RESCUE.

"The drying up a single tear has more
Of honest fame than shedding seas of gore."—BYRON.

"HETTY GOODENOUGH, you'll have to interfere, and set your foot down firmly too, or the child's health will be ruined for life," remarked that young lady to herself, stealing another and another furtive glance at the wan, thin cheeks of Floy Kemper. "Why, she's but the ghost of the pretty girl the expressman brought here two months ago."

The Christmas holidays were near at hand, and for weeks past orders for party-dresses, head-dresses, opera cloaks, etc., had poured in upon the establishment till, as Mrs. Sharp said, they were driven almost to distraction.

It was now near midnight following one of the hardest days of the season, and all the weary toilers save these two had left the work-room to seek the rest so sorely needed.

"Floy," said Hetty aloud.

They had long since taken up the habit of calling each other by these familiar names.

"Well, Hetty?" and the girl, who was busily engaged in looping up the folds of rich silk and lace on an over-skirt, with delicate blossoms wonderfully real in their loveliness, looked up from her work with a faint smile.

"Do give that up for to-night; you've done too much to-day by a great deal."

"But it can't be helped while so many are hurrying us so for their dresses, and this will be done now in a few minutes."

"The heartless creatures!" ejaculated Hetty. "There's nothing hardens the heart like love of dress, Floy; I'd rather be—what I am—worked half to death—than a butterfly of fashion. Well, if you're determined to finish that, I must come and help you."

"Thank you," said Floy. "What makes you so good to me, Hetty?"

"It's odd, isn't it? but somehow I took a fancy to you the first minute I set eyes on you."

"And you've been the one bright spot in my life here ever since."

Hetty looked both touched and gratified.

"There, it's done at last!" she said presently, holding up their finished work, gazing at it admiringly for an instant as she shook out the rich folds; then carrying it to a closet, she hung it up carefully, shut and locked the door, putting the key in her pocket, and came back to Floy.

"What is it?" she asked almost tenderly, for Floy sat in a despondent attitude, her elbow on the table, her cheek on her hand, while her eyes, gazing into vacancy, had a deeply sad, far-away look.

"I was only thinking," she answered with an effort to speak cheerfully; but her voice broke, and a sudden gush of tears followed the words.

"Don't mind me! I—I didn't mean to!" she faltered, dashing away the bright drops and vainly struggling to recover her composure, as Hetty dropped on one knee at her side and put her arms affectionately about her.

"You're just worn out ; that's one trouble, but I'm afraid not the only one. I'm not curious, and don't want to obtrude myself into your confidence, but if you want sympathy—I'd be ever so glad to give it. I—I've thought sometimes 'twould do you good to unburden your heart to some one. You're homesick, I'm sure of that, for I know the symptoms. The home folks ought to write to you oftener than they do. I've noticed the postman has brought you only two or three letters since you came, and one of those was from an attorney at law."

"Yes, and the others were from one who is a dear, kind friend, but has no drop of my blood in her veins. Hetty, I never had a sister or brother. Last year—oh ! only four short months ago—I was a petted only child, the darling of the best, kindest, dearest of parents ; now—I am alone—all alone ! The grave closed over them both in one day."

The last words were scarcely audible, but Hetty's quick ear caught them, and her warm heart bled for the bereaved one. She clasped her more closely in her arms and wept with her.

"Poor dear, poor dear !" she said, "what a pleasant home you must have had with them ! Wouldn't it do you good to talk of it to me ?"

Floy felt that it would, and in trembling, tearful tones drew a bright picture of the happy home of her childhood, the tender parental love and care that had made it such in no ordinary degree.

Hetty was just the deeply-interested, sympathizing

listener the poor heart craved, and the outpouring relieved it of half its load.

"What a change for you—coming here!" was Hetty's comment; "and how well you have borne it! so patient, so uncomplaining, so diligent, and faithful! I hardly know how you can have sufficient energy and ambition."

"A strange remark coming from you," returned Floy, smiling faintly as she wiped away the tears she had been shedding to the memory of the dear ones gone, "you who seem to me to be the very embodiment of energy and ambition."

"Ah, I'm used to the life, and I have an object. poor mother has only me to relieve her of her heavy burdens; love of her lightens toil wonderfully!"

"Love of Another too, Hetty; isn't it so? And I too can rejoice in the hope that He is pleased when I strive to do my work faithfully, because it is of His appointment, and be patient under trial, because He sends it."

Hetty silently pressed the hand she held, a tender moisture gathering in her eyes.

"And—yes, I will tell you, for I am sure you are a true friend, one worthy of my confidence. I have another object in life besides the necessity of earning my own support."

And in a few brief, eager sentences, a light shining in her eyes, a tender smile hovering around her full, red lips, Floy told of her hope that she had still a mother living, and should some day be able to search her out.

Hetty listened to he tale in almost breathless surprise and deligh'.

"You'll find her!" she cried, "you'll find each other—I'm sure of it."

"And so am I at times, but I seem to make no progress of late. I so seldom get out even into the street, or go anywhere that I am likely to meet strangers."

"You ought to be in the store," said Hetty musingly; "perhaps that can be managed by and by, and in the meanwhile I'll be on the lookout for you. You resemble her?"

"Yes, allowing for the difference in age. Oh, it seems to me I should know the face if I saw it!"

It was past midnight now, and as the girls must be up by five o'clock in the morning, it behooved them to retire at once.

They bade each other good-night and stole softly upstairs, Hetty stopping on the third floor while Floy went on up to the attic.

It was indeed a change from her old home in Cranley to this that hardly deserved the name, and not more the change in the accommodations and surroundings than in the life she led—leisure, petting indulgence, tender, watchful care in the one; in the other incessant toil, seldom rewarded by so much as a word or smile of approval, very plain fare, her happiness evidently a matter of indifference to all about her except warm-hearted, sympathizing Hetty.

But Floy had borne it well; silent and abstracted she often was, scarce hearing the idle chatter of the others, but always diligent and faithful in the performance of the tasks assigned her; no eye-service was hers, and though often very weary and heart-sick, no complaint passed her lips or could be read in her countenance; what her hand found to do she did with her might, and having, as Mrs. Sharp discovered ere she had been in the house a week, a decided genius for cutting, fitting, and trimming, she had been worked very hard, and was already secretly esteemed an invaluable acquisition to the establishment.

She was breaking down under the unaccustomed strain; she needed the generous, varied, and nutritious diet, the abundance of fresh air and exercise, and somewhat of the rest and freedom from care of the olden time.

Mrs. Sharp was slow to perceive this, but Hetty had suspected it for days past, and to-night had become fully convinced.

She did not lie awake thinking of it, for, like Floy, she was weary enough to fall asleep the moment her head touched the pillow, but it was her last thought on lying down, her first on awaking, and she sprang up, saying half aloud:

"It shall be attended to, and this very day, sure as you're born, Hetty Goodenough!"

"What, Hetty?" asked her mother drowsily.

"Can't wait to explain now, mothery; the clock's striking five; will another time. Just turn over and take another nap while Patsy and I get breakfast."

"It's a shame! I ought to get up and let you nap it a little longer. What is it Shakespeare says?" muttered Mrs. Goodenough sleepily, turning over as she was bidden to do.

Hetty laughed low and musically as she threw on a wrapper, caught up a shawl, and hurried from the room. She was a power in that house, and knew it too. Mr. Sharp was a penniless dependent upon his wife, who, starting in business with a very small capital, had managed by dint of great exertions to add something to it, and at the same time to support the family and educate their children.

No easy life was hers, as Hetty said; she had shown herself neither prudent nor sharp when she consented to take such a Thorne to her bosom as the lazy, supercilious, self-indulgent husband who, while looking down with contempt upon her from the lofty heights of his intellectual superiority, whether real or fancied, was yet none too proud to live upon her hard earnings; and instead of showing any gratitude for the favors heaped upon him, was perpetually grumbling and finding fault.

His wife bore with and excused him on the plea of ill-health; but Hetty's opinion, not always kept entirely private, was that he was quite as capable of exertion as the rest of them if he would only think so, and that if by any possibility he could be forced to leave his bed at the early hour set for the rest of the family, and then to go to work with a will at something useful and remunerative, it would have an excellent effect upon him both mentally and physically.

But alas! she had not the power to enforce her cure, and he went on from day to day dozing away the precious morning hours, often the afternoon also, then sitting up far into the night at some literary work that never paid. Sometimes it was an English grammar that was never finished, at others an essay on some subject in which the public could not be brought to take an interest.

He was soured by disappointment, considering himself a very ill-used man, and could not be made to see that the trouble lay in his selfish determination to do only what he liked, whether it would or would not pay and enable him to support himself and family.

Mrs. Goodenough, nominally at the head of the housekeeping department, lacked her sister's native energy, and was really out of health, and the greater part of that burden was assumed by Hetty, who was a perfect embodiment of vigor and efficiency.

Hetty had charge of the millinery part of the concern also, including a store in which she had invested a few hundreds inherited from her father, bringing to the business also a thorough knowledge of the trade.

She kept the accounts too, and was in fact quite as much the mainspring of the whole establishment as Mrs. Sharp herself, if not more so.

And this was well for the employees, since it was by Hetty's oversight of marketing and cooking that the table was supplied with a sufficiency of wholesome, well-prepared food, and meals were served with the regularity so necessary to health.

She could not wholly save them from being overworked, or indeed herself either, but the hours of labor were sometimes abridged by her thoughtful kindness in exerting her influence to that end.

CHAPTER XVIII.

A CRUEL BLOW.

"Our first love murdered is the sharpest pang
A human heart can feel."—YOUNG.

FLOY came down to breakfast with a violent headache. She said nothing about it, but her look of suffering and want of appetite did not escape Hetty's watchful eye, and made her more determined than ever to come speedily to the rescue.

The opportunity offered shortly after the conclusion of the meal. Leaving her mother and Patsy to clear it away, Hetty hurried into the store. It was still too early to open, but there were accounts to be looked over and things to be set right before she would be ready for customers.

She had not been there long when Mrs. Sharp came in with the over-skirt she had helped Floy to finish the night before.

"See, Hetty, what do you think of this?" she asked, with a pleased look. "Some of Miss Kemper's work. She really has a wonderful amount of taste."

"Yes, I think so; it's perfectly lovely, Aunt Prue; you never had an apprentice before, or a journey-woman either, for that matter, who could trim half so prettily or had so many original ideas about it."

Mrs. Sharp assented, shaking out the dress and

gazing admiringly upon it as she turned it this way and that to note the effect.

"Yes," she said complacently, "we've secured a real treasure in her, and I never shall regret having consented to take her."

"She's worth taking care of."

"Of course she is, Hetty; but what do you mean by that?" asked the aunt sharply.

"That she isn't getting sleep enough, or fresh air or exercise enough; that this work, work, work, from early morning until late at night, is breaking down her health, and we'll have to manage differently as far as she's concerned, or we'll have her dying on our hands."

"Dear me, Het," in a vexed tone, "you have a way of putting things so strongly, and in such a sudden fashion too, that I declare it nearly knocks one down! She's no more overworked than you or I."

"Perhaps not; but we're used to it, and naturally stronger, I think. Besides, we don't sit so steadily, but are here and there, all over the house, and in and out too, shopping or marketing."

"Well, it can't be helped while we're so driven with work."

"Better spare her for an hour or two every day now than lose her services for weeks or maybe altogether."

Mrs. Sharp tossed the dress on to the counter and sat down with her hands folded in her lap. For a moment she seemed lost in thought, her countenance expressing a good deal of annoyance.

"I generally send Annie Jones home with finished

work," she said presently, "because she's not good for much else; but if Miss Kemper is really in such pressing need of air and exercise, she may take that duty sometimes. I don't believe, though, that she'll be willing; she is too high in her notions."

"She is a lady, and would of course feel it somewhat of a trial to her pride," said Hetty, "but I believe she is too sensible and right-minded to refuse, when it's so necessary for her health."

"Well, we'll see."

Floy was called and the question laid before her.

The result was as Hetty had predicted—an evident struggle with pride, then a thankful acceptance of the offer. Health was far too valuable to be lightly thrown away, and—ah, how many strange faces would present themselves to her view in the houses to which she was sent, on the sidewalks, and in the street-cars, and who could tell that the one she so longed to find might not be among them!

It was assigned to her to carry home the work she had completed the night before, and when the late hour arrived at which a fashionable lady might be supposed ready to receive such a call she set out upon the by no means agreeable errand.

The air was keen and cold, but the sun shone brightly, and she found her walk of some half dozen squares bracing and enjoyable.

It was to a very handsome residence in a fashionable quarter of the city that she had been sent.

The servant who answered her ring left her standing in the hall while he carried away the package she had brought. Presently he returned with a request that she would follow it.

A CRUEL BLOW.

"Miss Carrie wants you to see it tried on, so's you can fix it if 'tain't all right," he said.

He led her up a flight of marble stairs, broad and low, with an elegantly-carved balustrade, and over softly-carpeted floors to a richly-furnished boudoir, where three young girls, in elegant morning dresses, lounged upon the sofas, taking their ease as though life had no serious duties for them and time were given only to be frittered away.

Floy was conscious that the three pairs of eyes were levelled at her on her entrance, but bore the ordeal with quiet dignity.

"Ah, you're the young person sent from Mrs. Sharp's, I presume?" said one, laying aside a novel. "I'm glad she didn't disappoint me. Will you please undo it?" pointing to the parcel lying on an ottoman. "I must try it on and let you see that it's all right before you go."

She spoke as if addressing a menial, and Floy's cheek burned; but she silently did as requested.

The wrappings were removed, and in a moment all three of the young ladies had started to their feet with exclamations of "Lovely!" "Charming!" "Exquisite!"

"I shall run into the next room and put it on!" cried the owner.

"And I'll help you, Carrie," said one of the others.

"No, no, Bell, thank you! you and Laura stay here and let me burst in upon you in full bloom," she answered laughingly. "But you may come," nodding graciously to Floy. "I'll need your assistance. I'll carry this lovely over-skirt; you may bring the rest."

The bedroom to which she conducted Floy was, in

the richness and luxury of its furnishing, quite in keeping with the boudoir.

The change of dress was quickly made, Floy adjusting the rich folds of the new gown, and making one or two little alterations in the looping or the position of the flowers to suit the taste of the wearer.

"Wait here a moment while I show myself to my friends," said the latter when all was done.

She sailed away into the adjoining room, and Floy heard the exclamations.

"Oh, charming, Carrie!"

"And so becoming! I declare, Cal, even Espy Alden would find you irresistible in that!"

"Why not say Will? he's to be here next week—coming home with Fred to spend the holidays. They're college chums, you know."

The light, joyous laugh that accompanied the words seemed to say that she considered him as already secured.

Floy heard it all, and a pang shot through her heart.

Espy Alden! her own Espy! it could be no other, for it was no common name.

Faint, giddy, sick at heart, trembling in every limb, she dropped into a chair and hid her face in her hands. She thought she had resigned him, yet oh, what anguish that another should have won her place in his heart!

No tears came to her burning eyes, but she was half frightened at the pallor of her face as, on raising her head again, she caught sight of it in a mirror on the opposite wall. She hastily drew down her veil to hide it.

The talk was going on in the next room, and every word came distinctly to her ear.

"What's he like?"

"Oh, you haven't seen him, Bell? There, what do you think of him? It's not a bit flattered; is it, Laura?"

"No; don't do him justice. No photograph could, for he's much handsomer when he's talking and laughing than when his face is at rest."

"That's so, and he's a splendid talker; quite an artist too, Fred says. But now tell me if you think all these flowers are disposed to the very best advantage."

The rest of the chat was about the dress, and fell utterly unheeded upon Floy's ear.

An artist, so handsome, so good a conversationist—it could be no other than her own Espy—hers from her very babyhood. And this girl had his likeness—no doubt given by himself. What could it mean if not that they were betrothed? Well, what right had she to blame him? None, none, for she had voluntarily resigned him; and yet, and yet—oh, her heart was like to break!

"What's the matter? are you ill?" she heard a voice asking at her side—the voice of the girl who had won him from her.

"Yes," she answered faintly, "I—I've been up very late for several nights; work is so pressing just now, and I rose this morning with a terrible headache."

"Ah, that's too bad! I wouldn't be a dressmaker for anything in the world. Well, I suppose you'd like to go, and there is no need for you to stay any longer. Tell Mrs. Sharp I'm delighted with the dress. Have you the bill with you?"

Floy produced it, receipted and signed; the money was paid, and she took her departure.

The keen, frosty air was no longer refreshing as she retraced her steps; it seemed rather to chill her to the very bones.

Hetty had asked her to come in through the store. Some customers were just passing out as she reached the door. Hetty glanced toward her on her entrance.

"Why, how dreadfully you look!" she exclaimed. "I haven't managed right. I shouldn't have let you go for such a walk when you'd eaten hardly a mouthful of breakfast."

She threw an arm about Floy's waist as she spoke, and drew her into a small room back of the store, where the making and trimming of bonnets was carried on. Several girls were working busily at the end nearest the window.

"Sit down here by the register and warm yourself," said Hetty, gently forcing Floy into a large arm-chair.

"No, no, I must go up to the work-room at once," answered the weary, half-fainting girl; "you know all hands are needed—"

"You'll just sit there till you're well warmed and have had a cup of tea," said Hetty with authority. "The Thorne is but just done his breakfast; there's a good fire in the kitchen, and—I'll be back in two seconds. Don't you dare to move till I come." And shaking her finger threateningly, she rushed away through a door opening into the dining-room.

Her promise was not fulfilled to the letter, but scarce five minutes had elapsed when she returned with a cup of fragrant tea and two or three slices of thin, daintily browned and buttered toast, all fresh from the fire.

The tray, covered with a snowy napkin, was quickly placed on a stand close at Floy's side, and Hetty ordered her, in a tone of good-humored authority, to eat and drink.

She tried to speak her thanks, but her lip trembled and tears came instead of words.

"There, now, my dear, don't emulate the folly of Oliver Twist over his water-gruel," said Hetty jocosely. "I think you'll find this fare somewhat more tempting than his ; but salt water won't improve it. You see," bending low and speaking in a whisper, " I've cribbed a little from the store of dainties provided for the Thorne and served it upon part of my own breakfast set, generally reserved for high days and holidays. Now I must leave you, for there's a customer," and she hurried into the store.

The fragrance of the tea was appetizing. Floy tasted it, then broke off a bit of the toast, and presently discovered that, whatever might have been the original cause of her headache, an empty stomach had not a little to do with it now.

The slight refreshment made it possible to force herself to work, though in other and happier days she would have been deemed too ill for any place but bed.

The pain in the head was partially relieved, but that of the heart remained unassuaged ; and though it cost a painful effort, it was perhaps well for her that she was compelled to give her mind to the details of her employment, cutting, fitting, and trimming through all the long hours of the day and evening, till nature was so thoroughly exhausted that sleep came the moment she lay down to her rest, two hours earlier than on the previous night—the result of Hetty's kindly interposition.

It was the same through the remainder of the week ; every day some errand to take her out for a breath of fresh air, every night an hour or two added to her time for rest ; also her bed was removed to a warmer and purer atmosphere, Mrs. Goodenough and Hetty taking her into their room, which was heated by a furnace in the cellar and was better ventilated than the crowded room overhead.

Floy was very grateful, especially when the added luxury of some degree of privacy was given her by the kindness of Mrs. Goodenough in curtaining off the corner where her bed was placed.

The beneficial effect of these changes was soon apparent in Floy's increased appetite and brighter looks.

On the ensuing Sabbath she felt herself able to go to church, which had been the case only once before since her coming to the city, all the other Sundays finding her so worn out with the week's work as to be compelled to spend the day in sleeping off her exhaustion.

She went alone ; and not wishing to attract observation, slipped quietly into a pew near the door.

The services had not yet begun, and her thoughts had flown far away to the dear ones worshipping in the upper sanctuary, when suddenly they were recalled to earth. A rustle of silk, and three gayly-dressed young girls swept up the aisle closely followed by two young men, the foremost, Espy Alden, stepping so close in passing that she could easily have laid her hand upon his arm.

Her heart gave a wild bound as she recognized him, but he did not see her.

She said to herself she was glad of it, yet it pained her to her heart's core. Had he no eyes for any one but Miss Carrie Lea? Surely if his heart were loyal as of yore to his first love, he would have felt her presence near. It had seemed ever so in those earlier days.

He sat where she could see his side face, and many a furtive glance fed her hunger for the old love, a consuming fire that pride—her woman's pride—vainly strove to trample out. Ah, it was the only earthly love left her, and it had been so sweet!

CHAPTER XIX.

A GREAT SURPRISE.

> "Thinkest thou
> That I could live and let thee go,
> Who art my life itself? No, no!"—MOORE.

THE moment the benediction was pronounced Floy left the church and walked rapidly away, turning the first corner she came to, nor paused nor slackened her pace till she reached Mrs. Sharp's door.

"Had you a good sermon?" queried Hetty at the dinner-table.

"Yes," Floy answered absently.

"It does not seem to have refreshed you much," sneered Mr. Sharp, with a keen glance at the pale, sorrowful face whereon the traces of tears were very evident. "I would prescribe a nap instead, next Sunday."

"Don't tease her, Thorne," said Mrs. Goodenough, "she's been trying to do her duty like a Christian. What is it Shakespeare says?"

"Madam, let me counsel you to purchase a copy of the works of that immortal bard, and study it for your own edification, for ours, and for that of the world at large," he returned lotftily and with a contemptuous wave of the hand, as he passed his cup to be refilled.

Hetty flushed indignantly.

"It might be for your edification, no doubt," she retorted ; " this passage for one—'Conceit in weakest bodies strongest works.' "

"Hush, hush, child ! that's too strong," said her mother, taking the cup. "But unasked advice isn't apt to be welcome, Thorne ; what is it Shakespeare says ?" and the tea-pot she had just lifted was set down again while she seeemd lost in contemplation. "Ah ! I have it :

" ' I pray thee cease thy counsel,
Which falls into mine ears as profitless
As water in a sieve.' "

Mr. Sharp rose, and, pushing his plate angrily away, strode from the room. Mrs. Sharp looked annoyed, but made no remark, contenting herself with a reproachful glance at her sister and niece.

Hetty accepted her share with extreme nonchalance. As for the other delinquent, she was too much elated by her successful quotation to heed so trifling a matter as the passing displeasure of her sister—a displeasure, too, which, as she shrewdly suspected, was more than half assumed for the mere sake of appearance.

That was the fact, and yet there was a real vexation to Mrs. Sharp in what had occurred, because she would have to bear the brunt of his ill-humor.

With that unpleasant conviction weighing upon her, she breathed a heavy sigh as she, too, left the table and the room.

"Poor Aunt Prue !" said Hetty, looking after her. "What a sad misnomer was her name when she undertook the care and support of—"

"Hush, hush, child!" interrupted her mother.

"Well, well, I must try to keep my opinions to myself," pursued the girl, with a serio-comic expression, "but I can't help feeling sorry for her, or glad for ourselves, that we'll get no more Sharp prickles from the Thorne to-day. He's bound to spend the rest of it in a fit o' the pouts, and will not darken these doors till noon of to-morrow."

Mrs. Sharp found her Thorne lying on a couch in their chamber, literally pouting like the great baby that he was.

"My dear," she said soothingly, "you mustn't mind that saucy girl; she isn't worth it, and—"

"No, I suppose not; but if you cared a penny for me you'd send her away at once, or rather would have done so long ago."

"But, unfortunately, Thorne, we can't do without her, and, still more unfortunately, she is perfectly aware of the fact, and doesn't scruple to take every advantage of it."

"'Where there's a will there's a way,' Mrs. Sharp, and if you were the right sort of wife you'd never sit by and see your husband insulted at his own table as I have been to-day."

"His own table indeed!" thought she; "it's more Hetty's than his; more mine than hers. But—ah, well, I must even make the best of a bad bargain."

And going into an adjoining room, she presently returned laden with delicacies—fine confections and tropical fruits—which she pressed upon him, saying, "You made such a poor dinner; hardly eat enough to keep a bird alive; do try to eke it out with these.

These grapes are splendid, so are the oranges and bananas, and I never saw finer candies."

"I don't want them," he said shortly; "if things are to be locked up and kept from my knowledge till it suits you to bring them out, I'll not touch them."

At this she was justly indignant, and, losing all patience, informed him that "since he was determined to 'bite off his nose to spite his face' he was entirely welcome to do so."

"To think that I should ever have married a woman who can use such vulgarisms as that!" said he, turning his back on her.

"Better be vulgar than wicked!" she retorted, "and the way you're behaving is downright wicked—such temper and ingratitude! If you were a child I should say you wanted a good spanking, and I rather think so as it is. If I were you I'd really try to put away childish things."

"You, who can be guilty of such extravagance as this, do well to reprove me, your liege lord," he remarked with bitter sarcasm. "Cast the beam from your own eye, and you may perhaps see clearly to pull the mote out of mine."

"My liege lord indeed!" she repeated scornfully; "rather my— But I will not bandy words with you, and, lest I should be too strongly tempted to do so, shall leave you to pout it out alone."

So saying, she gathered up her rejected dainties and swept from the room, leaving him to repent of his refusal at leisure, for no child could be fonder of sweets than he.

All that day and the succeeding night Espy was present in Floy's dreams whether sleeping or waking

Nor were they happy dreams, for they seemed to take him farther and farther from her. Yet she strove to be cheerful in the presence of others, and only Hetty suspected how hollow was the pretence. Monday passed by, bringing no unusual event. On Tuesday, at a late hour in the morning, she was again directed to go to the residence of the Leas; this time to fit a dress for Carrie's mother.

"Mrs. Lea is not quite ready for you yet, miss," said the servant who answered her ring. "She says you'll be so good as to wait till she sends for you. Just walk in here, please," he added on his own responsibility, perceiving that he was addressing a lady, and throwing open the door of the library as he spoke.

Floy stepped in, the door closing behind her, and instantly became aware that the room had an occupant, and only one—a young and handsome man, seated comfortably in an easy chair by the fire, and busied with the morning paper.

He looked up; the paper was suddenly flung aside, and in an instant he had caught both her hands in his, his face all aglow with delighted surprise.

"Floy, Floy! have I found you at last? Oh, darling, can you, will you forgive those cruel words of mine? Ah, if you knew how bitterly they have been repented!"

It was her own Espy again. Tears of joy rained down her cheeks; she could not speak for emotion; but she did not repulse him as he took her in his arms and folded her to his heart with many a tender caress, whispering the while, "Floy, Floy! my own darling, my own little wife!"

"No, no, not that!" she sobbed. "Oh, Espy, Espy, we must part!"

"For a little while—only for a little while—dearest."

"Your parents—have they relented?" she asked, wiping the tears from her eyes and gazing steadily into his.

His cheek flushed.

"I shall be of age in a few weeks, and be my own master," he said, drawing himself up proudly.

"But not mine," she said very low—so low that he scarcely caught the words—and gently releasing herself from his embrace.

He flushed more hotly than before. "Oh, Floy, have I ever seemed to think it? Nay, have I not rather been your devoted slave?"

"You were always good to me, Espy; always watching over and caring for me, and ready and anxious to give me the best of everything. Oh, I shall never, never forget your goodness! no, not even if—"

"If what, Floy?"

"Even though another has—has won you—"

"No, no, never!" he cried, taking her hands again. "I never have, never can love any one but you. Why should you think it?" and he gazed searchingly into her eyes.

Then she told him something of what she had involuntarily heard a few days previous while waiting in Carrie Lea's bedroom.

He was indignant and evidently surprised to learn that the girl had his photograph; puzzled, too, to conjecture how it had come into her possession.

"It must have been somehow through her brother," he said after a moment's thought. "But, Floy, I have never paid her any particular attention," he added with deprecating look and tone.

"I believe you fully, Espy," she replied, with a confiding smile; "but since I have released you from your engagement to me—"

"I do not accept my release," he interrupted impulsively, "and that being the case, I am answerable to you for my conduct toward other women."

She shook her head, and was opening her lips to speak again, when the sound of approaching steps prevented. She drew hastily away from Espy's side, and, seating herself by a window, seemed to have her attention fully occupied with something that was going on in the street.

The door opened.

"Miss, Mrs. Lea, says you'll please walk up now to her dressing-room."

Espy, standing before the grate with his back to the door, turned at the words and made a stride forward, his face blazing with indignation, but only to see Floy's black skirt vanish through the door, which instantly closed between them.

"What does it mean?" he asked himself half aloud; "I thought she was merely making a morning call, but that fellow spoke to her as if she were a menial like himself."

There was a sound of light laughter and gay girlish voices on the stairway, and in the hall without, the door again opened, and the smiling face of Miss Carrie Lea looked in.

The sleigh's at the door, Mr. Alden, and we're all ready, waiting for you."

He had engaged to drive out with the ladies at that hour in Mr. Lea's fine sleigh, behind his handsome, spirited bays ; and anxious though he was beyond expression to snatch another interview with Floy by intercepting her as she should leave the house, he felt compelled to go, not being able on the spur of the moment to think of any plausible excuse.

Since there was no alternative, he made the best of it ; with smile and jest handed the ladies to their places, tucked the buffalo-robes carefully about them, took his seat by Carrie Lea's side, and drove off, fervently hoping that something would occur to cause a speedy return

CHAPTER XX.

A SUDDEN SUMMONS.

"I tell thee life is but one common care,
And man was born to suffer and to fear."—PRIOR.

MRS. LEA's dressing-room was gorgeous with crimson and gold; they were the prominent colors of its adornment, from the velvet carpet on the floor to the gayly-frescoed ceiling.

The lady herself, arrayed in a morning robe of dark blue silk, and wearing a great quantity of heavy jewelry, reclined upon a crimson-satin-covered couch. She evidently belonged to the shoddy aristocracy, and her sallow, slightly-wrinkled face expressed nothing but supercilious pride and fretful discontent.

She greeted Floy with an angry nod and the question: "What's the reason Mrs. Sharp sends you instead of coming herself? You can tell her I don't like such treatment, and I consider that my money is as good as any other body's. She says in her note you can fit as well as she can; but I don't believe it; it stands to reason that a 'prentice-girl couldn't do as well her mistress."

Floy's cheek flushed, but she stood with an air of dignity, silently waiting for the end of the tirade, then quietly asked:

"Am I to fit your dress, Mrs. Lea?"

"Can you ? that's the question."

"You have Mrs. Sharp's opinion in regard to my ability. I can only say that I am ready to do my best, or to return to her with your message, as you please."

"Well, I guess you may cut and fit the lining, and I can judge by the looks of it whether to allow you to go on and do up the job. Eliza," turning to her maid, "bring the things. You know where they are."

Floy had not been invited to sit down, but feeling ill able to stand, quietly took possession of the nearest chair.

Mrs. Lea elevated her eyebrows and muttered something angrily about "impudence and upstarts, and some folks making themselves very much at home in other folks' houses."

Floy seemed not to hear, but kept her seat till the maid returned with the required articles, and Mrs. Lea was ready to stand up and be fitted.

This proved a tedious and trying process to both, by reason of Mrs. Lea's impatience and captiousness ; but at length Floy's efforts resulted in so signal a success that she was graciously permitted, in Mrs. Lea's phrase, "to go on and do up the job."

"Why, it fits elegant !" she exclaimed at the final trying on. "I declare Mrs. Sharp couldn't a done it better herself, and you may tell her I said as much."

Floy was gratified, for the Leas were among Mrs. Sharp's best customers. Her patience and forbearance had been sorely tried, but had not failed, and now she was rewarded for the restraint put upon herself.

Her pulses quickened as she passed the library door in going out, though she knew Espy was not there now, for she had heard the departure of the sleighing party, and they had not returned.

Another hour had slipped away before they came, and Espy was met at the door by a telegram to the effect that his mother was lying dangerously ill, and he must hasten home without delay if he would see her alive.

Espy read it at a glance; and turning a pale, agitated countenance upon the servant, who stood waiting,

"I must be gone at once," he said.

"Yes, sir; I expected as much, and I've packed your valise, sir; here it is all right—everything in it that you'd left in your room."

"Thank you; it was very thoughtful and kind. I will have to leave my adieus to the ladies and gentlemen with you. Tell them I have been suddenly summoned home. My mother is very ill, and I shall have barely time to catch the train. Good-by."

And dropping a dollar into the man's hand, Espy seized the valise and rushed away in hot pursuit of a passing street-car.

Even at that moment of grief, anxiety, and haste, he remembered with a sharp pang that this sudden departure robbed him of the opportunity to obtain another interview with Floy or to learn her address.

During the two hours' drive his thoughts had been so full of her, their late interview, and plans for securing another, that he found no little difficulty in attending to the small talk of his companions, and was more than once rallied by them upon his absence of mind.

It was the more annoying since he was the only gentleman of the party, young Lea being confined to his room that day with a severe cold.

Great were the chagrin and disappointment of Carrie when she heard of Espy's abrupt departure. The others cared less, as she had managed to monopolize almost all his attentions.

Floy's heart meanwhile was in a tumult of mingled emotions—joy that she had heard from Espy's own lips the assurance of his faithfulness to her, sorrow that duty seemed still to forbid their betrothment.

Well was it for her in those days that necessity compelled her to constant employment, and that much thought had to be given to her work.

The diversion of her mind from her cares and griefs was further assisted by the occurrences of the next day.

It was two hours since the early breakfast at Mrs. Sharp's, and in the work-room all was life, activity, and bustle: the buzz of three sewing-machines, the busy hum of voices giving and asking instructions, the click of the scissors cutting out garments and their trimmings, making a confusion of sounds.

Floy, putting the finishing touches to the rich silk she had fitted yesterday for Mrs. Lea, was wondering if she should be commissioned to carry home this dress, her heart trembling with mingled pleasure and pain at thought of a possible meeting with Espy if sent upon that errand.

A loud peal from the door-bell made her start,

and set all her nerves tingling, she scarce knew why.

"The postman," said Mrs. Sharp; "more orders, I presume. Here, give it to me, Patsy," as the little maid appeared with a note in her hand. "Yes, just as I thought. Run back to your work, Patsy. No, make yourself decent first; I won't have customers driven away by such a fright answering the bell."

With the open note in her hand, Mrs. Sharp hurried into the store to consult with Hetty.

"Here's a note from the Madame—wanting a dress fitted to-day, and made this week; with all this holiday work on our hands, giving us hardly time to breathe! But it's like her—always choosing my busiest time. Did you ever know it to fail?"

"Never! so we ought to be used to it by this time."

"What do you advise?"

"Madame is too valuable a customer to lose."

"Yes, indeed."

"I'd send Floy. No one else is competent except yourself."

"That's true; yes, she'll have to go, though I don't know how to spare her here."

Hastening back to the work-room,

"Is that dress done, Miss Kemper?" she asked.

"I'm just setting the last stitches," was the reply.

"Well, the minute you're done put on your things and take it home; then go on from there to the address I shall give you. She's a good customer—rich, middle-aged, queer, and must be humored in her notions. She thinks she must have a new dress immediately, though she has fifty already. You'll probably have to stay two or three days, as she will have her gowns made in the house, and a great deal of work put on them."

Floy obeyed, nothing loath, for she was weary enough of the monotony of her life and the disorder, hurry, and bustle of the work-room.

"Any change," thought she, "must surely be for the better."

As she passed though the hall at Mr. Lea's, after attending to her errand, she overheard the inquiry of a gentleman at the door for Mr. Alden, and the servant's reply,

"He's left the city, sir; went off yesterday in a mighty big hurry. Had a telegram that somebody was sick at home."

The words went through Floy like a shot. For an instant she was near falling, but recovering herself, she hastily drew down her veil and stepped past the servant into the street.

The gentleman was already gone, and she too went quietly on her way—seeming quiet outwardly, but in great tumult of feeling.

"Was it Espy's father who was so ill? Would he now relent? Would he die?"

In either case the bar to her own and Espy's happiness would be removed. She was horrified at the thrill of pleasure that thought brought with it: that she could be glad of the death of another! Silently asking forgiveness, cleansing, help, she hurried onward.

There was now neither hope nor fear of meeting

Espy. Was she glad? was she sorry? Truly she did not know. Then she thought of him bereaved of a parent, and her tears fell fast. Who knew better than she the anguish of such a loss? Ah, if she could but save him this great sorrow!

Madame Le Conte lived in the suburbs of the city in a large, handsome dwelling on the shore of the lake, of which there was a fine view from the whole front of the house. The street-cars, however, carried Floy to within a square of the place, and it was still comparatively early when she reached it.

Her ring was promptly answered by a pretty, neatly-attired Irish girl, rosy and smiling.

"Is it the dressmaker from Mrs. Sharp's that the Madame's expecting?" she inquired without waiting for Floy to tell her errand. "Well, I'm glad to see you, miss, for you've a purty face, and are a nice-lookin' lady intirely, besides that the Madame would a been awful vexed if you'd disappointed her. But just step this way, intil the dining-room; for the Madame's not up yet—she don't rise mostly afore nine o'clock—and me orders was to give you your breakfast the first thing."

"I have breakfasted, thank you, and—"

"Yes, miss, but sure don't we all know what onchristian hours they kape down there? giving ye yere breakfast afore six o'clock. An' sure ye've been walkin' and ridin' in the cowld, keen air o' the streets till folks would think ye'd be as hungry as a wolf."

As she spoke, she led the way through the great wide hall with its broad staircase, past open doors that gave glimpses of spacious, elegantly-furnished apartments, to a cosey, sunshiny breakfast-parlor, where a glowing grate, with an easy chair beside it and a little round table daintily spread with snowy drapery, cut glass, silver, and Sevres china, and set in a large bay window where some rare plants were blooming, and whence could be caught a view of the rolling waters of the lake, were very suggestive of ease and enjoyment.

"There, miss, wad ye ax a swater place to eat in?" queried Kathleen, watching with delight Floy's face brighten with pleased surprise as she glanced from side to side of the cheery room.

"No, indeed."

"Well, it's meself that wouldn't. Now just sit ye down in that big chair by the fire and take off your things and warm yerself while I fetch in the breakfast."

Very willingly Floy accepted the invitation.

"A very pleasant beginning," she thought as she felt the genial warmth of the fire; "the Madame must be both kind and generous. But I must not expect to find roses without thorns anywhere in this world; ah, no! but I will try to take quietly and thankfully the sweet and bitter as they come."

There was no bitter in the breakfast presently served by the smiling Kathleen: fragrant, delicious coffee, richly creamed and sugared; the sweetest of butter, elegant hot rolls, a tender beefsteak—all done to a turn.

Floy had not thought of hunger till food was offered her, but to her surprise found no lack of appetite for the tempting fare set before her.

She had hardly begun her meal when, at a whining sound, Kathleen opened the door leading into the hall and admitted a curly lap-dog as white as snow, a beautiful little creature.

"Why, Frisky, you're late till yere breakfast the day!" said Kathleen, stroking it gently. "See, miss, isn't he a purty crayther? his coat's so fine and soft and glossy!"

"Like floss silk," said Floy. "Is he the Madame's pet?"

"Yes, miss, that he is, the darlint! an' we all make much of him, an' it's spoilt he is intirely, the crayther. He's come fur his breakfast, miss; he's been used to ating in here with his misthress, an' niver a bit will he ate in the kitchen, such a grand gintleman as he is; so will ye plaze to excuse us if I bring his mate in here and feed him afore ye?"

"Certainly," returned Floy, with a smile. "I should like to see him eat."

"Thank ye, miss," said Kathleen, setting two more chairs up to the table, of one of which Frisky instantly took possession, then whisking into the kitchen and back again, bringing a plate of meat quite as carefully prepared as the one she had set before Floy.

"You see it's kapin' it hot for him I've been, miss," she explained, seating herself in the other chair and beginning to cut the meat up into small bits. "It must be hot, and cut fine, or he won't touch it; and, more nor that, he'll not ate a mouthful if ye don't sing to him all the time."

"Indeed!" exclaimed her listener in surprise.

"Yes, miss, it's thrue as prachin'; just see now!

we always have to feed him wid a silver fork too." And taking up a bit in her fingers she offered it, saying coaxingly, " Ate it now, me jewel ; it's illegant, tender, and swate."

He did not so much as sniff at it, but looked her steadily in the face, with a little growl, as much as to say, " Do you mean to insult me ?"

She began to sing, still holding the bit of meat in her fingers and bringing it a little nearer to his nose.

He snapped at her with a short, sharp bark, and, laughing, she took up another piece with a silver fork, and silently offered it.

He only repeated his growl.

She began her song again, still holding out the piece on the fork, and he took it at once and devoured it greedily.

The door opened, and a comely woman, older and more staid in appearance than the merry, talkative Kathleen, came in, asking in a tone of irritation,

"What's the matter here? what are you doing to Madame's pet? she sent me down to see if he was getting abused."

"Niver a bit at all, at all, Mary, me dear ; sure an' it's mesilf that likes the little baste wid it's cunnin' thricks too well to abuse it, let alone that I'd niver hurt a livin' crayther. Och, ye varmint ! take it, will yees ?" offering another choice morsel ; " can't yer see with half an eye that even the like o' me can't talk an' sing both at onct ? It's worse than a babby yees are ! Tra, la, la, la, la la !"

"Ten times worse!" observed the older woman testily, "but nothing to compare to his mistress, she's more trouble than forty babies ; never a wink o' sleep do I git till long after midnight."

"An' do ye think, Mary, me dear, it's much slape ye'd get wid forty babbies to the fore?" queried Kathleen, ceasing her song for a moment. "But I'm forgetting me manners. It's the young lady that's come to make the Madame's dress, Mary," she added, with a nod of her head in Floy's direction.

"How do you do, miss?" said Mary civilly. "Don't be discouraged at what I've been saying ; the Madame has her good points as well as other folks ; you'll find her unreasonable and hard to please sometimes, but she'll make it up to you ; she's very generous and free with her money."

In reply Floy, having finished her meal, intimated that she would like to get to work at once.

"Then come with me ; I'll take you to the sewing-room and give you the skirts to work at till Madame is pleased to be fitted," returned Mary, leading the way.

This, too, was a bright, cheery, prettily-furnished room, and Floy was not sorry to be left alone in it for the next hour. Quietness and solitude had become rare luxuries in the busy, crowded life of the homeless young orphan.

How quiet the house was! were there no children in it? No, surely only a childless woman could be so foolishly fond of an animal as this Madame evidently was.

CHAPTER XXI.

GHOSTS OF THE PAST.

> "Oh, it comes o'er my memory
> As doth the raven o'er the infected house."
> SHAKESPEARE, *Othello*.

No wonder Floy found the house so quiet. Madame's dressing-room, adjoining the one where she sat, was tenantless, the lady herself sleeping soundly in the bedroom beyond, Frisky curled up by her side, and Mary dozing on a sofa near by, while Kathleen had locked up her kitchen and gone out upon some household errand.

As the clock on the mantel struck ten Madame awoke.

"Mary!" she called plaintively, "Mary, why did you let me sleep so long?"

"Because if I had not you would have reproved me for waking you," returned the maid, shaking off her drowsiness and assuming a sitting posture upon the sofa.

"Mary, you are impolite, not to say unkind and disrespectful, to answer me so," whimpered the mistress, applying a handkerchief to her eyes. "You don't appreciate all I do for you. It isn't every girl that can live in the luxury you do—fed and clothed like a lady—and lay by her five or six dollars every week too."

"That's true enough, Madame; but I'm sure I earn it all, and you know as well as I that you couldn't get anybody else to serve you as much to your liking for twice the money. What will you be pleased to have for your breakfast?"

"Nothing," returned Madame, sobbing behind her handkerchief.

"How will you have it prepared?" asked Mary with unmoved gravity.

Madame burst into a laugh. "I'll have a broiled sweet-bread, hot buttered muffins, coffee, and marmalade."

"Shall I prepare it?"

"No, ring for Kathleen."

Mary touched the bell.

"What gown will Madame be pleased to wear?" she asked, bringing a basin of water and a towel to the bedside.

"That blue silk wrapper. Has Mrs. Sharp come?"

"No, but she has sent a young girl to work for you. I left her in the sewing-room making your skirts."

"The top o' the mornin' to yees, Madame!" cried Kathleen, coming in fresh and rosy from her walk. "I hope ye're aisy, an' feel like atin' a big breakfast. Ye breathe aisier nor ye do sometimes."

Madame was seized at that moment with a wheezing asthmatic cough.

"I had a bad night," she said pantingly, "and have no breath to spare. Tell her what to get me, Mary."

Thirty years ago Madame Le Conte was a slender, graceful girl, with a clear olive complexion, delicate features, ruby lips, bright black eyes, and lively, engaging manners ; now she was an overgrown, gross-looking, middle-aged, or rather elderly, woman, immensely fat, tortured with asthma, gout and sundry kindred ailments, dull, heavy, and uninteresting, nervous, irritable, childishly unreasonable and changeable, full of whims and fancies—a wretched burden to herself and all about her.

Rolling in wealth, she constantly sighed over the sad fact that there were none of her own kith and kin to inherit it, and that the service rendered her was not the service of love, but merely of self-interest.

Mary, her personal attendant, had been with her many years, thoroughly understood her ways, and knew how to minister to her wants as no one else did ; and quite aware of the fact, sometimes took advantage of it to scold her mistress when much tried by her unreasonable demands, threatening to leave, and occasionally even refusing to obey orders, when Madame would angrily dismiss her, but on being seemingly taken at her word, would relent, burst into tears and pathetic entreaties, and buy a reconciliation with fair promises, increased wages, or expensive presents.

Madame wore a cork hand ; how she had come to be deprived of her good right hand no one knew or dared ask, for she was extremely sensitive in regard to her loss, and would not endure the slightest allusion to it. Mary removed the artificial limb at night and replaced it in the morning without question or comment, and made it part of her business to divert the idle curiosity of others from this deformity of her mistress. This she did without waiting for instructions; for Mary had a heart, and often pitied the poor rich cripple from its very depths.

"Yes, she had a bad night, so don't make her talk any more," she said to Kathleen as she carefully laved her mistress's face and hand. "She'll have a broiled sweet-bread—"

"No, no, let it be stewed; I'll have it stewed," interrupted the Madame.

Mary completed the bill of fare as given by her mistress a few moments before, and Kathleen turned to go, but had scarcely reached the door when she was called back.

"Waffles, waffles, Katty," wheezed her mistress.

"Yes, ma'am; and muffins too?"

"No—yes, yes. Go, and make haste; I'm starved."

Kathleen had reached the head of the stairs when she was again recalled, and tea and cream-toast substituted for coffee, muffins, and waffles; then the Madame thought she would prefer chocolate, and finally decided that all three should be prepared, toast and muffins also, and she would take her choice.

Even Kathleen's almost imperturbable good-nature was somewhat tried. Her face clouded for a moment, but all was sunshine ere she reached her kitchen again, where she flew nimbly about, executing the latest orders of her capricious mistress, saying laughingly to herself:

"Sure an' it's me that 'ud better make haste afore she has time to change her mind again; for it won't be long it'll take her to do that same."

There was a knock at the side gate, and Kathleen flew to open it, the rose on her cheek deepening and her pretty blue eyes dancing with delight.

"It's only me, Kathleen, me darlint!" cried a cheery voice.

"Sure and don't I know your knock, Rory?" she responded, drawing back the bolt and admitting a strapping young Irishman. "But come into the kitchen; I've got the Madame's breakfast over the fire, and can't stop here to spake two words to ye," she added, running back, he following close at her heels.

"Has the Madame sint down her orders yet?" he asked, sitting down beside the fire and watching the girl's movements with admiring eyes.

"No; she's just up, and I'm thinking the horses'll be likely to rest till after dinner anyhow, for she's got a dressmaker at work makin' up that illegant silk she bought yesterday, and she'll be wantin' to get fit, you know."

"Av coorse. Well, I'm contint, since me wages goes on all the same, an' maybe I'll have the more time to sit here with you."

"Maybe so, and maybe not," said Kathleen, turning her muffins; "they'll maybe be wantin' me up there to run the machine."

"I wish it was to make a silk gown for yersilf, jewel; the Madame's got a plinty now, and all the fine dresses as iver was made couldn't make her look half as purty as you do in that nate calico. Things isn't avenly divided in this world, Kathleen, mavourneen."

"Sure now, Rory, the good things isn't all on one

side, afther all," returned Kathleen, laughing. "Wouldn't the Madame give all her fine dresses, and silver and goold too, for my health and strength or yours?"

"That she would; or for your illegant figger and purty skin that's just like lilies and roses, and your eyes that shine brighter than her diamonds."

"Whist!" cried Kathleen, hastily lifting her coffee-pot from the fire just as Mary opened the dining-room door with the query:

"Is breakfast ready?"

"Everything's done to a turn," said Kathleen. "And here's Rory ready to carry it up, if ye like."

"No, she has changed her mind; she'll eat in the breakfast-room. Rory's to bring her down in the elevator, and take her up again in it when she's done."

When Madame had duly discussed her breakfast, and recovered breath after her ascent to her private apartments, Floy was summoned to her presence.

The young girl came quietly into the dressing-room, where the lady reclined in a large easy chair.

Madame started at sight of her, uttering a low exclamation.

"Who are you?" she asked, her voice trembling a little as she spoke, "and what is your name?"

"I am one of Mrs. Sharp's apprentices, and my name is Florence Kemper. I have cut and basted the lining of your dress; shall I fit it on you now?"

"Yes—no; Mary will put it on me and see if it is all right. Mary knows my ways."

Madame's tone was still agitated, and she seemed flurried and uneasy under Floy's glance.

The girl noted it, and with true delicacy turned her eyes in another direction while Mary performed the required service.

Madame stood up before the glass. "I think it fits, Mary, doesn't it?"

"I think not quite. Shall Miss Kemper look at it?"

Madame assented, and Floy's nimble fingers were presently busied about her, she meanwhile earnestly regarding the reflection of the young face in the glass.

It seemed to have far more interest for her than the fit of the new gown, though ordinarily she was eager as a child in regard to any new article of dress.

"Does it satisfy you now, Madame?" asked Floy at length.

The Madame started as if waking from a dream, glanced at the image of her own portly figure, and responded with a hasty "Yes, yes, it is all right! Child, you look tired, wretchedly tired—almost ill. You must rest. Sit down in that chair, and Mary shall bring you some refreshments."

"Many thanks, but I have no time for rest; these are busy days for dressmakers," Floy answered, with a sad smile, thinking of the piles of dress patterns still untouched, and garments in various stages of completion, in Mrs. Sharp's work-room.

"Sit down!" repeated the Madame, with an imperious gesture; "I am used to obedience from all in this house. Just slip my wrapper on again, Mary, and then go to my closet and bring out all the good things you can find."

Mary obeyed, nothing loath, for she too felt drawn

to the young stranger, and Floy presently had spread before her a tempting variety of cakes, confectionery, and tropical fruits.

In vain she protested that she was not hungry; Madame would not be content till she had seen her eat an orange and a bunch of grapes, and put a paper of candies into her pocket.

For the rest of the day the Madame insisted upon occupying an easy chair in the sewing-room, where, with Frisky curled up in her lap and the latest novel in her hand, she furtively watched Floy's movements, and when she spoke, listened with ill-concealed eagerness to every tone of her voice.

Floy, whose thoughts were far away, was scarcely conscious of this strange interest taken in her, but Mary noted it with wonder and growing curiosity shared by Kathleen, who had been, as she anticipated, summoned to the work of running the machine. They telegraphed each other with nods, winks, and smiles, neither the Madame nor Floy perceiving.

"The sun has set, and it is growing dark," remarked the Madame, closing her book and breaking in on a long silence. "You are straining your eyes in your efforts to thread that needle, Miss Kemper. Come, put up your work and rest a little, while Mary and Kathleen prepare our tea."

"Thank you, Madame," said Floy, "but Mrs. Sharp would not approve of so early a rest, and if I may have a light I will go on with the work."

"Tut! tut! *I'm* mistress here, and I'll have no such overwork!" was the quick, imperative rejoinder. "I'll make it right with Mrs. Sharp, paying for the time all the same."

Floy submitted, repeating her thanks, for to the over-strained eyes and weary frame a little rest was most refreshing.

The work was neatly folded and laid aside. Mary and Kathleen tidied the room, gathering up the shreds of silk and lining, and putting things in place ; then receiving orders from Madame for a delicious little supper to be served in her dressing-room for Floy and herself, they went down to prepare it.

A bright fire in an open grate filled the room with ruddy light, and Floy was glad that the Madame refused to have any other for the present.

Very sad, very quiet the young girl felt, thinking of Espy and his sorrow ; and taking, in obedience to her employer's direction, an easy chair by the window, she gazed out musingly upon the lake, whose dark, restless waters were now faintly illumined by a line of silver light along the eastern horizon.

"The moon's about to rise," wheezed her companion. "I like to watch it as it seems to come up out of the water. Did you ever see it ?"

"No, Madame," returned the girl, smiling slightly, "Mrs. Sharp's apprentices have little time or opportunity to observe the beauties of nature."

"But Sundays—you do not work then ?"

"No, Madame, but they find me weary enough to go very early to bed."

"Ah, too bad, too bad ! But look, look ! what a shame to be deprived of so lovely a sight as that !" cried the Madame as the queen of night suddenly emerged from her watery bed, flooding the whole scene with mellow radiance.

"It is very beautiful," murmured Floy, sighing softly to herself.

How often in the happy days gone by she and Espy had enjoyed the moonlight together!

"I would not stay there if I were you," pursued the Madame. "Why should you stay where you are so badly treated? Why should any one?"

"Because, Madame, it is there I must gain the knowledge that is to enable me to earn my bread."

"A hard thing for a lady to do. Any one can see you are a lady—your speech, your manners, your appearance, all tell it. But, ah well, you have youth, good looks, health! and though I'm rich, I'd be only too glad to exchange with you," and in her wheezing tones, and with many a pause for breath, the Madame went on to give a long account of her sufferings by day and by night.

Floy listened with a patient attention and sincere sympathy such as the Madame, in her loneliness, was little accustomed to.

"It must be very dreadful to have so many ailments," she said feelingly. "I don't know how I could bear your difficulty of breathing even, without any of the others."

The Madame started, sat upright, and looked earnestly at the girl, while tears gathered in her eyes.

"Your voice is like a half-forgotten strain of music," she said, sighing; "and your face—ah, it seems as if I must have seen it in the long ago, the happy time when I was young and life full of sunshine and flowers. Alas, child!" she added, sinking back upon her cushions again, "as the years roll on how the sunlight gives place to clouds and darkness.

and the flowers fade and die! would that I could be young again!"

"Were you always happy in your youthful days, Madame?"

There were tears in the low, sweet voice that put the question.

"No, no; indeed I believe I sometimes thought myself quite wretched!" exclaimed the Madame; "but I see now what a fool I was."

"Supper is ready, ladies," announced Mary, throwing open the door of communication with the dressing-room. "Shall I wheel you in, Madame?"

With a peevish reply in the negative the Madame rose and waddled to the table, preceded by Frisky, for whom a chair had been placed at her right hand.

Floy was invited to the seat opposite her hostess, and, conscious of being a lady, accepted it with no feeling of surprise that it was accorded her. In fact, her thoughts were again far away, and scarcely to be recalled by the tempting nature of the repast or the magnificence of the solid silver and rare old china.

Fortunately she was not called upon to talk or to listen, as Frisky was taking his supper after the same manner in which he had eaten his breakfast, Kathleen attending to him while Mary waited upon the table.

The Madame ate and drank enormously, paying no heed to an occasional reminder from Mary that she would have to suffer for her over-indulgence.

"You are a cruel creature! you would deprive me of the only pleasure left me in life!" she at length exclaimed passionately, as the girl almost absolutely refused to help her for the sixth time to fried oysters.

"Madame," replied Mary firmly, "you know the doctor has forbidden them altogether, and that an hour or two from now you'll be abusing me for letting you have any at all."

At that the Madame rose, angrily pushed back her chair and retired in a pet to her room.

CHAPTER XXII.

REMORSE.

" Remembrance wakes with all her busy train,
 Swells at my breast, and turns the past to pain."
                                        GOLDSMITH.

MADAME LE CONTE did not appear again that evening.

Floy returned to her work upon the new gown immediately upon leaving the table, and did not lay it aside again until the clock struck ten.

Then Kathleen showed her to an adjoining bedroom, whose appointments seemed to carry her back to the happy days when she was the loved and petted only child of well-to-do parents. Less than a year ago she had seen the last of them, but how far, far away they already seemed!

The young heart was sore with grief and care, and not for itself alone. But the worn-out body must have rest, and all was soon forgotten in sound, refreshing sleep.

She woke in the dull gray light of the winter morning and sprang up instantly, half trembling with affright at thought of the lateness of the hour.

At Mrs. Sharp's, breakfast was long since over. To-morrow was Christmas, and, though not expecting either to go out or to receive company at home, the Madame must have her new dress to wear on that occasion.

But no one found fault with Floy; the buxom Kathleen had an excellent breakfast ready for her, and greeting her cheerily with "The top o' the mornin' to ye, miss," waited upon her with a smiling face.

She took her meal alone, as on the previous day, and had the cosey work-room to herself for a couple of hours; then the Madame waddled in, wheezing and groaning, dropped into a chair, and told a pitiful tale of her wearisome night and Mary's crossness, weeping and sighing as she talked.

Floy pitied and tried to console her, but fortunately found it necessary to say but little, as the lady talked on with scarcely a pause except for breath, and presently fell to petting and caressing her lapdog, then to examining the dress, commenting with much satisfaction upon its beauty and probable becomingness, querying whether it could be finished that day, and consulting Floy about the style of trimming.

Floy advised a deep, heavy silk fringe to match in color, or of a little darker shade.

The Madame caught at the idea, and Mary, coming in at that moment, was sent to order the carriage that she might go at once and select it herself.

Frisky pricked up his ears, gave a short, joyous bark, ran to the window overlooking the side entrance, and jumped upon a chair whence he could see into the street.

"See that, miss?" queried the laughing Kathleen, who was present, engaged in running the sewing-machine as on the day before. "The little baste knows more'n a babby. He always rides with the Madame, an' whin he hears the carriage ordered he's ready for a start. He'll stay there watchin' now till it comes."

"Yes," said the Madame, overhearing the remark, "he's the most intelligent little creature you ever saw, and the prettiest. I wouldn't part with him for any money—the darling! Now, Mary," as her maid re-entered the room, "dress me at once."

"Certainly, Madame. What will you be pleased to wear?"

"That green silk suit and the green velvet hat," answered her mistress, waddling into the dressing-room; "gloves to match, and my emerald set, earrings, pin, and bracelets, and a point-lace collar and sleeves. Get out one of my worked white skirts too, and a pair of silk stockings and gaiters."

"It's very cold, Madame; the wind from the lake cuts like a knife, and you'll suffer in thin shoes," Mary objected to the last clause of the order.

"Lamb's-wool stockings, then, and kid boots."

Bureau-drawers, wardrobe, and closets were laid under contribution, and the Madame's toilet began.

It had progressed to the putting on of her hat, when, glancing in the mirror, she suddenly changed her mind.

"Green doesn't become me to-day," she said, "why didn't you tell me? Take it off at once."

"Tell you? much good that would have done!" grumbled Mary, removing the obnoxious hat; "you wouldn't have believed me."

"Get out my black velvet hat and a black silk suit," said her mistress, ignoring the impertinent rejoinder.

"You'll not have time for your shopping if you wait to dress again, Madame," objected the girl; "it is already half-past eleven, and the days are short. Your black velvet cloak and hat will not look amiss with the green dress."

The Madame yielded to these suggestions all the more readily because at that moment a joyous bark from Frisky announced that the carriage was in waiting.

He sprang from the chair, rushed down to the outside door, and scratched and whined there till Kathleen ran down and opened it for him, when he immediately took possession of one half of the back seat, leaving the other for his mistress, who presently followed, having reached the lower floor, not by the stairs, but by the elevator, carefully lowered by the ever-ready Kathleen.

Mary, without whom the Madame never stirred from the house, took the front seat, a handsome afghan and wolf-skin were tucked carefully about their feet by Rory, and the carriage drove off.

For a short space the Madame puffed and wheezed in silence, then she spoke:

"We'll get the fringe first, and have it sent up; then the Christmas gifts. Mary, what do you think Miss Kemper would like?"

"How should I now, Madame? I'm not acquainted with the young lady's tastes," returned the maid snappishly.

She had a raging headache, the result of an almost sleepless night spent in efforts to undo the evil effects of the rich, heavy, evening meal, indulged in by her wilful charge.

The Madame, who was feeling depressed and hysterical from the same cause, put her handkerchief to her eyes, shed a few tears, and whimpered:

"It's shameful the way I'm treated by you, Mary. There aren't many ladies who would put up with it as I do."

"Handkerchiefs are always acceptable," remarked the delinquent, ignoring the reproach, but giving the suggestion in answer to the query. Then, by way of salve to her conscience, she added: "It's like your generosity to think of making a present to a stranger."

This restored the Madame to good-humor. She was generous, and she liked to have full credit for it.

The day was very cold but clear and bright, and the city was full of life and activity. Vehicles jostled each other in the streets, pedestrians hurried hither and thither along the sidewalks, there was a grand display of holiday goods in the windows, and the stores were crowded with purchasers.

The bustle and excitement were agreeable to Madame Le Conte, and she found much enjoyment in selecting her gifts and paying for them from her well-filled purse.

Meanwhile Floy toiled on at the dress, her thoughts now with Espy in his anxiety and grief, now dwelling mournfully upon the past, memory and imagination bringing vividly before her the loved faces that should gladden her eyes no more on earth, and causing her to hear again each well-remembered tone of the dear voices now silent in the tomb.

She longed to seek out a solitary place and weep,

but the luxury of tears was not for her; she forced them back, silently asking help to obey the command to be ever "rejoicing in hope, patient in tribulation."

Hope! ah, she had not lost that even for this life. Espy still lived, still loved her; they might yet be restored to each other. And her mother—that unknown yet already dearly-loved mother—who should say how soon she would be given to her prayers and efforts?

Her needle flew more swiftly, while a tender, loving smile played about her lips and shone in her dark, lustrous eyes.

The Madame came home panting and wheezing, but elated with her success in shopping. She was quite ready for Christmas, and it might come as soon as it pleased. But—ah, there was the dress!

"Are you going to get it done to-day?" she asked, sinking into a chair in front of Floy, and glancing anxiously from her to the garment and back again.

"I shall try, Madame, but fear it is doubtful," Floy replied, raising her eyes for an instant to her interrogator's face.

The Madame started, changed color, and seemed quite agitated for a moment. Then recovered herself.

"The girls shall both help you," she said, "and you won't mind working in the evening, will you? You'll not need to go back to Mrs. Sharp's to-night, will you?"

"No, Madame; and I may as well work late here as there."

The Madame thanked her, and left the room with a mental resolve that the girl should not lose by her willingness to oblige.

"I'm worn out, Mary," she said to her maid, who was bestowing in a closet in the dressing-room the numerous parcels which she and Rory had just brought upstairs; "change my dress for a wrapper, and I'll lie down and take a nap while you and Katty help with the dress. You're not too tired, I suppose?"

"No, of course not; it isn't my place ever to be too tired for anything you wish done," grumbled Mary, putting the last package upon the closet shelf and closing the door with a little more force than was necessary.

Then half ashamed of her petulance, in view of the generous way in which her mistress had just been laying out money in gifts for herself and her brother, "I'll do my best, Madame," she added in a pleasant tone, "but I hope you'll take a light supper to-night for your own sake as well as mine."

"I'm quite as anxious to rest well at night as you can be to have me, Mary," returned the Madame in an injured tone, as she sat down and began herself to unfasten and remove her outer wrappings.

"Yes, I suppose so, Madame, and you must excuse my free speaking," responded Mary, coming to her assistance.

The Madame's enormous weight made her a burden to herself, and the unwonted exertion of the day had wearied her greatly. Comfortably established on a couch in her bedroom, she presently fell into a sleep so profound that she was not disturbed when her maid stole softly in at nightfall, drew the curtains, lighted the gas, and retired again.

But a moment later the Madame awoke with a low cry, and starting to a sitting posture, rubbed her eyes and glanced hurriedly about the room.

"Ah," she sighed, sinking back again, "it was a dream, only a dream! I shall never see her more! My darling, oh, my darling! How could I be so cruel, so cruel! Pansy, Pansy! And I am so lonely, so lonely! with not a soul in the wide world to care for me!"

Sobs and tears came thick and fast; then she rose, slowly crossed the room, turned up the gas, and unlocking her jewel-box, took from it a small, plain gold locket attached to a slender chain.

It opened with a touch, showing a sweet, sunny child face, with smiling lips, soft, wavy brown hair, and large, dark, lustrous eyes.

The Madame wept anew as she gazed upon it, and her broad breast heaved with sigh after sigh.

"So many years! so many years!" she moaned, "and my search has been all in vain. Ah, dear one, are you yet in the land of the living? My darling, my darling!" and the tears fell in floods.

But at length growing calmer, she restored the trinket to its place, turned down the gas, and staggering to an easy chair beside the window, dropped heavily into it.

Her breath came pantingly, the tears still stood in her eyes. She wiped them away, and drawing aside the curtain, looked into the street.

The moon had not yet risen, but the lamps were lighted, and there was a clear, starlit sky. She could see the passers-by as they hurried on their way, now singly, now in groups of two or more ; mostly well, or at least comfortably, clad, and carrying brown-paper parcels suggestive of the coming festivities.

A confectionery on the opposite corner was ablaze with light, showing a tempting array of sweets in the windows. It was crowded with customers, and there was a constant passing in and out of cheerful-looking men and women and bright-eyed, eager children.

Presently a slender figure, apparently that of a very young girl, very shabbily dressed in faded calico and with an old shawl thrown over her head caught the Madame's attention.

She came suddenly around the corner, and though shivering with cold, her thin garments flapping in the wind, stood gazing with longing eyes upon the piles of fruit, cakes, and candies. The Madame's eyes filled as she noted the child's hungry look and scant clothing. With a great effort she rose and threw a shawl about her shoulders ; then she went to a drawer in her bureau where she kept loose change, and returning, tapped on the sash, threw it up, and called to the girl, who had not moved from her station on the other side of the street.

She turned, however, at the sound of the voice, and seeing a beckoning hand, crossed swiftly over.

"Stand under here and hold out your shawl," wheezed the Madame. "There ! now run back and buy yourself a lot of goodies for Christmas."

"Thank you, ma'am, oh, thank you !" cried the child as the window went down again, and the Madame dropped into her chair, wheezing and coughing, to find her maid close at her side.

"Madame, are you mad?" exclaimed Mary. "Your bare head out of the window this bitter cold night. Well, if either of us gets a wink of sleep it'll be more than I expect!"

The Madame's cough forbade a reply for the moment.

"I'll get you your drops," said Mary, running to a closet where medicines were kept. "I can't imagine what on earth induced you to do such a foolish thing. Why didn't you ring for me?"

"Never mind," panted the Madame; "you seem to forget that I'm my own mistress, and yours too. Is the dress nearly done?"

"We can finish it by sitting up, if you'll let Katty wait on you. All the machine stitching's done, and only Miss Kemper and I can work on it now; so Katty's gone down to get you some supper."

"I don't want any."

"But you know, Madame, you'll be ill if you don't eat; fasting never agrees with you, no more than over-eating."

Kathleen came in at that moment bearing a tempting little repast upon a silver waiter, which she set down before her mistress.

The Madame at first refused to eat, but presently, yielding to the combined entreaties and expostulations of the two, made a very tolerable attempt. Kathleen was retained to wait upon her, and Mary was directed to assist Floy until the gown should be completed.

"You're looking very tired," the latter remarked, as Mary resumed her seat by her side.

"Not a bit more'n you do, miss," said the girl,

with a compassionate glance at Floy's pale cheeks and heavy eyes. "Dear me! don't you think riches harden the heart? There's the Madame has a dozen elegant silk dresses, good as new, if she has one, yet we must both wear ourselves out to get this done for to-morrow, though there won't be a soul besides ourselves here to look at it, unless the lawyer or doctor should happen to call, which ain't in the least likely, seein' it's a holiday."

"Perhaps, then, we may consider ourselves blest in being poor," Floy returned cheerfully; "and which of us would exchange our health for the poor Madame's wealth?"

"Not I, I'm sure," said Mary, shaking her head; "she's worth her thousands, and has everything that money can buy, but she has never an hour's ease or happiness."

Both were too weary, Floy too heartsore, to be in a talkative mood; so they worked on in silence till startled from it by a sudden loud peal from the door-bell.

"Who can that be?" exclaimed Mary, laying down her work and glancing at the clock on the mantel; "half-past nine, and we never have any callers of evenings. There," returning to her work at the sound of the opening and shutting of a door, followed by footsteps hastily descending the stairs, "Katty's gone to answer it."

The next minute Floy felt a light tap on her shoulder, and looked up to find Hetty's bright, cheery face bending over her.

"Ah, I've surprised you! Thought I should. Hope the shock will be good for your nerves,"

Hetty said, laughing in a pleased, kindly way at Floy's start and joyous exclamation :

"Oh! is it you? how glad I am!"

"Yes; John and I have come to take you home."

"John?"

"One of Aunt Prue's boys. The children have come home for the holidays—but wouldn't Araminta take my head off if she heard me say that! She's the youngest, has arrived at the mature age of fifteen, and considers herself wiser than her parents or 'than ten men that can render a reason.' Come, put on your things, my dear."

"I wish I could, but I have engaged to finish this to-night, and there's a full hour's work on it yet."

"Not if I help," said Hetty, pulling off her gloves and taking a thimble from her pocket. "I'll call master John up and give him a book. You see I came prepared for emergencies."

"He won't like it, will he?"

"He's a dear good fellow, and would do more than that for me ; or for you when he knows you."

CHAPTER XXIII.

OLD FRIENDS AND NEW.

"All things, friendship excepted,
Are subject to fortune."—LILLY.

THE hands on the dial-plate of the clock pointed to quarter-past ten as Hetty's nimble fingers set the last stitch in the gown and Floy drew on her gloves, having already donned hat and cloak in obedience to orders.

"Done!" cried Hetty, putting her needle in the cushion and her thimble into her pocket. "Now, John, make way with these few basting threads while I put on my duds, there's a good soul!"

John—a well-grown lad of seventeen, in looks a happy mixture of father and mother, in character an improvement upon both, having his mother's energy without her hardness and closeness—laid down the paper he had been reading, and with the smiling rejoinder, "Pretty work to set a man at, Het!" was about to comply with her request when Mary, coming in from her mistress's bedroom, her hands full of packages, interposed:

"Oh, never mind them! I'll have them all out in the morning before the Madame's up. Here, Miss Goodenough, Miss Kemper, and Mr. John, she charged me to give you each one of these.

They're boxes of fine candies. She always lays in a great store of them about Christmas."

"Ah, ha!" cried John as the street-door closed on him and his companions, "won't I have the laugh on Lu to-night, Het? He'd never have let me be your gallant if he'd thought there was a box of candy to be won by it."

"A good thing he didn't; he'll manage as it is to get enough to make himself sick," she returned somewhat scornfully.

"It was so kind in you to come for me," remarked Floy. "How did you happen to do it, Hetty?"

"Because we wanted you—mother and I at least —and we thought it was getting too late for you to come alone."

Floy was very weary in body, inexpressibly sad and weary in heart and mind. She strove to shake off her depression and respond to Hetty's merry mood; but in vain. She could not banish the thick-coming memories of other holiday seasons made bright and joyous by the gifts, and still more by the love, of those of whom she was now bereaved by death and enforced separation.

Ah, what of Espy to-night?

Hetty read something of this in the sad eyes, and her mood changed to quiet, subdued cheerfulness.

They entered the house quietly, letting themselves in with a latch-key, and passed into the room back of the store.

Floy uttered a slight exclamation of pleased surprise as John turned up the light.

The room had put on quite a festive appearance; all signs of work had vanished, and it had been made neat and orderly, and its walls tastefully decorated with evergreens.

"John's doings," said Hetty, pushing a cushioned arm-chair nearer the fire. "Sit down here, my dear, and we'll have some refreshments shortly; you see the kettle's boiling, and the coals are just splendid, and we can take our time, as we're not obliged to rise early to-morrow.

"Toast and tea, Jack, my boy; you and I know how to make 'em," she went on, throwing off cloak and hat, and producing the requisite articles from a closet beside the chimney.

"I've already had three good meals to-day," observed Floy, smiling slightly.

"What of that? four or five hours of hard work since the last, beside a brisk walk and a ride through the cold, ought to have made you ready for another," returned Hetty, giving John the toaster and a slice of bread, then putting on the tea to draw.

"Have you nothing for me to do?" asked Floy.

"Yes; warm yourself thoroughly. Ah, what a good forgettery I have of my own! Here's something else to employ you. A bit of Christmas in it, I suspect," she ran on, taking a letter from the mantel and putting it into Floy's hand.

A flush of pleasure came into the young girl's cheek as she recognized in the address the writing of her old friend Miss Wells, but faded again instantly, leaving it paler than before.

What news did this missive bring? would it tell her of Espy, and that sorrow and bereavement had befallen him?

She broke the seal with a trembling hand. Ah, if she were only alone !

But Hetty and John, busy with their culinary labors, might have been unconscious of her existence for all the notice they seemed to be taking of her movements.

She opened the letter. A pair of black kid gloves and a folded bank-note fell into her lap ; but without waiting to examine them, she glanced her eye down the page.

It was a kind, motherly letter, saying a great deal in few words ; for Miss Wells had but little time to give to correspondence.

"She sent a trifling gift just to assure her dear child of her loving remembrance, and she inclosed ten dollars, fearing her purse might be low (she had not forgotten how it was with herself in the days when she was an apprentice and getting nothing but her board for her work) ; and if Floy did not like to take it as a gift, as she would be only too glad to have her do, then let it stand as a loan."

"How kind, how very kind !" thought Floy.

Yes, her purse was very low, and such a loan from such a source was very acceptable. Ah, here was Espy's name ! He had been called home to see his mother die ; she had had a stroke of paralysis, but the case was not hopeless ; she might linger a good while, and perhaps get about again.

Floy breathed more freely.

There were just a few more lines.

"Dear child, sorrow and care will sometimes press heavily ; you will sadly miss the old loves ; but take heart : 'He careth for you,' He who loves you with a greater, tenderer love than a mother's, and hath all power in heaven and in earth."

"Good news, I see! and I'm real glad for you, poor child!" said Hetty softly, as she handed Floy a cup of fragrant tea and a slice of hot buttered toast, and in so doing caught the look of sweet peace and joy in the dewy eyes lifted from the letter to her face.

"Good news? oh, yes indeed! that I'm not forgotten, that I'm loved and cared for still by—"

"Ah, yes, don't I know how nice it is to be remembered by home friends when you're far away!" Hetty put in quickly, as the low, tremulous tones faltered and fell, and Floy hastily drew out her handkerchief to wipe away the tears she could not keep back.

"I too," said John, buttering his toast and taking a sip of tea; "a fellow gets awfully homesick sometimes at school, and a letter such as you, for instance, dash off once in a while, Het, does him a world of good."

"News from home," whispered Floy to herself, as she laid her weary head upon her pillow; "yes, from my Father's house; a sweet message from my Elder Brother on the throne, reminding me anew that He cares for me; how strange that, knowing that, I can ever be sad and anxious!"

It was the last waking thought. But, alas! what a pang of remembrance came with the first moment of returning consciousness! One year ago how loved and cared for, to-day how lonely and forsaken!

Ah no, not that! "He careth for you," sweetly

whispered the Comforter to her aching heart, and she was comforted.

A few quiet tears dropped upon her pillow, but they were not all of sadness.

A faint rustling sound came from the bed on the other side of the room, then a whisper from Hetty.

"Merry Christmas, mothery! how are you this morning?"

"Oh, I'm splendid! I'm going to say everything's splendid now. Merry Christmas to you too. I wish I had a million to give you."

"A million of what, mothery?" laughed the girl.

"Dollars, to be sure! But what is it Shakespeare says?"

"Don't know, mothery; but it's getting light, and I must get up and see about breakfast."

"Yes, and we're to have Indian; Thorne insisted on it."

"What in the world is that?" thought Floy, raising her head to look at Hetty, who was making a hasty but very quiet toilet.

"Merry Christmas and Happy New Year!" they cried simultaneously, ending in a merry laugh.

"We'll exchange Yankee sixpences when we get our faces washed," said Hetty. "Breakfast in twenty minutes precisely. Indian all hot and hot!" and with the last word she darted from the room.

"Thorne gives a good bit o' trouble one way and another," observed Mrs. Goodenough, who had risen also and was dressing much more deliberately than Hetty had done; "he'll have what he wants in spite of everything (in the line of trouble to other folks 'specially). But then there ain't many that's equivalent to him in learning. There isn't anything but what he's read ; he knows everything. So it's quite natural Prue should be proud of him and spoil him with humoring all his whims."

"Do we all breakfast together this morning, Mrs. Goodenough?" asked Floy.

"Yes ; but I'm going to wear this thick wrapper ; it's not handsome or dressy, but the comfort supersedes the outward appearance."

With this remark she left the room.

Floy was glad of the few moments of solitude thus afforded her. It was growing light, and she found time before the call to breakfast for another peep at her precious letter. She hurried down at the first stroke of the bell, anxious to avoid meeting the Sharps on the stairway.

Patsy, in her ordinary soiled, frowsy-headed, slipshod condition, was setting the chairs up to the table, on which Mrs. Goodenough and Hetty were arranging an unusually inviting meal.

"Don't delude yourself with the hope that you are about to be regaled upon pound-cake, Miss Kemper," remarked Hetty, placing a loaf of hot corn-pone near Floy's plate, another at the farther end of the board.

"No, it's only Indian," said Mrs. Goodenough, "but it's splendid, and more than equivalent to pound-cake for breakfast."

"Yes indeed," said Floy, "*I* greatly prefer it, at any rate ; I'm extremely fond of good corn-bread."

"Well, Hetty's is always superior to the best."

"Superior to the best, eh?" sneered the Thorne, as with pompous air he came leisurely in and took his accustomed seat. "Madam, that is a contradiction in terms."

"Well, if it isn't good enough for you, you needn't eat it," she returned indifferently ; "but let's sit down and begin while it's hot."

The Thorne was evidently in no holiday mood. "Where are the children ?" he demanded, with a scowl, glancing about upon the empty seats as he took up the carving knife and fork.

"Don't wait for them ; they'll be here presently," said his wife.

"Presently, madam !" he growled ; "they ought to have been ready an hour ago. You are bringing up your children to ruinous habits of self-indulgence."

"Example is better than precept," Hetty could not help remarking.

"And pray, miss, what do you mean by that ?" he asked, turning almost fiercely upon her.

"Surely a man of Mr. Sharp's talent and erudition can have no difficulty in understanding words so simple," she replied, with a twinkle of fun in her eye.

"Come, don't let's quarrel to-day of all days in the year," put in her mother good-humoredly. "Here's John, anyhow," as the lad came briskly in with a "Merry Christmas to you all !"

"Where have you been, sir, that you are so late to this very late breakfast ?" asked his father, ignoring the greeting.

"Round to the grocer's on the corner, sir."

"Doing an errand for me," said Hetty, "and he's not to be scolded ; for if it hadn't been for him—getting me kindling to hurry up my fire, and assisting in various ways—breakfast would have been later than it is."

"Where now, Prudence?"

Mrs. Sharp had risen hastily and pushed back her chair.

"I must go up and see if Araminta is sick, Thorne; the poor thing was too tired yesterday with her journey to do anything but lounge about."·

"Humph! I dare say; you are ruining that child with your coddling."

"Ah, here she comes! Lucian too," said Mrs. Sharp in a relieved tone, resuming her seat as the door opened and a girl of fifteen, looking only half awake and far from neat, in a loose, somewhat soiled morning dress and hair in crimps, came languidly in, followed by a lad some four years older, the veritable counterpart of his father in appearance and manners.

The latter had a scowl and rebuke for each, which were received as matters of course.

"Don't scold 'em, Thorne," said their aunt; "the poor things have so much book attention when they're at school!"

"You're rather late, children," the mother remarked, helping them bountifully; "times are changed since you were little things. Then we could hardly keep you from waking us too soon Christmas morning."

"That was when we were children indeed, and hung up our stockings," said Lucian, "and didn't know what was in them. Now you just give us the money and let us buy for ourselves."

A loud peal from the door-bell sent Patsy flying

out to the hall. She returned in a moment with a letter, two packages, and the morning paper.

"For me! I know they are!" cried Araminta, waking up. "Here, Patsy, give them to me. Dear me, no! how provoking! they're every one directed to Miss Kemper," and she looked around inquiringly.

Upon that John introduced the two, and Floy's property was somewhat reluctantly resigned to her.

She had finished her meal, and, asking to be excused, was leaving the room, when an exclamation from John, who was glancing over the paper, stayed her steps.

"Lea! what Lea is it, I wonder?—'was arrested yesterday on a criminal charge, and has committed suicide. His affairs are found to be hopelessly involved.'"

"Doesn't it give his Christian name?" asked Mrs. Sharp, with interest.

"Yes: Abner."

"Just so; there's a good customer lost!" she exclaimed in a tone of vexation.

"And they were so rich!" remarked her sister; "what turns of the wheel of fortune! What is it Shakespeare says?"

Floy hurried away to the privacy of Hetty's parlor, sighing softly to herself, "Poor Miss Carrie! Ah, there are heavier trials than mine!"

Half an hour later Hetty looked in. "May I see what Santa Claus has sent you?"

"Yes, indeed. A dozen beautifully fine handkerchiefs, with Madame Le Conte's card—"

"Just like her! she's the soul of generosity so far as money is concerned."

"And a letter—such a nice one—and some warm stockings of her own knitting from my kind old friend Mrs. Bond," concluded Floy.

"How splendid!" said Hetty. "You shall sit here and answer it, and the other if you like, while I see about dinner; and this afternoon we'll take a walk and look at the fine things in the shop windows."

CHAPTER XXIV.

GILDED MISERY.

> "Thinking will make me mad : why must I think
> When no thought brings me comfort?"

MADAME LE CONTE was suffering from her imprudent exposure on Christmas-eve. She had taken cold, and her increased difficulty of breathing had robbed both herself and Mary of the greater part of their night's rest.

The gift of a black silk dress and a few trinkets mollified the maid's ill-humor, but Madame was sadly depressed in spirit.

"Go downstairs and enjoy yourself, Mary," she said when she had sent away her almost untasted breakfast. "I'm poor company for any one, and prefer to be alone."

"Let me read to you," said Mary, taking a new book from the table. "This book is lively and interesting."

"I don't care to hear it."

"Then here's the morning paper."

"Take it and read it yourself. I tell you I wish to be alone. Go! I'll ring when I want you." And Madame waved her hand imperiously.

She was in her dressing-room, a cheery apartment elegantly furnished with every appliance for comfort and convenience ; a velvet carpet of exquisite design covered the floor, lace and damask draped the windows; one or two fine paintings adorned the delicately-tinted walls; articles of virtu were scattered here and there; everything the eye rested on was beautiful and appropriate.

Her easy chair was drawn up before the fire (she loved open fires, and had them in every room much frequented by herself), and on a costly Persian rug at her feet Frisky lay sleeping, her only companion since Mary had gone out in obedience to her order, softly closing the door behind her.

Perhaps there were few sadder hearts to-day in all the great city than that of this rich but childless and lonely woman. She sat with her hands folded in her lap, sigh after sigh heaving her bosom, and tears trickling down her cheeks.

"Remorse, remorse!" she whispered almost under her breath; "can there be anything worse? Oh, Pansy, my little Pansy! where are you? living or dead? Are you poor and suffering? Oh, come back, come back to me, and gladly, gladly will I share with you all I have!"

Covering her face with her handkerchief, she sobbed aloud, her whole frame shaking with the violence of her emotion.

This lasted several minutes; then, gradually growing calmer, she wiped away her tears, rose, went to her jewel-box, and possessing herself of the little locket she had been looking on the previous night, returned to her chair by the fire, touched the spring, and again gazed mournfully upon the pretty child-face.

She sat there for hours with the locket in her hand, sometimes looking at the picture, dropping tears upon the sweet face, pressing it to her lips; at others lying back among her cushions with closed eyes, while quick-coming memories of the past thronged through her brain.

At length Mary became alarmed, and ventured in without being summoned.

Her mistress was again gazing at the miniature, and seemed unconscious of her entrance until she stood close at her side.

"A thousand pardons for intruding upon you, Madame," said the girl, "but I grew frightened lest you had been taken suddenly ill and were not able to ring."

"See! look! tell me if you see any resemblance to any one," said the Madame huskily, holding out the picture, the tears stealing down her cheeks.

"No-o, Madame," returned the maid doubtfully, gazing upon it with some surprise that she had never been shown it before—she who had deemed herself fully acquainted with the contents of her mistress's jewel-box.

"No?" cried the Madame irritably. "Look again. Well? Speak out; do not fear to offend."

"That young girl we had here yesterday—"

"Well? well? go on; what of her?" asked the Madame, fairly struggling for breath in her excitement.

"I can imagine she might have looked like this years ago."

"Yes, yes! I have thought so too;" and tears rained down the Madame's cheeks.

Mary's curiosity was strongly excited, but she indulged in no questions or remarks in regard to the original of the picture; she had learned long since that her mistress would tolerate no prying into the secrets of her past life. She waited a moment in silence, then said soothingly, "Come, Madame, cheer up. Just consider how much you have to make you happy. Look at this beautiful room, this grand house—all your own; your elegant dresses too; your silks and laces and jewels; your fine carriage and horses; Katty and Rory and me to wait on you, and your loads of money. Why, Madame, who would not be glad to change places with you?"

"You, Mary?" she asked, with sudden impulse, extending her maimed limb toward the girl, her breast heaving with sobs, her eyes full of passionate sorrow; "say, would you give your good right hand for all my wealth? to say nothing of my struggles for breath, and all the rest of it?"

"I—I don't know—"

"I know you would *not!* Then don't talk to me of how fortunate I am," she said, heaving a deep sigh as she drew back the hand, laid her head against the cushions, and averted her face.

"Ah, well, Madame, none of us can have everything," observed the girl, "and we must all make the best of our lot. There's some that's sick and crippled, and poor too; not a bite or sup, or fire to keep 'em warm this cold day. And we've everything that's good downstairs, thanks to your generosity and your full purse. Now what will you have for dinner?"

"Dinner!" Madame turned her head away with a look and gesture of disgust as if loathing the very thought of food, and by an imperative wave of the hand indicated that it was her pleasure that her maid should consider herself dismissed from her presence.

Without another word Mary promptly left the room, but within half an hour returned, accompanied by Kathleen, the two bringing with them materials for a most tempting meal, which they quickly spread out upon the table, and presently found means to induce their mistress to eat of, with very considerable appetite.

The Madame's mental anguish had been real, but the violence of the paroxysm was over for the time, and the long-indulged love of the pleasures of the table asserted its sway.

But the poor lady's enjoyments were few; she was an educated but not an intellectual woman, and cared little for any books except novels of the most frivolous and sensational class; she had no friends, hardly an acquaintance in the city, having purposely avoided society from extreme sensitiveness regarding the loss of her hand—a loss which had befallen her prior to the removal of herself and husband to Chicago. And she was also a stranger to the consolations of religion

CHAPTER XXV.

STITCH, STITCH, STITCH.

"The web of our life is of a mingled
Yarn, good and ill together."—SHAKESPEARE.

"I'M afraid I've taken you too far: you look dreadfully tired!" said Hetty, as she and Floy reached home after their walk.

"No, don't worry, I've enjoyed it very much; a walk on an agreeable errand, and in pleasant company, is such a rare treat nowadays. It's only a headache," Floy answered, trying to smile.

"*Only* a headache! I call that worse than only being tired. I'm real sorry for you. Just go into my parlor and take off your things and lie down on the lounge. You'll be nice and quiet there, and you're not to mind the supper-bell. I'll bring you a cup of tea and some toast."

Rest and quiet. They were what the weary frame, the aching head, and homesick heart craved just then above everything else that seemed attainable.

Ah, were even they within her reach? Sounds of wrangling and strife assailed her ears as she neared the door of the little back room where Hetty had entertained her the previous night. Opening it, this was the scene which presented itself:

The gas was blazing high, and just beneath it Araminta lolled back in an arm-chair, her feet propped up on the seat of another, and a paper-covered novel in her hand, which Lucian, standing over her puffing away at a cigar, seemed to be trying to wrest from her.

"See here, Miss Mintstick," he was saying, "I got this out of the library for my own enjoyment, so just give it up."

"You hateful fellow!" she cried, "you know I can't bear to be called that, and I'll just tell mother of you if you don't stop it."

"Oh, it's a baby, is it? and mustn't be teased," he said jeeringly; whereat Araminta burst into tears, and again threatened to "tell mother of him."

"Come, it's quite too young to read novels," he said, with another and successful effort to take it from her.

"So are you too, Miss Lucy Ann! There! take that!" she retorted, giving him a resounding slap upon the cheek.

Flushing crimson, he seized her by the wrist.

"See here, young woman!" he hissed in a tone of concentrated fury.

But becoming suddenly aware of Floy's presence, and that she was standing gazing upon them in disgust and astonishment, he turned shamefacedly away, muttering, "A man can't stand everything!" and would have beaten a hasty retreat, but encountered his mother in the doorway.

"What is the meaning of all this?" she asked sharply. "What are you two quarrelling about? I'm ashamed of you! And the room full of tobacco-smoke, the gas turned on full head! you'll ruin me!"

She turned it lower as she spoke ; then catching sight of Floy, now seated on the lounge taking off her gloves,

"Don't mind 'em, Miss Kemper," she said; "they're fond of each other for all."

"I'm not a bit fond of Lucian!" whimpered Araminta, "he's so rude and bearish; so different from the nice young men one reads about in books. He snatched that book away from me, and nearly broke my finger off."

"You look pale, Miss Kemper. I hope you're not going to be sick," remarked Mrs. Sharp as Floy rose to leave the room. "We'll have to be up and at work betimes to-morrow. There are a number of dresses to be finished, and only ourselves to do it, for the other girls won't be back till Monday."

"It's only a headache and the tobacco-smoke, I think," Floy answered in a patient tone. "I'll go up and lie down on my bed, and perhaps it will pass off."

And so the weary round of ceaseless toil was to begin to-morrow! Ah, well! she would struggle on in hope; perhaps better days would come. And to-morrow would be Saturday, the next the blessed day of rest, God's own gift to the toil-worn and weary.

Mrs. Sharp, Hetty, and Floy had need of it after the labors of the intervening day; the last-named more especially, as having feebler powers of endurance than the other two.

Lucian and Araminta were pressed into the service, but, with their whimpering, dawdling ways, proved of small assistance. John was a far more efficient aid; ran the sewing-machine for hours, doing the work well, and lightening their labors with his cheery good-nature and innocent jests.

As the clock told the hour of midnight Floy stuck the needle in her work and began to fold it up.

"Ten minutes more would finish that, Miss Kemper, so that it could be sent home in the morning," said Mrs. Sharp persuasively.

"I am very, very weary, Mrs. Sharp," returned the young girl respectfully; "yet to accommodate you and the customer I would work on a little longer, but it is already the Lord's day, and the command is, 'In it thou shalt not do any work.'"

A portentous frown was darkening the face of her employer, but it changed to an expression of enforced resignation as Hetty said:

"You're right, Floy. Aunt Prue, I can't go on any longer; and indeed what right has anybody to ask us to work as late as this?"

Mrs. Sharp sat in moody silence for a moment, but, being greatly fatigued herself, presently acquiesced and followed their example, remarking:

"Well, well, girls, I don't blame you. There really is no use in killing ourselves, for nobody'll thank us for it."

"Whatever should I do without you, Hetty!" said Floy as they two went up the stairs together.

Monday morning brought a note that greatly vexed Mrs. Sharp, but to our heroine seemed a Heaven-sent relief.

To the usual discomforts of the work-room were now added almost incessant squabbling between Lucian and Araminta, the whining complaints of the latter and the sickening scent of the cheap cigars frequently indulged in by the former.

She had been asking herself how all this was to be endured until next Monday should take them back to their studies ; and now came the answer—this request of Madame Le Conte for her services during the whole week.

The lady desired some alteration in the trimming of the new dress, and had other work which only Miss Kemper could do to suit her.

Mrs. Sharp fumed and fretted, grumbled and scolded, yet nevertheless the request was promptly granted.

"Sure an' I'm plazed to see ye, miss!" was Kathleen's smiling greeting as she admitted Floy. "The Madame's been wearyin' for ye, and couldn't be aisy at all, at all, till she'd got the note sint to tell ye to come. Will ye have a bite o' breakfast?"

Floy declined, and was then requested to walk right up to the sewing-room.

She found Mary there, and receiving directions as to the wishes of the Madame, who had not yet risen, settled herself to her work with an odd feeling of being at home.

"The Madame has taken a wonderful fancy to you, miss," remarked Mary, gazing earnestly at the young girl, and thinking her more than ever like the miniature in her mistress's locket.

"Has she?" Floy asked in some surprise.

"Yes ; and I hope you'll try to cheer her up, miss ; she's been dreadfully downhearted of late, crying 'most all day Christmas."

"No wonder; she seeems to suffer so much, and to be so alone in the world, poor thing!"

"Yes, that's it; she often cries by the hour; and when I ask what's the matter, she says, 'I haven't a soul in the world to care for me, Mary; my family are all dead and gone.' Poor creature! it's sad enough, and I ought to be patient with her; but indeed, miss, it's often enough to try the patience of a saint—the way she goes on, wantin' to be dressed a half a dozen times a day, and wakin' me up to wait on her every hour in the night. There's her bell now, and I must be gone."

"Poor woman!" sighed Floy to herself. "I wonder if she knows of the Friend whose love is everything to me now? I wish I could tell her what comfort and rest it gives."

The Madame was still in bed. Frisky had crept in beside her, and Mary found her petting and caressing him.

"My pretty pet! my little darling!" she was saying, "you at least love me. And I love you, precious little beauty. Ah, Mary," to her maid as she caught sight of her, "so there you are! Just bring the darling's silver bells, and a pink ribbon to tie them with. He wants them, I know he does, the pretty pet!"

Mary obeyed, fastening the string of tiny, tinkling bells about the dog's neck, and could not refrain from joining her mistress's laugh over his evident delight in his finery.

"Has he had his breakfast, Mary?" the Madame inquired with solicitude, "and did he eat with appetite? You know I thought him dull and droopy yesterday."

"Yes, Madame, I know; but I'm sure, as I told you then, it was nothing but want of exercise and over-eating."

"Nonsense, Mary! you forget that he takes an airing with me almost every day."

"No, Madame, but I should say he needed more than that. Yes, he had his breakfast, and eat a plenty."

"That is well. Has Miss Kemper come?"

Mary answered the query, and made a report of the work and directions she had given Floy, at the same time busying herself in assisting the Madame with her toilet.

That week was a busy one to Floy, yet restful also, albeit she was somewhat sated with the Madame's company, often wearying enough to those who must listen to her complainings and submit to her whims.

Yet she was at times quite entertaining. Frisky's little tricks, too, were really very amusing. Besides, Floy had every day several quiet, usually solitary hours—while the Madame slept—was fed upon the fat of the land, and retired to bed reasonably early each night.

On returning to Mrs. Sharp's, she was not grieved to learn that the young people had already left for school.

Work slackened slightly for a few weeks, then again, as the spring season opened, they were almost overwhelmed with it.

And this was the state of affairs until the fervid

heats of summer began to drive the fashionables away from the city.

Even then there was small respite, for some left unfinished dresses to be sent after them, and many who remained behind wanted work done also.

In all this time Floy had heard but once from Cranley—a few lines from Miss Wells telling of the death of Espy's mother, and that he had gone she knew not whither.

"Gone!" Floy's heart almost stood still with grief and pain; but the next instant gave a quick, joyous bound at the thought, "It may be he has but come here in search of me."

And for days and weeks every peal from the doorbell made her heart beat fast and sent a quiver through her nerves.

But he came not; and remembering that he could have no clue to her residence unless through the Leas, who had disappeared from society and probably from his knowledge, she called herself a fool for having indulged any such expectation.

The poor girl had grown very weary in body and mind, and oh, so homesick! Ah, could she but go back for a little while to the old haunts and look again upon the dear graves of her loved ones! But for that she had neither time nor means.

One day in July there came a summons for Floy from Madame Le Conte; bereavement had come upon the wealthy widow, so the note stated, and Floy's services were wanted in the making up of mourning.

"Bereaved!" the girl said to herself in surprise;

"she told me she had not a relative or friend in the world."

"Humph! I was giving the Madame credit for being considerate for once in her life in choosing a slack time to send for you, Miss Kemper," said Mrs. Sharp, refolding the note and tossing it from her after reading it aloud, "but it being a death, of course she didn't choose."

"It'll be a change for you, and I hope will do you good," said Hetty, who had for some time past noticed with concern Floy's increasing languor. "You've found the heat of the city hard to bear, not being used to it as we are; and this—so far out, and close to the lake shore too—will be like a taste of the country."

"Yes," remarked Mrs. Goodenough in her slow way, "it's quite a providence. What is it Shakespeare says? or is it in the Bible now?" she queried meditatively.

"What, Aunt Sarah?" asked Araminta pertly, while Lucian "Haw hawed!" and exclaimed in loud, rough tones:

"Well, I declare, Aunt Sarah! it's a sin and a shame that you haven't a full set of Shakespeare's works, seeing there's nobody tries to quote him oftener."

The young people were at home again for the summer holidays; the time was directly after dinner, and all the family, excepting John and his father, were in the sitting-room at the moment.

Hetty treated the rude boy to a severe look, and seemed more than half inclined to box his ears.

"Well, it's quite true that my memory isn't what

it used to be," sighed her mother, "but it's something about the wind and the shorn lamb, and I rather think it's in the Bible."

"It's Sterne, mother," said Hetty. "'God tempers the wind to the shorn lamb.'"

"But it doesn't suit," laughed Araminta, "for Miss Kemper has an awful lot of hair, and if she was shorn it's so dreadful hot to-day that anybody'd be glad to get where the wind would blow on 'em."

"Be quiet, children!" said Mrs. Sharp. "Miss Kemper, I s'pose you'd better go at once."

CHAPTER XXVI.

THE MADAME AT HER SOLICITOR'S.

"The miserable hath no other medicine
But only hope."—SHAKESPEARE.

"THE Madame bereaved! of whom, I wonder?" mused Floy, riding along in the almost empty street-car. "Has she discovered the existence of a relative only to see him or her snatched away by death? Ah, poor woman! so unhappy before, what will she be now?"

Leaving the car, the young girl quickly passed over the short intervening distance, and glancing up at the Madame's house as she approached it, saw that the shutters of every window were bowed with white ribbon, while several yards of white cashmere tied with the same were hanging from the bell-pull.

"A child!" said Floy to herself in increasing surprise, as she went up the steps and gave a very gentle ring.

The door was opened as usual by Kathleen, who recognized our heroine with a faint, rather watery smile.

"I'm plazed to see you, miss."

"Who is dead, Kathleen?" Floy asked as she stepped in and the door closed behind her.

"Sure, miss, an' it's just himself—the Madame's pet, that was always wid her night an' day; an' it's just breakin' her heart about him she is, poor dear, that hasn't a chick nor a child left! An' it's sad an' sore me own heart is whin I think o' niver seeing the little baste at its purty thricks no more."

"Frisky, her lap-dog!" exclaimed Floy. "I thought it must be a relative."

"Yes, miss, an' sure she always thrated the little baste like a Christian, an' she's kapin' on wid that now it's dead."

"What ailed it?"

"Well, miss, the docther he said 'twas just laziness and over-feedin'—only he put it into grand words, you know—and the Madame didn't like it; but it's dead an' gone he is, annyhow, the purty darlint!"

"Is it Miss Kemper?" asked Mary, appearing at the head of the stairs. "Please walk right up, miss."

Floy was ushered at once into the Madame's dressing-room, where she found that lady weeping bitterly over her dead favorite as it lay stiff and stark in her lap.

"He's gone, Miss Kemper!" she sobbed, looking up piteously into Floy's face, with the tears running fast down her own; "he's gone, my pretty darling—the only thing I had left to love, and the only one that had any love for poor me!"

The young girl scarcely knew what consolation to offer; she could only express her sympathy and hope that he might be replaced by another as pretty and playful.

"Never, never!" exclaimed the Madame indignantly; "no other ever could or ever shall fill his place.

And he shall have a splendid funeral," she went on, with a fresh burst of grief, " the finest casket money can buy, and a white satin shroud ; a monument over his dear little grave too ; and I'll put on mourning as I would for a child."

For a moment Floy was silent with surprise ; then recovering herself,

"This is handsomer than satin, Madame," she said, gently touching the silky floss of the dog's own natural coat ; "and what a pity to bury it : would it not be better to have it stuffed ? for then you need not lose your pet entirely, but can keep him here, caress him, and deck him with ribbons as you have been used to doing."

"Bless you for the suggestion!" cried the mourner, drying her tears. "So I can ; and it will be better than hiding him away out of my sight."

"Mary, you needn't send the order for the casket or the digging of the grave ; but, instead, go out at once and inquire who is the best taxidermist in the city."

Left alone with the Madame, Floy set herself to the task of persuading her out of the absurd notion of putting on mourning, her main argument being that it was an unwholesome dress and the lady's health already poor enough.

"That is true ; nobody knows what I suffer every day of my life," assented the Madame ; "and as I'm not going to quite lose the darling," hugging the dead dog lovingly in her arms as she spoke, "I'll give it up ; that is, I'll wear white instead ; and you shall stay all the same and make me some lovely white morning dresses, tucked, ruffled, and trimmed with elegant lace."

"How immense she will look in them!" was Floy's mental comment; but she wisely kept her thoughts to herself.

In the mean time Mary was executing her commission with such promptness and energy that within an hour Frisky's remains had been taken away—the Madame parting from them with many tears and caresses—and the insignia of mourning removed from the outside of the house.

"I don't know how to thank you enough, miss," the maid said aside to Floy. "It was just awful to me—the idea of a grand funeral for a dog, and all the neighbors lookin' on an' thinkin' us a pack o' fools. I wish in my heart you lived here all the time, for you can do more to make the Madame hear reason than all the rest of us put together."

"Can that be so?" said Floy. "I should not have expected my influence to be nearly so great as yours."

"Nor I," said the maid, and Floy wondered at the earnest, curious gaze she bent upon her.

Mary was thinking of the miniature to which the young girl bore so strong a resemblance; but perceiving that Floy observed her scrutiny, she turned hastily away and left the room.

Several times afterward, during this sojourn in the house, Floy was aware of a repetition of Mary's fixed, searching look, and that the Madame also, in the pauses of her grief, regarded her more than once in much the same manner.

Each time it struck our heroine as strange, but she soon forgot it in thoughts of Espy or the lost parent of whom she was still in quest.

Now that she had not Frisky to take her attention, the Madame took to poring over the miniature again, often weeping bitterly the while ; sometimes Mary overheard such murmured words as these :

" Pansy, Pansy, my little Pansy ! Oh, I can never forgive myself ! My darling, my darling !"

One morning Madame Le Conte awoke with a sudden resolution, and surprised her maid with an unusual order.

" Mary," she said, " I shall call upon my solicitor to-day. Tell Rory to have the carriage at the door at eleven o'clock. Then bring me my breakfast and dress me at once for the street."

"What's up now?" inquired Mary of herself as she hastened downstairs in obedience to the order ; "is she going to make a will and leave a lot of money to that pretty Miss Kemper? And all because she looks like that picture in the locket? Well, well, if it had only happened to be me now, how lucky 'twould have been !"

Having come to her resolve, Madame Le Conte was in feverish haste to carry it out, scolded because her breakfast was not ready on the instant, and fretted and fumed over her toilet, accusing Mary of being intentionally and exasperatingly slow.

But the maid bore it with unruffled equanimity, perhaps looking to the possibility of a fat legacy.

The Madame entered her carriage in a tremor of excitement and haste, which, however, calmed down somewhat during the drive.

Arrived at their destination, Mary assisted her to alight and ascend the three or four steps leading into the hall of the building.

"Stop! it is this first door," said the Madame, panting and wheezing, slight as the exertion had been. "Wait a minute till I recover breath. I want a private interview, and you will stay outside. Rap now."

Mary obeyed, and hearing a loud "Come in!" opened the door and stepped back to let her mistress enter.

"Ah! Madame Le Conte! how d'ye do?" said the lawyer, rising and offering a hand to his rich client; then, with a sudden recollection, dropping it at his side and contenting himself with pushing forward an arm-chair.

"Sit down, Madame," he said. "You are quite a stranger here, but I have been out of town, and may have missed a call from you."

"No," she panted, "I've—not—been here since I saw you last."

"Ah? Well, my dear Madame, what can I do for you to-day?"

"You have heard nothing—learned nothing yet?"

"Nothing whatever, as I am sorry to say."

She sighed deeply.

"I think I should give it up," he said.

"No, no, no!" she cried with vehemence. "I would have you renew and redouble your efforts."

"What can I do that has not already been done?"

"I don't know, but you must try to think of something. Write a new advertisement; send it to every paper in the land."

"It will be putting you to very great expense, and uselessly, I am almost sure."

"That is my affair," she wheezed, wiping the perspiration from her face with a delicate cambric handkerchief.

"Certainly," he replied, with a slight bow of acquiescence ; " the money is your own to use as you please, but it is a pity to throw it away. And how long have we been engaged in this search ?"

"Ten years !" she sighed half despairingly ; "but," brightening a little, "we've almost let it drop for months past. I'd nearly lost heart, but we must begin again and never mind expense. I'd give half my fortune to succeed."

"I wish you may ; though I have not much hope of it, I must confess," he answered indifferently, " but of course your instructions shall be promptly carried out."

CHAPTER XXVII.

THE LONG-LOST DEED.

*"Thus doth the ever-changing course of things
Run a perpetual circle, ever turning."*

HETTY and her mother had taken advantage of the slack time to pay a long-promised visit to some friends in the country, leaving to Mrs. Sharp the oversight of domestic affairs and the care of the store, with such assistance as she could get from Araminta and Lucian, who were home for the summer vacation.

John was, as usual, spending his vacation in farm work, while all the apprentices and journey-women had left for the time being, except our heroine and Annie Jones, who was an orphan and had neither home nor friends to go to.

These two were kept pretty steadily employed upon the few dresses of customers still on hand, and in preparing Miss Sharp's wardrobe for another year at boarding-school.

One morning Floy, who had been left for an hour or more sole occupant of the work-room, was startled by the sudden entrance of Annie in a state bordering on distraction.

"Oh, what shall I do! what shall I do!" she cried, wringing her hands and pacing the floor to and fro with rapid steps, while great tears rolled down her cheeks. "Oh, Miss Kemper, can you help me?"

"What is it, Annie?" Floy asked, stopping the machine which she was running at the moment, and turning upon the girl a look of mingled surprise and pity. "Stop crying and tell me, and I will certainly help you if I can. Have you offended Mrs. Sharp?"

"Oh, yes, and worse than that: she says I've robbed her; but oh, I haven't! I wouldn't steal a pin from anybody. But she won't believe a word I say, and she says if I don't find the five dollars pretty quick she'll have me arrested and taken to prison; and Lucian wants to go off for a policeman right away. Oh dear, oh dear!"

The girl's distress and agitation were so great that Floy had some difficulty in coming to a clear understanding of her trouble; but at length, by dint of soothing and questioning, she learned the facts, which were these:

Annie had been sent to carry home some finished work, taking with her a receipted bill for thirty dollars, her instructions being not to leave it unless it was paid.

The woman, a Mrs. Collins, a new customer, handed her twenty-five dollars, saying that she would pay the rest at another time; and the girl, from stupidity, carelessness, or bashfulness, allowed her to retain the bill.

Mrs. Sharp sent her back for it, but the woman refused to give it up, and, to the astonishment and dismay of the poor child, stoutly asserted that she had paid the whole.

And now Mrs. Sharp accused Annie of retaining the missing sum, and with much anger and indignation declared that she would send her to prison unless she made good the loss within an hour.

"Oh, Miss Kemper," sobbed the girl in conclusion, "I haven't a dollar or a friend in the world! and if I lose my character what will become of me? Nobody'll trust me, and I can't get work, and I'll just have to starve."

"I'm very sorry for you," said Floy; "but trust in the Lord, and He will help you; and if you are innocent, He will bring it to light some day."

"If I am innocent! oh, Miss Floy," sobbed the girl, "you don't think me a thief, do you?"

"No, Annie, I don't, if that's any comfort to you, poor child!"

"I'm glad of that!" Annie said, a gleam of pleasure flitting over her tear-swollen face, then burst out again, "But oh, what shall I do? Oh, if I only had five dollars! Miss Floy, can you lend it to me? I'll pay it back some day, and never, never forget to ask God to bless you for your kindness."

"I would if I could, Annie, but I haven't half that sum," Floy was beginning to say, when a sudden recollection stopped her.

In the old pocket-book found upon Mr. Kemper's person after his death, and kept by her as a sacred relic, she had safely stowed away the golden half-eagle he had given her but a few moments before the awful accident that had made her an almost penniless orphan.

For herself she would not have spent it unless reduced to the last extremity of want; but her noble, generous heart could not withstand Annie's appeal.

"Wait here a moment; I will see," she said in tremulous tones, and hurried from the room.

Up to her own she ran, locked herself in, opened her trunk, and, diving to the bottom, drew forth the old, worn, faded pocket-book.

For a moment she held it lovingly in her hand, hot tears rushing to her eyes as she thought of that terrible scene enacted scarce a year ago.

But the present was no time for the indulgence of grief. She undid the clasp and looked for the treasure she had come to seek.

"Where was it? with fingers and eyes she examined each division, yet without success. Had she been robbed? A sudden pang shot through her heart at the thought.

But oh no, that could not be! The lining was much torn, and the coin had doubtless slipped in between it and the outside.

She ran her fingers in and felt it there, and—something else: a memorandum or bill probably. She pulled at it, tore the lining a little more, and finally drew out a bit of folded paper that looked like a leaf torn from a note-book.

Her heart gave a wild throb, and in her excitement the paper slipped from her fingers and fell to the floor. She stooped and clutched it hastily, eagerly, as if she feared it would even yet escape her; then, with a strong effort at composure, opened out the folds with her trembling fingers.

One glance told her that it was in very truth the long-sought deed of gift.

She did not wait to read it in detail, but scanned the lines hurriedly. The name—her mother's name and her own—was what she sought; and there it was—" Ethel Farnese"—perfectly legible, though evidently written with unsteady fingers, as of one in great agitation of mind.

"Ethel Farnese!" repeated Floy half aloud, letting the paper fall into her lap and clasping her hands together over it, while with a far-off look in her lustrous eyes she gazed into space. "Ethel Farnese! and that is who I am; who she was when she gave me to them! Ethel Farnese! I seem to be not myself at all, but somebody else. How strange it all is! just like a story or a dream." And for a moment she sat with her head upon her hand, overcome by a curious sense of loss and bewilderment. Was she the same girl who had come into that room ten minutes ago?

Then a thought struck her. "The will! might it not have shared the hiding-place of the deed? Oh, what joy if she could but find *that!*"

She caught up the pocket-book again, the color coming and going in her cheeks, her heart beating so fast she could hardly breathe, and with remorseless fingers tore it apart till not a fold or crevice remained unexplored; but alas! without any further discovery.

"Ah, he never made it!" she sighed sadly to herself, as she had done months before.

She restored the pocket-book to its place, with the deed of gift safely bestowed inside, locked her trunk, and with the gold piece in her hand returned to the work-room.

Annie, pacing to and fro with agitated steps, was still its only occupant. "Oh, I thought you'd never come!" she cried, stopping in her walk and turning eagerly to Floy. "Have you got the money for me? What's the matter? you look as if something had happened."

"I have the money—a five-dollar gold piece which I value so highly as a keepsake that I would not spend it for myself unless I were in absolute danger of starvation," Floy said, answering the first query, ignoring the other; "still I will lend it to you if necessary to save you from arrest. But, Annie, wouldn't your paying the money to Mrs. Sharp look like an acknowledgment that you had really kept it back, as she says?"

"I don't know; maybe it would," sobbed Annie, "but she'll send me to jail if I don't. I don't like to take your keepsake either; but oh dear, oh dear! what shall I do?"

At that moment Mrs. Sharp came hastily into the room. She was a quick-tempered woman, but not hard-hearted, and, her anger having had time to cool, began now to relent toward the friendless girl who had offended her. Still she did not like to retreat from the position she had taken.

"Well, Annie, what are you going to do?" she asked in a tone whose mildness surprised the child. "I hope you've concluded to give up the money you've held back from me. You may as well, for it won't do you any good to keep it."

"Oh, I would if I had it!" sobbed Annie, "but that woman never gave me a cent more than what I handed to you; and if you don't believe me you can search me and my trunk."

"Humph! there are other places where you could hide it," was the quick, sarcastic rejoinder.

"Miss Kemper," turning to Floy, "what do *you* think of this business?"

"I cannot believe that Annie would rob you, Mrs. Sharp, though she did wrong in leaving the bill contrary to directions, and therefore might in strict justice be required to make good your loss," said Floy. "And I think she is willing to do it if it were in her power; but you know she has no money, and no way of earning any just now."

"Well, she soon will be getting wages," said Mrs. Sharp meditatively, "and if she'll agree that I shall keep the first five dollars—"

"Oh, I will, I will!" interrupted Annie, catching eagerly at the suggestion and clasping her hands in passionate entreaty, "indeed I will, if you'll only believe I didn't take it, and let me stay on here! And I'll never forget your kindness."

Mrs. Sharp gave a somewhat ungracious consent that it should be so; and hearing a customer enter the store, hurried back to wait upon her, while the relieved Annie dried her eyes and took up the work she had dropped when sent upon the unfortunate errand.

That she was spared the parting with her prized souvenir was certainly a pleasure and relief to Floy, but the remembrance of that was soon lost in the excitement of her recent discovery; her thoughts were full of it, and with joy she said to herself, "Here is another step taken toward the finding of my mother. I am more convinced than ever that she still lives, and that the good God who has helped me thus far will finally guide me to her; for now, knowing the name she once bore, I can advertise in a way much more likely to attract her attention."

But here a great obstacle—the want of money—presented itself, and the girl's busy brain set to work to contrive ways and means to earn the needful funds.

The treasured half-eagle would not go very far, and it, she quickly decided, must be kept as a reserve in case of dire necessity.

The question arose in her mind whether she should now drop her adopted name and resume that which was hers by right of birth.

But such a course would involve explanations and confidences which she did not care to give to those about her—these people who would feel no interest in them or in her but that of idle curiosity. Hetty was the only member of the family who knew, or had ever shown any desire to know, anything of Floy's history or hopes, and our heroine quickly decided that until Hetty returned this secret should be all her own.

CHAPTER XXVIII.

MESSRS. TREDICK & SERVER.

"How sudden do our prospects vary here!"—SHIRLEY.

But Floy's resolve was destined to be speedily swallowed up in the current of swiftly-coming events.

Only two days later, after some hours spent down town in the fatiguing business of shopping for Araminta Sharp, going from store to store in search of exact matches in dress goods, trimmings, and ribbons, she was standing on a corner waiting for a street-car, when a ragged little newsboy accosted her with:

"I say, miss, won't you buy one o' these here papers?" running over the names of several of the dailies; "I hain't sold none to-day, and if I don't have better luck Teddy an' me (that's my little lame brother) we'll have to go hungry and sleep in the street."

"That would be hard. Give me one, I don't care which," Floy said hastily, signalling the approaching car.

"Thank 'ee, miss!" said the boy as she dropped the pennies into his hand.

Seated in the car, she scanned the news items, skipping the police reports and the details of "the murder," read the editorials, then ran her eye down the columns of advertisements.

It lighted on something that nearly startled her into an outcry. Could it be? did not her eyes deceive her?

She closed them for an instant in her excitement, almost holding her breath, while her heart beat tumultuously, the color came and went on her cheek, and she trembled until the paper shook in her hands; then opened them again to see it still staring her in the face—that name, her name, which only two days ago she had learned was hers.

"If Ethel Farnese—wife or widow of Adrian X. Farnese, and formerly of Jefferson, Clinton County, Indiana—or her heirs will open communication with Messrs. Tredick & Server, Attorneys at Law, No. —— —— Street, Chicago, they will learn something to their advantage."

How much that short paragraph told her! how much that was to her of intense interest, of great importance: her father's Christian name, the former residence of her parents, and that some one else (who could it be?) was engaged in the same quest as herself!

Unless (but the idea of such a possibility did not occur to her at the moment, and when it did was quickly discarded) some other Ethel Farnese than her mother were intended.

No one was observing our heroine, no one noticed her agitation, and she had time to partially recover from it before facing the uncongenial and indifferent inmates of the house which was her temporary home.

Though inwardly in a whirl of excitement, she contrived to preserve a calm exterior while in the presence of the family, giving sufficient attention to the duties required of her to go through them in a creditable manner.

But it was a great relief when at last she was left free to follow her own inclinations and could seek the solitude of the room which she occupied alone in the absence of Mrs. Goodenough and Hetty.

This was not till her usual hour for retiring, but in her present mood sleep was simply out of the question. She sought her pillow indeed, but lay awake the greater part of the night thinking, planning, and full of conjectures as to the revelations which the near future might have in store for her.

She had no earthly friend to go to for advice, but had learned to seek guidance and direction from that Friend who is ever-present with His children wherever they may be.

From early childhood she had always known her own mind, and circumstances during the past year had done much to develop and increase this natural tendency to self-reliance and independence of thought and action.

She rose in the morning with her plans arranged, and quite ready to carry them out with promptness and decision. As a preliminary she surprised Mrs. Sharp by telling her as she rose from the breakfast-table, after an almost untasted meal, that she must have the day to herself; she had some matters of her own to attend to, and knew she could be spared, the sewing for Araminta being about done and nothing else at all pressing.

Hardly waiting for a reply, in her haste and excitement, she left the room.

"Well, I declare! mighty independent, to be sure!

What's in the wind now, I wonder!" exclaimed Mrs. Sharp, setting down the cup she had just lifted to her lips, and looking after Floy's retreating figure.

But Floy did not hear. Repairing to her own room, Floy arrayed herself in her best attire—a suit of deep mourning, simply made and inexpensive, but very pretty and becoming—and, armed with all the documents at her command which could help to establish her identity, wended her way to the street and number named in the advertisement.

She had no difficulty in finding the place; the name of the firm was on the outside of the building, and repeated on the first door to the right as she passed into the hall.

A voice bade her enter in answer to her knock. She did so with a noiseless step and quiet, lady-like air.

The room was of good size and handsomely furnished; evidently Messrs. Tredick & Server were a prosperous firm.

They were both there, seated each at his own desk. Both looked up and bowed good-morning, while one, the nearest to her, Mr. Server, as she afterwards learned, rose and handed her a chair, asking, "What can I do for you, Miss—"

"Ethel Farnese," replied Floy as he paused for the name, her cheek flushing, the low, sweet tones of her refined voice slightly tremulous.

What audacity it seemed in her thus to take quiet possession of a name she had never before so much as heard pronounced!

At that both lawyers pricked up their ears, a look of surprised satisfaction coming into their faces.

"Indeed!" said Server, extending his hand; "then we are most happy to see you. But can it be the Mrs. Ethel Farnese for whom we have been so long advertising? so young—her daughter, perhaps?"

"For her or her heirs, was it not?" Floy quietly asked.

"Ah, yes, certainly! and you bring proofs of your identity, doubtless? You come from your mother? or—"

He paused, glancing inquiringly at her deep mourning.

"Yes; I have documents to show—a story to tell," Floy said, ignoring the last query; "have you leisure to hear it now?"

"We have; no time like the present," said Server briskly, drawing his chair nearer, while his partner came forward with an air of keen interest and joined them.

"Allow me to introduce Mr. Tredick, Miss Farnese," said Server; "and now let us proceed to business," he added as Tredick, having shaken hands with Floy, took a seat at his side. "What have you to show us?"

"This," replied Floy, putting the deed of gift into his hand.

He examined it curiously.

"Ah! your mother gave you away?" he said, elevating his eyebrows and glancing inquiringly at her as he passed the paper on to Mr. Tredick.

"You shall hear how and why presently," she said. "First let me prove that I am the child adopted by Mr. and Mrs. Kemper," and she handed

Mr. Server a package, saying, "These are letters addressed to me by my legal adviser, Mr. Crosby, of Cranley, Iowa."

"What! my old friend Crosby?" exclaimed Mr. Tredick. "Ah! I know his hand, and if he indorses you you're all right. Yes, yes, these are genuine!" he added, glancing over the letters as Server opened and spread them before his eyes. "I see they are directed and addressed to Miss Floy Kemper; and he alludes here to your search for your mother. My dear young lady, let us have your story. Your mother, I conclude, is still living? My client will be overjoyed to hear it."

"I do not know; I hope so, sir," Floy answered with emotion.

Then calming herself by a determined effort, she went on to give a brief statement of such facts as were necessary to establish her own identity, vindicate her mother from any suspicion of want of love for her child, and show what reason there was for believing, or at least hoping, that she still lived.

She passed very lightly over her own sorrows, and said nothing of her struggles with poverty.

They heard her to the end without interruption, and evidently with deep interest, especially as she detailed her efforts to trace her lost parent, and what she had learned of that parent's history while doing so.

Their faces lighted up with satisfaction as she closed with the information gleaned from Mrs. Dobbs.

"Ah!" cried Mr. Tredick, rubbing his hands and showing a fine set of false teeth, "I begin to see a little light. You deserve a great deal of credit for your exertions—the energy and wisdom with which they have been made, Miss Farnese."

"It was God's good providence, sir, not any wisdom of mine," she answered with quiet simplicity.

"May I ask if you were brought up by the Kempers with the knowledge that you were their child only by adoption?" queried Mr. Server.

"I had not the slightest suspicion of it till my— Mrs. Kemper revealed the fact to me with her dying breath," Floy answered in a voice that trembled with almost overpowering emotion.

"Pardon me," he said, with a touch of compassion in his tones and a second glance at her mourning dress, "your loss has been recent, I fear?"

She bowed a silent assent.

"And you were ignorant of your true mother's name?" pursued Mr. Tredick, modulating his voice to express sympathy in her sorrow; "had you not then this deed of gift in your possession?"

Floy told of her vain search of last year, and her recent discovery.

"Are you now satisfied of my identity?" she asked.

"Perfectly; and it is your turn to question us. Do you not wish to learn who has been engaged in the same quest as yourself?"

"I do indeed!" she replied with earnest animation.

"Your mother had a sister," he said. "The two were entirely alone in the world after the death of their parents, which occurred before your mother— the younger one—was quite grown up. In time both married. The husbands quarrelled, the sisters became estranged (each, it is to be presumed, taking part with her husband), and there was a separation. Your father carried his wife off to parts unknown, and the sister, my client, has heard nothing of her since, though for the last ten years, during which she has been a wealthy, childless widow, she has used every effort to find her. All this occurred before your birth, and she is still in ignorance of the fact that her sister ever became a mother."

Floy sat with her hands clasped in her lap, her large, lustrous eyes fixed intently upon the speaker, her breathing hurried, the full red lips slightly parted, a rich, varying color on her softly-rounded cheek.

"She is very pretty," thought Server, watching her furtively ; "very like the descriptions I have heard of Mrs. Farnese."

Mr. Tredick paused, and the girl drew a long, sighing breath.

"Where is my aunt ? When may I see her ?" she asked, vainly striving to be calm and composed.

"She is in this city. I will send for a hack and take you to her at once, if you will allow me to do so."

CHAPTER XXIX.

A THORNY ROSE.

"There's a divinity that shapes our ends,
Roughhew them how we will."—SHAKESPEARE.

"YOUR aunt is an invalid, I regret to say," Mr. Tredick remarked as they drove rapidly through the streets, "and we must not come upon her too suddenly with this good news. I shall have to ask you, Miss Farnese, to take a seat in the parlor below while I seek a private interview with her in her boudoir."

Our heroine bowed in acquiescence, and he went on:

"It will not take long to break the matter to her, and you are not likely to be kept waiting many minutes."

"Please do not concern yourself about that," she said; "I should prefer to be kept waiting for hours rather than run the slightest risk of injury to the only relative I am certain of possessing in all the world."

The girl seemed composed—the lawyer thought her so, and rather wondered at such an amount of self-control in one so young—but inwardly she was full of agitation and excitement.

Her lonely heart yearned for the love and companionship of kindred, yet dreaded to find in this unknown relative one who might prove wholly uncongenial and even repulsive. She remembered that she was not yet of age, and was about to place herself under authority of which she knew nothing. There might be conflict of tastes and opinions on very vital subjects. Yet she had no thought of drawing back. She had weighed the matter carefully, viewed it in all its aspects, had decided that this was her wisest and best course, and was ready to pursue it unfalteringly to the end.

So wholly absorbed in these thoughts and emotions was she that she took no note of the direction in which they were moving, nor what streets they traversed.

The carriage stopped. Mr. Tredick threw open the door, sprang out, and, turning, assisted her to alight.

He led her up the steps of a large and handsome dwelling, and rang the bell. She glanced about her, and started with surprise. The street, the house, everything within range of her vision, had a strangely familiar look.

They had reached the suburbs of the city, and before them—as they stood on the threshold, looking out toward the east—lay the great lake, quiet as a sleeping child, under the fervid rays of the sun of that still summer day, one of the calmest and most sultry of the season. A second glance around, and Floy—as we must still call her—turned to her conductor with an eager question on her lips.

But the door opened, a smiling face appeared, and a cheery voice exclaimed :

"Is it you, Misther Tredick, sir? Will ye plaze to walk in, and I'll run up an' tell the Madame.

She's dressed and ready to resave ye, by good luck.

"An' the lady too," added Kathleen, catching a sight of Floy, but without recognizing her, her face being partially concealed by her veil.

"Step intil the parlor, both o' yees, plaze, an' who shall I say wishes to see the Madame?" she asked, with another and curious glance at the veiled lady.

"Mr. Tredick," said that gentleman, giving her his card; "don't mention the lady at all. She will wait here till I come down again. Just tell the Madame that Mr. Tredick wishes to see her a moment on business."

But Mary's voice spoke from the stairhead, "Katty, the Madame says ask the gentleman to walk right up," and Mr. Tredick, hearing, awaited no second invitation.

Floy's brain was in a whirl.

"The Madame? the Madame?" she repeated in low, agitated tones, dropping into a chair in the luxuriously-furnished parlor, but with no thought of its richly-carved, costly wood and velvet cushions. "My aunt must be visiting here. But 'twas for the Madame he asked, 'twas the Madame he wished to see! Can it be that she—she is— Yes, it must—it is!"

She hid her face in her hands, with a slight shudder and something between a groan and a sigh.

The poor Madame had never been an attractive person to Floy; she was not one whom she could greatly respect or look up to for comfort in sorrow, for guidance in times of doubt and perplexity.

In finding her she had not found one who would at all fill the place of the parents she mourned, and whose loss had left her without an earthly counsellor, an earthly prop.

In the bitterness of her disappointment she learned how much she had been half unconsciously hoping for. The pressure of poverty had been sorely felt by the young girl during these past months, but was as nothing to the yearning for the tender love and care and happy trustfulness that had been the crowning blessing of earlier days

CHAPTER XXX.

PANSY.

"A hundred thousand welcomes : I could weep,
And I could laugh ; I am light and heavy : welcome !"
SHAKESPEARE.

MADAME LE CONTE received her legal adviser that morning in her boudoir, rising from her easy chair in her eager haste to learn if he were the bearer of tidings, and coming forward to meet him as he entered.

"What news, Mr. Tredick ? I see in your face that you have some for me !" she cried, almost breathless with excitement and the exertion, slight as it was.

"Ah ! are you so skilled in reading faces ?" he returned playfully. "Well, I own that I have a bit of news for you—good news as far as it goes. But let me beg you to be seated and calm yourself before I proceed further."

"Oh, go on, go on ! don't keep me in suspense !" she cried in increasing agitation, sinking into her chair again and pointing him to a seat as she spoke.

"Remember it is good news," he repeated, taking up a large feather fan and beginning to fan her flushed cheeks, while Mary brought her smelling-salts and asked if she would have a glass of water.

She made a gesture of refusal, and pointed to the door opening into her dressing-room.

The girl at once obeyed the hint and went out, closing the door after her.

"Now, Mr. Tredick, speak, speak!" exclaimed the Madame imperatively. "Have you heard anything of—of—"

"Your sister? No—yes; that is, nothing recent, but I have just learned that she has a daughter living at no great distance from this. Shall I send for the girl?"

"Send for her? How could you wait to ask? Why did you delay a moment when you know that I'm dying with longing for the sight of somebody who has a drop of my blood in her veins?" she interrupted in great excitement and anger.

"Only for your own sake, Madame," he answered deprecatingly. "Knowing the precarious state of your health—"

"Oh, don't stop to talk!" she cried, half rising from her chair. "Where is she? She must be sent for this instant! As if I could wait, and my sister's child within reach! Mary must run down and order the carriage at once."

"Softly, softly, my dear Madame," he said soothingly. "I have anticipated your wishes so far as to make arrangements for the young lady to be here within an hour from this time," consulting his watch, "and in the mean while I must lay before you the proofs of her identity, and have your opinion as to their being altogether satisfactory and convincing."

"Oh, if you have decided that they are, it's quite sufficient," she answered with a sort of weary impatience; "you would be less easily deceived than I."

"But we may as well fill up the time with the examination; and you will be glad to learn something of your sister's history after your separation?" he remarked persuasively, taking from his pocket the papers Floy had given him.

"Ah, yes, yes!" she cried with eagerness. "I did not understand that you had that to communicate to me. Ah, Pansy, Pansy! my poor little Pansy!" and covering her face with her handkerchief, she sobbed convulsively.

"Come, my dear Madame, cheer up!" he said, "she is still living—"

"Oh, is she? is she?" she again interrupted him, starting up wildly. "But why don't you go on? why will you keep me in this torturing suspense?"

"I am trying to go on as fast as I can," he said a little impatiently. "I was about to correct my last statement by saying we have at least reason to hope that your sister still lives, and that we shall yet find her."

"But the girl—the daughter—have you seen her? and doesn't she know all about her mother?"

"No, Madame; but if you want to hear the facts, as far as I have been able to gather them, your best plan will be to listen quietly to what I have to say. There is quite a little story to be told, and one that cannot fail to be of interest to you."

Of interest! The Madame almost held her breath lest she should lose a syllable of the narrative as he went on to describe the scenes enacted in the shanty inn and depot at Clearfield Station, in which her sister had borne so conspicuous a part.

Then he showed her the deed of gift.

"Yes, yes," she said, pointing to the signature, "that is my poor Ethel's handwriting. I should recognize it anywhere. It was always peculiar. Oh, where is the child?"

"Downstairs in the parlor. Shall I call her? shall I bring her to you?"

She was too much moved to speak. She nodded assent.

In a moment more Floy stood before her.

The Madame gave a cry of mingled joy and surpise, and held out her arms.

"Is it you—*you?* oh, I am glad! I am the happiest woman alive!"

Floy knelt down by her side and suffered herself to be enfolded by the stout arms, pressed against the broad breast, kissed and cried over.

She had meditated upon Madame's sufferings from loneliness and disease till her heart was melted with pity. She had thought upon the fact that the same blood flowed in their veins—that this was the sister, the only, and probably dearly loved, sister of the unknown yet beloved mother of whom she was in quest—till a feeling akin to affection had sprung up within her.

"My poor dear aunt," she whispered, twining her arms about the Madame's neck and imprinting a kiss upon her lips, " what a dreary, lonely life you have had! God helping me, I will make it happier than it has been."

"Ah, yes, child!" returned her new-found relative, repeating her caress with added tenderness; "and you, you poor darling! shall never have to toil for your bread any more. Ah, what a delight it will be to me to lavish on you every desirable thing that money can buy! It is Miss Kemper, but it is my little Pansy too; did I not see the likeness from the first?" and the tears coursed down the Madame's swarthy cheeks.

"Why do you call me that?" asked Floy.

"It was my pet name for my sister. She was so sweet and pretty, so modest, gentle, and retiring. And she called me Tulip, because, as she said, my beauty was gorgeous, like that of the flower. You would not think it now; there's not a trace of it left," she added, with a heavy sigh and a rueful glance into a pier-glass opposite.

It was all quite true. Nannette Gramont (that was the Madame's maiden name) had a sylph-like form, a rich brunette complexion, sparkling eyes, ruby lips, a countenance and manners full of vivacity and mirth.

Now she was dull and spiritless; her eye had lost its brightness; the once smiling mouth wore a fretful expression; the smooth, clear skin had grown sallow and disfigured by pimples and blotches not to be concealed by the most liberal use of powder and rouge, poor substitute for the natural bloom which had disappeared forever under the combined influence of high living, indulged temper, remorse and consequent ill-health, far more than advancing years.

"You were not alike then?" Floy said, with a secret sense of relief.

"No, no! never in the least, in looks or disposition. I was always quick-tempered and imperious, Ethel so gentle and yielding that we never quarrelled—never till—ah, I cannot endure the thought of it!" And burying her face in her handkerchief, the Madame wept bitterly.

For a moment there was no sound in the room but her heavy sobbing, Floy feeling quite at a loss for words of consolation; but at last she said softly:

"One so gentle and sweet would never harbor resentment, especially toward a dear, only sister."

"No, no; but it has parted us forever—this unkindness of mine! And it may be that she—my sweet one, my dear one—has perished with want, while I rolled in wealth. Ah, me! what shall I do?"

"I believe she is living still, and that we shall yet find her!" cried Floy, starting up in excitement and pacing to and fro, her hands clasped over her beating heart, her eyes shining with hope.

"It may be so," said the Madame, wiping away her tears. "Child, would you like to see your mother's face?" She drew out of her bosom the little gold locket which of late she had worn almost constantly, and opening it, held it out to Floy.

In an instant the young girl was again on her knees at her aunt's side, bending over that pretty child-face, one strangely like it in feature and coloring, yet unlike in its eager curiosity, its tremulous agitation, the yearning tenderness in the great, dark, lustrous eyes.

"How sweet! how lovely!" she said, raising her eyes to her aunt's face again. "But ah, if I could see her as she was when grown up!"

"Look in the glass and you will," said the Madame.

Floy's face flushed with pleasure.

The Madame opened the other side of the locket.

"This was of me, taken at the same time," she said, displaying the likeness of a girl some six or eight years older in appearance than the first; bright and handsome too, but with a darker beauty, and a proud, wilful expression in place of the sweet gentleness of the other. "Our mother had them painted for herself. After her death I claimed the locket as mine by right of priority of birth, and though Pansy wished very much to have it, she yielded to me for peace's sake, as usual."

"You, too, were a very pretty child, Mad—" Floy broke off in confusion.

"Aunt Nannette," corrected the Madame, with a slight smile, passing her hand caressingly over the soft, shining hair of her newly-found niece. "Aunt Nannette, or simply auntie, as you like, my little Pansy."

There was an earnest, unspoken entreaty in Floy's eyes as she glanced from the locket to her aunt's face.

"There is hardly anything I would refuse you, little one," the Madame said in answer, "but this I cannot part with. I will have them copied for you, though; and the locket itself shall be enough handsomer to more than compensate for the pictures being only copies of the original."

CHAPTER XXXI.

A WONDROUS CHANGE.

" Herein fortune shows herself more kind
Than is her custom."—SHAKESPEARE.

MR. TREDICK, having accomplished his mission by breaking the good news to Madame Le Conte and ushering Floy into her presence, quietly withdrew, and, leaving a message with Mary to the intent that he would call again the next morning, returned to his office.

This was a memorable day in Floy's life, the turning of a new page in her history.

Mary was presently despatched with a note to Mrs. Sharp briefly stating the facts, and with orders to bring away the few effects of the young girl which were there.

The news created a great sensation in the Sharp household, as Mary duly reported on her return, telling her story in a way which showed that she had keenly enjoyed her part in the scene, and that she was delighted to know that our heroine was no longer a mere transient sojourner in the Madame's house.

Floy, in her capacity of dressmaker, had won golden opinions from the servants, and both were scarcely less pleased than astonished at the strange turn affairs had taken.

"It's perfectly amazin', as I told 'em down there," said Mary in conclusion. "Who'd have thought that day you came here, lookin' so sweet and sad in your black dress, to make that new gownd for the Madame, that you'd more real right in the house than any of us except the Madame herself!"

"I hope she will never need to look so sad again," said Madame Le Conte, gazing with fond pride at the pretty face of her niece. "My dear, would you be willing to lay off your mourning now for my sake?"

The request caused such a flood of sad and tender memories that for a moment Floy was utterly unable to speak.

"I long to see you dressed as your mother used to be at your age," the Madame went on. "She usually wore white gowns with pink or blue ribbons, and it was sweetly becoming."

Floy conquered herself with a strong effort.

"I will, Aunt Nannette; I would do more than that to give you pleasure," she said, with a winning smile, though tears trembled in her eyes and a bright drop rolled down her cheek as she spoke.

Madame Le Conte saw it, and appreciated the sacrifice.

"Dear child!" she said, "I see you are going to be a great comfort to me. I am no longer alone in the world, thank fortune! nor are you. It was a happy chance that brought us together at last, wasn't it, dear?"

"A kind Providence, aunt," Floy responded in cheerful tones, "and I am very glad and thankful to know that I have at least one living relative in the world. And a good home," she added, with a bright smile. "I have not been cast adrift for a year without learning the value of that."

It was a double house, and Floy had been already assigned a suite of spacious, elegantly-furnished apartments on the opposite side of the hall from the Madame's own, and also told that she was to be joint mistress with her aunt, take the oversight of the domestic affairs, order what she pleased for her meals, and make free use of domestics, carriage and horses, the grand piano in the parlor, the library—in short, everything belonging to the establishment.

Floy was touched by this kindness and generosity of her aunt, and felt that she might well be willing to make some sacrifices to confer pleasure in return. This feeling was increased tenfold by the occurrences of the next day.

Mr. Tredick called according to appointment, was for a short time closeted with the Madame in her boudoir; then Floy was summoned to join them, when, to her amazement, she learned that her aunt had made over to her property in bonds, stocks, and mortgages to the amount of one hundred thousand dollars.

The girl's first impulse was to return it with the idea that Madame Le Conte was impoverishing herself, and forgetful that other heirs might yet be found. Grateful tears filled her eyes; she was too much overcome to speak for a moment.

"It is a very generous gift," the lawyer said, looking at her in surprise at her silence.

"Generous? it is far too much!" Floy burst out, finding her voice. "Dear aunt, what have you left for yourself? and have you not forgotten that my mother may be living and may have children by her second husband, who will be quite as nearly related to you as I?"

"No, child, take it. I have plenty left for myself and them," the Madame answered, with a pleased laugh.

"That is quite true, my dear young lady," remarked Mr. Tredick; "for though I consider this a generous gift for Madame Le Conte to bestow during her lifetime, it is not one fifth of what she is worth."

Floy rose hastily and came to the side of her aunt's easy chair.

"Ah, little one! are you satisfied now to take and enjoy it?" the Madame asked, touching the fair young cheek caressingly as the girl bent over her with features working with emotion.

It was not so much the abundant wealth so suddenly showered upon her as the affection she saw in the act of its bestowal which overcame Floy, so sweet was love to the lonely heart that for a year past had known so dreary a dearth of it.

"I will, dear auntie," she said, smiling through her fast-falling tears. "But what return can I make for all your generous kindness?"

"My generous kindness!" the Madame repeated in a tone of contempt; then at some sad memory a look of keen distress swept over her face, and her voice grew low and husky. "It is a small atonement for the past," she said, "the past that car never be recalled!"

Mr. Tredick was busied with some legal document, and seemed quite oblivious of what was passing between the ladies. Presently he folded the paper up, handed it, with several others, to Floy with the smiling injunction to keep them carefully, inquired of the Madame if she had any further commands for him, and, receiving a reply in the negative, bowed himself out.

As the door closed on her solicitor, the Madame lifted a tiny silver bell from the table at her side and tapped it lightly.

"The carriage waits, ladies," said Mary, appearing in answer.

"Then we will go at once," returned her mistress. "Pansy, my dear, put on your hat."

A heavy rain during the night had wrought a sudden and delightful change in the temperature of the atmosphere; light clouds still partially obscured the sun, and a fresh breeze was blowing from the lake. The ladies had voted it a fine day for shopping, and decided to avail themselves of it for that purpose.

A few moments later they were bowling rapidly along toward the business part of the city in the Madame's elegant, easily-rolling, softly-cushioned carriage, drawn by a pair of handsome, spirited grays, the pride of Rory's heart.

They returned some hours after laden with great store of costly and beautiful things which Madame Le Conte had insisted upon heaping on her niece.

There were several ready-made dresses, and in one of these Floy made her appearance at the tea-table spread for herself and aunt in the boudoir of the latter.

The robe was white; a fine French muslin, trimmed with beautiful lace. Floy had fastened it at the throat with a pale pink rose, and placed another among the glossy braids of her dark brown hair.

"Ah, how lovely you look, my darling!" the Madame exclaimed, gazing upon her in delighted admiration. Then, the tears springing to her eyes, "I could almost believe that my little Pansy of other days stands before me," she said.

While they were at the table her eyes continually sought her niece's face, and when they left it she called for her jewel-box, saying, "You must let me add something to your attire, Pansy."

The Madame had a great fondness for gold and precious stones, and Floy's eyes opened wide in astonishment and admiration at the store of diamonds, pearls, rubies, emeralds, amethysts, and sapphires, adorning brooches, ear-rings, finger-rings, chains, and necklaces shortly spread before her.

"Have I not a fine collection?" asked their owner, gloating over them with intense satisfaction. "Take your choice, Pansy; take any or all you want; they will probably all belong to you some day."

"Oh, thank you! I should be astonished at such an offer, auntie, had you not already shown yourself so wonderfully generous," said Floy, coloring with pleasure. "But am I not too young to wear such things?"

"Not pearls, at all events," said the Madame, throwing a beautiful necklace, composed of several strands of very large and fine ones, about the young girl's neck, then adding bracelets, brooch, and ear-rings to match.

"Oh, auntie, what a present! they are too lovely for anything!" cried Floy in delight.

A WONDROUS CHANGE. 247

"This, too, you must have," said the Madame, putting a jewel-case into her hand.

Floy opened it with eager curiosity. It contained a gold chain and a tiny gold watch, both ornamented with pearls.

"Do you like it?" asked the Madame.

"Like it!" cried Floy; "I am charmed with it! I have always wanted a watch, but never had one. My dear adopted father had promised me one on my eighteenth birthday, but I was all alone in the world before that came," she added, her voice sinking low and trembling with emotion.

CHAPTER XXXII.

ETHEL AT HOME.

"Pleasures mix'd with pains appear,
Sorrow with joy, and hope with fear."—SWIFT.

MADAME LE CONTE had missed her afternoon nap, and was much fatigued by the unusual exertions and excitement of the day.

It was quite early when she dismissed her niece for the night—so early that as Floy (or Ethel, as we should perhaps now call her) passed into her own apartments and stood for a moment before a window of her bedroom looking toward the west, she saw that the glow of the sunset had not yet faded from the sky.

She, too, was weary, but felt no disposition to seek her pillow yet, though the bed with its snowy drapery looked very inviting.

She was glad to be alone; she wanted time to collect her thoughts, to compose her mind after the constant whirl of excitement of the past two days.

Her spirit was buoyant with hope to-night; she would find her long-lost mother, and Espy would find her; for that he would search for her, that he would be true to her, she never doubted.

And there was no bar to their union now; now that she was possessed of twice the fortune she had resigned, Mr. Alden would be only too glad to give consent.

The blissful certainty of that was the greatest happiness this sudden gift of wealth had brought or could bring to her.

But there were minor ones which she was far from despising. She thought with a thrill of joy of the ability it gave her to show her gratitude and affection to those who had befriended her in adversity, and to relieve poverty and distress.

And then the removal of the necessity of laboring for her own support—what a relief it was! what a delightful sense of ease and freedom she was conscious of, as, turning from the window, she glanced at her luxurious surroundings and remembered that she would not be called up in the morning to a day of toil; that she might choose her own hours for rising and retiring; that she would have time and opportunity for the cultivation of mind and heart, for the keeping up of her accomplishments, and for many innocent pleasures that want of means had obliged her to forego during the past year!

The communicating doors between her apartments stood wide open, giving a free circulation of air. She sauntered through the dressing-room into the boudoir beyond, a beautiful room looking out upon the lake.

A cool, refreshing breeze gently stirred the curtains of costly lace and kissed the fair cheek of our heroine as she ensconced herself in an easy chair beside the window, and, with her elbow on its arm, her chin in her hand, gazed out over the dark waters, where she could faintly discern the outlines of a passing row-boat and the white sails of two or three vessels in the offing.

A tap at the outer door, and Kathleen put in her head, asking:

"Shall I light the gas for you, Miss—Miss—"

"Ethel," returned her young mistress, smiling. "Not here, Katty, but in the bedroom. And turn it quite low. The moon will be rising presently, and I shall sit here till I see it."

If you'll excuse me, miss, but you do look lovely in that white dress and them pearls,." said the girl, stepping in and turning an admiring glance upon the graceful figure at the window. "They was just made for the likes of you, wid your shining eyes, your pink cheeks, and purty red lips, an' your skin that's the color o' cream an' soft an' fine an' smooth as a babby's."

Ethel shook her head and laughed.

"Ah, Katty, you have been kissing the blarney-stone," she said. "My cheeks are pale and my skin dark compared with yours. And your sunny brown tresses are far prettier, to my thinking, than my own darker locks."

"Och, Miss Ethel, an' it's mesilf that would thrade aven and throw in a thrifle to boot!" replied Kathleen, with a blush and a smile. 'But it's attendin' to yere orders I should be, and it's proud I'll be to attind to 'em if ye'll be plazed to ring whin I'm wanted," she added as she courtesied and left the room.

"They are certainly very beautiful," thought Ethel, looking down at the pearls on her wrist gleaming out whitely in the darkening twilight, "the dress, too, with its exquisite lace. And I— I seem to have lost my identity with the laying off of of my mourning!" And a tear fell, a sigh was breathed to the memory of those for whom she had worn it.

"Yet why should I grieve any longer for them, dear as they were to me?" she thought; "for them, the blessed dead whom I would not for worlds recall to earth."

A hush came over her spirit; she forgot herself and her changed circumstances as she seemed to see those beloved ones walking the golden streets, casting their crowns at Jesus' feet, and to hear the distant echo of their voices singing the song of the redeemed.

And one day she should join them there and unite in their song; but ah, what a long, weary road must be travelled first! how many foes there were to be overcome, how many dangers and temptations to be passed through on the way!

The Saviour's words, "How hardly shall they that have riches enter into the kingdom," came forcibly to mind, and she trembled at thought of her newly-acquired possessions, and lifted up her heart to Him for strength to use them aright.

Then she fell to considering the duties of her new situation, and saw very plainly that one of the first was to devote herself to the task of making her aunt as comfortable and happy as possible.

But she had been musing a long while: the moon rode high in the heavens, the night wind had grown cool and damp. She rose, dropped the curtain, and withdrew to her dressing-room to prepare for her night's rest.

No life is so dark as to be utterly without blessings, none so bright as to be wholly exempt from trials. Ethel's rose did not prove a thornless one. Madame Le Conte was exacting in her affection, and made heavy draughts upon the time and patience of her niece.

The young girl soon found that her cherished plans for the improvement of her mind must be given up, except as she could prevail upon her aunt to join her in the effort by listening to books worth the reading, which was very seldom, the Madame having no taste or appetite for solid mental food.

She wanted Ethel with her constantly in her waking hours, chatting with or reading to her, and her preference was always for the latest and most exciting novels.

Ethel grieved to learn, what indeed she had suspected all along, that her new-found relative was utterly worldly. Madame Le Conte had not entered a church for years ; and though a very handsomely-bound Bible lay on the table in her boudoir, it was never opened—never till Ethel's advent into the household ; but she was not long in persuading her aunt to permit her to read aloud to her a few verses every day.

The Madame consented to gratify her darling, but did not always take note of what was read. Still Ethel persevered in sowing the seed, hoping, believing that some day it would spring up and bear fruit.

She succeeded also, after some weeks of persistent effort, in coaxing the Madame to accompany her occasionally in her attendance upon the services of the sanctuary.

Ethel had been religiously brought up, had early

united with the church, and though but young in years, had attained, through the blessing of God upon the trials of the past months, to some maturity of Christian character; had learned in her own personal experience how sweet it is to cast all our burdens of sin and sorrow and care upon the Lord; how a sense of His love can sustain in every trial, temptation, and affliction.

And as day by day she perceived the restless unhappiness of her aunt, groaning and fretting under her physical sufferings, weighed down with remorse on account of something in her past life, Ethel knew not what, and sometimes full of the cares that riches bring, especially to such as find in them their chief treasure, she longed with an ever-increasing desire to lead the poor lady to this divine Friend and see her become a partaker of this blessed trust.

But the Madame foiled every attempt to introduce the subject, always broaching some other topic of conversation, or closing her eyes as if drowsy and politely requesting her niece to be silent that she might take a nap.

There were two other subjects that, for the first few months after they came together, the Madame avoided with more or less care—Ethel's previous life and her own; and perceiving her aversion, the young girl forbore to speak of them.

She did not, however, forget or neglect her old friends, but wrote to those at a distance of her changed circumstances, and, as the Christmas holidays again drew near, found great pleasure in preparing a handsome present for each.

Hetty and her mother were remembered in like

manner, and treated to an occasional drive in the Madame's fine carriage ; only occasional because they were so busy, and Ethel generally accompanied in her drives by the Madame herself, and her maid.

Hetty rejoiced greatly in the improved fortunes of our heroine, but not more than Miss Wells and Mr. Crosby. Both of these wrote, congratulating her heartily, and the latter added that he had vastly enjoyed communicating the tidings to Mr. Alden, and seeing him almost ready to tear his hair with vexation that he had been the means of keeping such an heiress, or perhaps rather such a fortune, out of his family, for Espy had gone and left no clue to his whereabouts.

CHAPTER XXXIII.

A LETTER, A STORY, AND A PROMISE.

"The love of gold, that meanest rage
And latest folly of man's sinking age."—MOORE.

MR. ALDEN was so chagrined, so deeply repentant, so anxious to repair the mischief he had done, that at length he wrote to Ethel himself, apologizing, begging her to forgive and forget, assuring her that his opposition to her union with Espy was entirely withdrawn—nay, more, that he was extremely desirous that it should take place, and entreating her to be kind to the lad should she ever meet or hear from him again.

Ethel was with her aunt in the boudoir of the latter when this letter was handed to her.

The weather was very cold, and a three days' storm had kept them within doors till the Madame had grown unusually dull and spiritless, weary of every amusement within her reach, and ready to snatch at anything that held out the least hope of relief from her consuming *ennui*. "Ah, a letter!" she said, with a yawn. "Pansy, you are fortunate! no one writes to me."

"Because you write to no one, is it not, auntie?" the girl asked playfully. "But will you excuse me if I open and read it?"

"Certainly, little one; who knows but you may find something entertaining? Ah, what is it? may

I hear?" as she saw the girl's cheek flush and her eye brighten, though her lip curled with a half-smile of contempt.

Ethel read the letter aloud.

Madame Le Conte was all interest and attention.

"What! a lover, my little Pansy!" she cried, "and you never to tell me of him! Fie! did you think I had grown too old to feel sympathy in affairs of the heart?"

"Oh no, Aunt Nannette! but—you have troubles enough of your own, and I did not think—"

"Ah, well, tell me now; a story, and above all a love-story—especially of your love—will be the very thing to while away these weary hours. And who knows but I may have the happiness of being able to help these poor divided lovers?" she added, touching Ethel's cheek caressingly with the fingers of her left hand, as she had a habit of doing.

"Ah, have you not helped us already?" said the young girl, smiling through gathering tears; "for I think he will come back some day and be glad to learn that there is no longer anything to keep us apart."

"Yes, I am sure of it. And now for the story."

"You shall have it if you wish, aunt," said Ethel earnestly, a slight tremulousness and a sound of tears in her voice; "but to give you the whole I must also tell the story of my childhood's days."

"Let me hear it, child! let me have the whole!" the Madame answered almost impatiently; and Ethel at once complied.

She began with the first meeting between Espy and herself when they were mere babies; drew a lovely picture of her life in infancy and early youth; described the terrible scenes connected with the death of her adopted parents and the circumstances that followed, including her formal betrothal, the search for the missing papers, the quarrels and estrangements, her visit to Clearfield, interview with Mrs. Dobbs, arrival in Chicago, the conversation in Miss Lea's boudoir, the sight of Espy in the church the next Sunday, her interview with him in Mr. Lea's library ; and, lastly, the manner in which she had learned the fact of his sudden departure from the city the very day that she first entered the Madame's house, coming there in pursuit of her calling as a dressmaker's apprentice.

It was a long story, but the Madame's interest never flagged.

"Ah," she said, drawing a long breath at its conclusion, and feeling for her niece's hand that she might press it affectionately, for it was growing dark in the room, "my poor child, what you have suffered ! How did you endure it all ? how did you have courage to give up the property and go to work for your living ?"

"It was God who helped me," said Ethel low and reverently, "else I should have sunk under the repeated blows that took all my earthly treasures from me. But He was left me ; the joy of the Lord was my strength ; and, dear aunt, there is no other strength like that."

Madame Le Conte sighed. "I wish I was as good as you are, my little Pansy," she said, stroking the young girl's hair caressingly. "But I intend to get religion before I die. I shall need it when it comes to that," she added, with a shudder.

"I need it to live by," remarked Ethel very gently.

> "Oh, who could bear life's stormy doom,
> Did not Thy wing of love
> Come sweetly wafting, through the gloom,
> Our peace-branch from above!'

"But, dear aunt, don't tell me I am good; I am not, and my only hope is in trusting solely in God's offered pardon through the atoning blood and imputed righteousness of Christ."

"You never harmed anybody, Pansy, and so I'm sure you are safe enough."

"That would not save me, aunt. 'Except your righteousness shall exceed the righteousness of the scribes and Pharisees, ye shall in no case enter into the kingdom of heaven,' Jesus said, and His own is the only righteousness that does that."

"And you've suffered so much!" the Madame went on maunderingly, "and I too—enough, I hope, to atone for all the evil I have done. Yes," moving the artificial hand slightly and bending upon it a look of aversion and pain, while her voice sank almost to a whisper, "I am sure my little Pansy would say so, cruel though it was."

"What was?" The words burst half unconsciously from Ethel's lips.

Madame Le Conte turned a startled look upon her.

"Not to-night, not to-night!" she said hurriedly. "To-morrow, perhaps. Yes, yes, you have confided in me, and I will not be less generous toward you. You shall hear all; and if you hate and despise me, I must even bear it as best I may."

CHAPTER XXXIV.

THE MADAME'S CONFESSION.

"Can wealth give happiness ? look round and see
What gay distress! what splendid misery !"—YOUNG.

ETHEL had never betrayed the slightest curiosity in regard to her aunt's crippled condition, not only refraining from asking questions, but with delicate tact seeming utterly unconscious of it ; but the Madame's words to-night, and the slight accompanying gesture, so plainly indicating that the loss of her hand was in some way connected with that past which so filled her with remorse, kindled in the young girl's breast a strong desire to learn the whole truth ; and since her aunt had voluntarily promised to tell her all, she did not feel called upon to repress the wish.

Mary's entrance with a light, and the announcement that tea was ready, prevented a reply to the remark with which the Madame supplemented her promise, and the subject was not broached again during the hour or two that they remained together after the conclusion of the meal.

But having withdrawn to the privacy of her own apartments, Ethel sat long over the fire in her boudoir lost in thought, vainly trying to conjecture what cruelty her aunt could have been guilty of toward the sister she seemed to remember with such tender affection.

"Hate her!" she exclaimed half aloud, thinking of the Madame's sadly-spoken words. "No, no, I could not do that, whatever she has done! I should be an ingrate if I could," she added, sending a sweeping glance about the elegantly-appointed room, and as she did so catching the reflection in an opposite mirror of a slight, graceful, girlish figure richy and tastefully attired, reclining at ease on the most comfortable of softly-cushioned chairs in front of a glowing, beautiful fire.

Without the storm was raging with increased violence; it seemed to have culminated in a furious tempest.

Absorbed in her own musings, Ethel had hardly been conscious of it before; but now the howling of the wind, the dashing of the waves on the shore, and the rattling of the sleet against the windows made her shiver and sigh as she thought of the homeless on land and the sailors on the water alike exposed to this wild war of the elements.

Ah, were Espy and her dear unknown mother among the number? What a throb of fear and pain came with that thought!

But she put it resolutely aside. She would hope for the best, and—there was One who knew where each of these loved ones was, and who was able to take care of them. To His kind keeping she would commit both them and herself, and go to her rest with the peaceful, confiding trust of a little child.

"Ah, little one, how did you rest?" was Madame Le Conte's morning salutation.

"Delightfully, auntie; dropped asleep the instant my head touched the pillow, and knew no more till I woke to find the sun shining in at the windows. And you? how did you rest?"

"Very little," the Madame sighed, shaking her head sadly; "my asthma was worse than usual, and would scarcely allow me to lie down."

"I am so sorry! But you are better?"

"Yes; the attack has passed."

The tempest was over, the day still, calm, and bright, but intensely cold, and the streets were so blocked up by a heavy fall of snow that going out was not to be thought of; nor were they likely to be troubled with callers.

"We shall have the day to ourselves," the Madame remarked as they left the breakfast-table, "and if you will invite me into your boudoir, Pansy, we will pass the morning there for variety."

"I shall be delighted to entertain and wait upon you, Aunt Nannette," Ethel answered, with a smile.

She was looking very lovely in a pretty morning dress of crimson cashmere, edged at neck and sleeves with ruches of soft, rich lace.

Having seen her aunt comfortably established in an easy chair, Ethel took possession of a low rocker near her side, and employing her busy fingers with some fancy work—a shawl of soft white zephyr which she was crocheting for Hetty—waited with outward composure, but inward impatience, for the fulfilment of yesterday's promise.

The Madame sat with her hands folded in her lap, her eyes gazing into vacancy, her breathing somewhat labored, her thoughts evidently far away. To Ethel's eager expectance it seemed a long time that she sat thus, but at length she began, in a low, even tone, much as if she were reading aloud, and with eyes still looking straight before her :

"I was eight years older than my sister Ethel, my little Pansy. There had been others, but they all died in infancy, and we two were the only ones left when our parents were taken. That was when Ethel was fourteen and I twenty-two.

"I tried to be a mother to her. I was very fond of her, yet now I can see that I always cared more for my own happiness than for hers—always wanted to be first, and to rule her.

"We lived in Jefferson, Indiana, a mere village, to which the family had removed shortly before the death of our father ; he and mother went very near together, both dying of congestive chills. We were left with a little home of our own and a modest competence, and we continued to keep house, a middle-aged woman who had been in the family from the time of my birth matronizing us and taking the oversight of domestic affairs."

Madame Le Conte paused for breath, and Ethel said softly, "Aunt, you have never told me the family name ; it seems odd enough that I should never have heard it—my own mother's maiden name."

"Gramont—Nannette and Ethel Gramont we were called, and I have always thought them very pretty names."

Again the Madame paused for a moment. Her voice trembled slightly as she resumed :

"It was something more than a year after we were left alone in the world that Rolfe Heywood came to Jefferson and opened a dry-goods store He was a fine-looking, gentlemanly fellow, some twenty three or four years old, I should think, well educated, of agreeable manners, and rather fond of ladies' society.

"I was pleased with him, and the liking seemed to be mutual. He became a frequent visitor at our house, and soon the girls began to tease me about him. He was said to be paying attention to me, and indeed I think he was at first, and I gave him some little encouragement—not much, for I had several suitors, and was naturally inclined to coquetry ; but I liked Rolfe Heywood best of all. I think partly because I was less sure of him than of the others, and that piqued my vanity and pride.

"He did not offer himself, but kept on coming to the house and making himself very much at home there. And so things went on for nearly two years, when all at once I discovered that it was Ethel he admired and wanted. She was seventeen now, and a sweeter, prettier creature you never saw. Ah, my darling little Pansy!"

Tears rolled down the Madame's cheeks. She hastily wiped them away.

"How did you make the discovery, aunt?" her niece asked in low but eager tones.

"By a look I saw him give her, and which she did not see. It made me furious at him, and I vowed he should never have her. I thought she did not care for him. I kept her out of his way as much as I could, and she made no resistance. But the more obstacles I threw in his way the more eager after her he became.

"At length we learned that he had sold out his business and was going to California, and now my eyes were opened to the fact that Pansy did care for him, she turned so white when she heard the news.

"But I said to myself that it was only a passing fancy, and she would soon forget him. I watched her constantly, and contrived never to allow them to be alone together.

"But one day—the day he was to leave—he called, and found her alone in the parlor. He had not been there ten minutes, though, before I hurried in, pretending to think his call was meant as much for me as for her, and was just in time to prevent a declaration of love which I saw he was beginning.

"It was his last opportunity, and he went away without telling her his feelings or learning hers. He held her hand lingeringly in parting, but I gave him no chance to speak.

"Poor thing! she drooped sadly when he was gone, but I took no notice, saying to myself, 'She'll get over it in time.'

"I thought he would write, and he did. I took his letter from the office, deliberately broke the seal, read it ('twas full of passionate love, and would have been a cordial to the poor darling's fainting heart), and answered with a cold rejection of his suit, imitating my sister's hand so perfectly that even she could hardly have recognized it as a counterfeit, and signing her name.

"Monsieur Le Conte was paying me attention at this time, having come to the place some months before. He was a handsome, middle-aged man, of courtly manners and considerable wealth. I found his company agreeable, and before we had been acquainted a year we were married.

"He had an intimate friend, a distant relative, Adrian Farnese, who came to see us shortly after our marriage, and who took a violent fancy to Ethel from the first moment he set eyes on her.

"He courted her assiduously, but she turned coldly from him and rejected his addresses again and again, much to my husband's annoyance and mine, for we both liked Adrian and desired the match.

"I undertook to reason with Ethel, saying everything I could think of in Adrian's favor. She heard me in sad silence, and when at last I insisted upon her giving me a reason for her persistent rejection, she burst into tears, crying out, 'Oh, how can I marry him when my heart is another's?'

"Then I twitted her with giving her heart unasked, said I knew it was to Rolfe Heywood she had lost it, but he didn't care for her now, if he ever had; that was plain enough from his silence. No doubt he had found a new sweetheart by this time—perhaps was already married.

"My poor little Pansy never answered back a word, but cried as if her heart would break."

The Madame's voice broke. She stopped, buried her face in her handkerchief, and sobbed aloud. Tears were stealing down the cheeks of her listener also, and for a moment neither spoke.

Then the Madame resumed her narrative:

"As I said before, Ethel and I were very different—she so gentle and yielding, so ready to think others wiser than herself; I proud and wilful, always made more determined by opposition. I resolved that she should marry Adrian Farnese."

"Oh, how could you be so cruel?" cried her listener.

"Ah, try not to hate me! I have suffered terribly for my fault, as you shall learn presently," said the Madame in piteous tones. "But how shall I tell of all my wicked unkindness to that poor child! I wrote a notice of the marriage of Rolfe Heywood, giving a fictitious name to the bride, and sent it to a paper published in New York. I was a subscriber, and when the number with the notice came I showed it to Ethel, saying, 'You see I was right. Rolfe Heywood cared nothing for you, and is already united to another.'"

"She turned deathly white, seemed about to faint, but recovering herself a little, hastily left the room.

"'Now,' I thought, 'she will presently give up and marry Adrian.' But she would not hear of it, and avoided him whenever she could without absolute rudeness.

"'No, she'll never give up while she knows Rolfe Heywood is alive,' I said to my husband one day.

"'Then we must make her believe him dead,' he answered.

"I was afraid to publish a false report of his death, but we got one printed on a slip of paper that had the appearance of having been cut from a newspaper, and I gave it to my sister. She swooned, and looked so deathlike, seemed so utterly crushed for days and weeks afterward, that I could scarcely refrain from telling her the whole truth. But the fear of my husband's displeasure, and the thought that if I did Rolfe Heywood would get her after all, restrained me. So I kept my secret, and tried to make all other amends in my power by being very kind and sympathizing.

"Ah, her gratitude for it was quite touching—almost harder to withstand than her grief!

"She seemed gradually to recover from the shock, but was never again the light-hearted, merry creature she had been before Rolfe Heywood went away."

"And she learned at last to love—?" Ethel broke off without pronouncing the name.

"She finally gave up to us and married him," sighed the Madame. "How much she loved him, if at all, I do not know. I tried to believe her not unhappy, and she made no complaint.

"However, they had not been married many months when a fierce quarrel arose between our husbands. It was about some money matters. I never fully understood it, but I then learned for the first time that it was more Pansy's little fortune Adrian wanted than herself, and that Monsieur Le Conte's influence was used in his favor because they had agreed that in that way he should cancel a debt owed to Adrian. Had I known this I would never have let them use me as their tool."

"And he was my father!" murmured Ethel in a pained tone.

"Yes, child, and you might justly hate me for giving you such a one!" exclaimed the Madame almost passionately. "I'm afraid he was a bad man. I fear he was unkind to my sister; but she was loyal to him, poor thing.

"When the quarrel arose between him and Monsieur Le Conte I sided with my husband, and went to Ethel with his version of the affair; but she would not listen to me.

"'I am his wife now,' she said; 'I will hear nothing against him. And you, Nannette, who brought about the match, should be the last to tempt me to do so.'

"I was very angry, and heaped bitter reproaches upon her," pursued the Madame, almost overcome by emotion. "She heard them in grieved silence, which somehow only exasperated me the more, and I said still harder and more cruel words. And so I left her."

For some minutes the room was filled with the sound of the Madame's sobs, and Ethel wept with her.

"It was our last interview," she began again in a broken voice. "A few days later her husband spirited her away no one knew whither, and from that day to this I have never heard a word from her or about her, except what I have learned through you —her child.

"I have now told you of my crime; I have yet to tell of its punishment. In spite of all my unkindness, I loved my sister; how dearly I never guessed till she was gone. I was nearly frantic at her loss, and at the thought of my last words to her.

"The world went prosperously with us so far as money was concerned. My husband invested my little fortune and his own partly in an oil-well, partly in a gold-mine in California, and we were wonderfully successful in both. But we were not happy. Remorse and anxiety about Pansy made me wretched and robbed me of my vivacity and my bloom. I grew dull and spiritless, and my husband began to neglect me and to seek the society of other women, whom, as he said, he found more entertaining.

"I sought forgetfulness in dress and all sorts of dissipation. I could not bear to be alone ; but sometimes Monsieur Le Conte's business would call him away for days and weeks together. I had no child, and I could not always go out or contrive to have company in the house ; and so at times I would try to drown my misery in the wine-cup.

"I did not become a drunkard, but two or three times I drank to intoxication."

She paused, and, with a downward glance at her mutilated limb, sighed heavily.

"One wild, stormy night I was quite alone," she continued. "The wind howled round the house like a legion of devils, as it seemed to me, and the air was full of eerie sounds. I had been more than usually depressed all day, and grew worse and worse as the hours crept slowly by. My husband I knew would not be home before morning ; one servant was away, and the other had gone to bed in a distant part of the house.

"I wasn't exactly afraid, but I kept thinking of Ethel, and how I had ill-used her, and that I should probably never see her again, till I was half crazed with remorse. At last I could not endure it any longer. I kept wine in a closet in my dressing-room ; I went to it, poured out and drank one glass after another till I was quite stupefied.

"The last thing I remember is dropping into a chair beside the fire—a low-down grate filled with glowing coals ; the next I knew I awoke in my bed, roused to consciousness by a sharp pain in my right arm.

"My husband, the servant-woman—who was crying bitterly—and two or three doctors were in the room. They were talking in low tones, and kept glancing at me.

"'What is the matter?' I asked; 'what have you been doing to my hand that it pains me so?' It was the surgeon nearest me who answered.

"'Madame,' he said in a compassionate tone, 'it was so badly burned that we were obliged to take it off.'

"'Off! burned!' I shrieked, wild with terror and despair.

"'Yes,' he said, 'your husband found you lying insensible on the floor, with your right hand in the grate and burnt almost to a cinder.'"

Ethel sprang up, threw her arms about the Madame's neck, and sobbed aloud.

"My poor, poor aunt!" she said when she could speak. "What a dreadful, dreadful thing it was! My heart aches for you! oh, how could you bear it?"

Madame Le Conte returned the caress, then Ethel resumed her seat.

"I could not escape it!" she sighed, "and I felt that it was a just punishment that deprived me of the hand I had used to forge the notices which robbed my sister of her lover.

"Remorse has tortured me horribly many a time since, but I never have resorted to the intoxicating cup to escape its stings.

"I gave up society from the time of my accident.

I could not bear the thought of exposing myself to the curious gaze and questioning of common acquaintances or of strangers.

"My husband pitied me very much, and never once said to me, 'It is your own fault,' as well he might. Finding how I shrank from meeting any one I knew, he proposed removing to this city, where we were entirely unknown, and I was glad to come. It is now ten years since he died, leaving me everything he possessed."

CHAPTER XXXV.

A FLITTING.

> " The keen spirit
> Seizes the prompt occasion, makes the thougnt
> Start into instant action, and at once
> Plans and performs, resolves and executes!"
> HANNAH MORE.

" AND all alone !" sighed Ethel, breaking the momentary pause that followed the concluding sentence of the Madame's story. " Ten years of utter loneliness, save the presence of hired servants—of constant ill-health and mental anguish, besides the dreadful loss of your right hand ! My poor, poor aunt, you have indeed suffered horribly and long !"

" Indeed I have, and I hope Heaven will accept it as some atonement ! Well, what is it, child : you deem it not sufficient ?" as Ethel turned upon her a pained, troubled look.

" Ah, Aunt Nannette," she said, " there is but one atonement for sin, even the blood of Christ."

" My sister, my gentle, forgiving little Pansy, would think I had endured far more than enough," sobbed the Madame in an injured tone, and almost turning her back upon her niece.

Ethel dropped her crocheting, rose hastily, and putting her arms about the Madame's neck, said soothingly, " Don't misunderstand me, auntie dear.

I did not mean—I could not feel for a moment that my mother or I could wish to add a feather's weight to all you have suffered, or help grieving over it, or wishing you might have been spared it."

"What then?" asked the Madame petulantly, and with a movement as if she would free herself from the enfolding arms.

"Only," Ethel said gently, withdrawing them and resuming her seat, "that sin as committed against God cannot be atoned for by anything that we can do or suffer."

"I shall try to sleep now, ' said the Madame, closing her eyes. "I am exhausted."

And truly she looked as if she were ; her face was haggard and old beyond her years, and her eyes were swollen with weeping.

Ethel's filled with tears as she gazed upon the careworn, miserable face, and thought how wretched she was in spite of all her wealth ; how her wounded spirit would keep her so, even could her hand and health of body be restored.

"Poor thing!" said the young girl to herself, "none but Jesus can do her good, and she will not come to Him."

Feigned sleep presently became real, and for an hour or more Ethel was to all intents and purposes as much alone as if she had been sole occupant of the room.

She did not move from her chair, but her fingers were busy with her crocheting, her thoughts equally so with the tale to which she had been listening.

It seemed to have made her acquainted with her mother, and she dwelt upon her character, as drawn by Madame Le Conte, with ever-increasing love and admiration.

How she pitied her sorrows—the separation from him who had won her young, guileless heart, the news that he was lost to her, then of his death! Ah how could *she* bear such tidings of Espy! He would never love another; but he might die. She shivered and turned pale at the very thought. Ah, God grant she might be spared that heart-breaking grief! But should it come, she would live single all her days; she could never be forced or persuaded to do as her mother had done; her nature was less gentle and yielding, better fitted to brave the storms of life. That loveless marriage! ah, how sad! how dreadful the trials that followed!

And her mother had married again. Rolfe Heywood was not really dead, and perhaps—ah yes, it must have been he who had found and won her, he the one whom she had always loved; Ethel was certain of it, certain that none but he could have reconciled her, the bereaved, heart-broken mother, to life, and so quickly gained her for his bride.

And had she forgotten her child in her new-found happiness? the child who was now searching so eagerly, lovingly for her? No, no, the tender mother-love could not be so easily quenched! No doubt unavailing efforts had been made to recover her lost treasure; and though other little ones had perhaps come to share that love, the first-born held her own place in the mother's heart.

"Oh, when shall I find her? how can I endure this waiting, waiting in suspense? 'Tis the hardest thing in life to bear!" she exclaimed half aloud, forgetting that she was not alone ; letting her work fall in her lap while she clasped her hands together over her beating heart and drew a long, sighing breath.

"What—what is it?" cried Madame Le Conte, starting from her sleep and rubbing her eyes. "Has anything happened?"

"No, nothing. How thoughtless I have been to disturb your slumbers!" Ethel said, rising, bending over her, and gently stroking her hair.

"Oh," sighed the Madame, "it is no matter! my dreams were not pleasant : I am not sorry to have been roused from them. But what is it that you find so hard to bear?"

"This suspense—this doubt whether my mother still lives ; whether I shall ever find her."

"We will! we must!" cried the Madame with energy, starting up in her chair as she spoke. "They say money can do everything, and I will pour it out like water!"

"And I," said Ethel low and tremulously, "will pray, *pray* that, if the will of God be so, we may be speedily brought together ; and prayer moves the Arm that moves the universe."

"And we will share the waiting and suspense together ; it will be easier than for either alone. But if you have found it hard to endure for one year, what do you suppose the ten that I have waited and watched have been to me?"

Many, many times in the next two years, while looking, longing, hoping even against hope for the finding of her mother and the coming of Espy, Ethel's heart repeated that cry, "Oh, this weary,

weary waiting, this torturing suspense! it is hard, hard to bear!"

Two years, and no word of or from either. Two years of freedom from poverty with all its attendant ills. Two years of abounding wealth.

But poverty is not the greatest of evils, nor do riches always bring happiness. Ethel's life during this time had had other trials besides the absence of those loved ones, and the uncertainty in regard to their well-being and their return to her.

Her days, and often her nights also, were spent in attendance upon her aunt, whose ailments seemed to increase, and who grew more and more querulous, unreasonable, and exacting.

Ethel bore it all very patiently, seldom appearing other than cheerful and content in her aunt's presence, though sometimes giving way to sadness and letting fall a few tears in the privacy of her own apartments.

There was a sad, aching void in the poor hungry heart which the Madame's capricious, selfish affection could not fill. A hunger of the mind, too, for other and better intellectual food than the novels she was daily called upon to read aloud for the Madame's delectation.

But, as says an old writer, "Young trees root all the faster for shaking," and the young girl's character deepened and strengthened under the trying but salutary discipline.

She was developing into a noble, well-poised woman, soft in manner, energetic in action, unworldly and unselfish to a remarkable degree. And making diligent use of the scraps of time she could secure to herself, she was accomplishing far more than she realized in the direction of mental culture.

On a bright, warm day in the latter part of April, 1876, Ethel sat in her boudoir looking over the morning paper. As usual, the advertisements claimed her first attention ; for who could say that Espy and her mother might not be searching for her in the same way in which she was pursuing her quest for the latter?

Ah, nothing there for her. The daily recurring disappointment drew forth a slight sigh. An additional shade of sadness rested for an instant upon the fair face, then was replaced by a most sweet expression of patient resignation.

The paper was full of the coming Centennial. She read with interest the descriptions of the great buildings and the many curious and beautiful things already pouring into them ; also of the preparations for the accommodation of the crowds of people from all parts of the world who were expected to flock thither.

A thought struck her, and her face lighted up ; her heart beat fast. She started to her feet, the paper still in her hand ; then dropping into her chair again, turned once more to the advertisements and marked one with her pencil, after which she sat for some moments in deep thought.

A tap at the door, and Mary, putting in her head, said, " The Madame wants you to come now, miss."

Ethel hastened to obey the summons.

Madame Le Conte was in her boudoir, receiving a professional call from her physician, Dr. Bland.

The doctor rose with a smile as the young girl entered, and offered his hand in cordial greeting.

She seemed to bring with her a breath of the sweet spring air, so fresh and fair was she in her dainty morning dress of soft white cashmere, relieved by a bunch of violets at the throat, and another nestling amid the dark glossy braids of her hair.

The easy grace of her movements, the brightness of her eyes, the delicate bloom on the softly-rounded cheek and chin, spoke of perfect health.

"You are quite well?" he asked, handing her a chair.

"Quite, I am thankful to say. No hope of finding another patient in me, doctor," she returned laughingly. "But what of Aunt Nannette?"

"I think she needs a change of air and scene. I have been trying to persuade her to go to Europe for the summer; or if she would stay a year, it would be better."

"Preposterous idea!" wheezed the patient. "Hardly able to ride down town, how could I think of undertaking to cross the ocean? Suppose there should be a shipwreck; immensely heavy, unwieldy, helpless as I am, I'd go to the bottom like a lump of lead. No, no, home's the only place for me."

"You will get no better here, Madame," said the doctor shortly.

"And we need not anticipate a shipwreck," said Ethel. "The sea air might do you great good."

"I tell you it's nonsense to talk of it!" returned the Madame impatiently.

The doctor rose and bowed himself out. Ethel ran after him, stopped him in the hall, and talked eagerly for a few moments.

"By all means, if you can persuade her; anything

for a change," he answered, bidding the young girl a smiling adieu.

She stood musing a moment when he had left her; then rousing herself, hastened back to her aunt, who said reproachfully:

"I wish you wouldn't run away and leave me alone, Ethel. I want to be read to."

"And I am entirely at your service," the young girl returned pleasantly, taking up the morning paper again and seating herself near the Madame's easy chair. "There are some articles here about the Centennial which I am sure will interest you."

She read with an enthusiasm that was contagious.

"What a pity we should miss it all!" exclaimed the Madame at length. "There will never be another Centennial of our country in my lifetime, or even in yours."

"No; and why should we not go, as well as others?" Ethel answered with suppressed eagerness.

"Impossible, in my invalid condition."

"Aunt Nannette," cried Ethel, throwing down the paper and clasping her hands together in her excitement, "people will be flocking there from all parts of the land and the civilized world. I have a presentiment that my mother will be there, and that we shall meet her if we go!"

"Child, child! do you really think it?" cried the Madame, starting up, then sinking back again upon her cushions panting and trembling.

"I do, Aunt Nannette, I do indeed! and we shall never, never have such another opportunity. And Espy, too, will be there—I know it, I feel it! He is an artist. Will he not have a picture to exhibit?"

"Yes, yes, I see it! we must go! But how can I? how can we manage it? I can never live in a hotel, never exist in a crowd; I should suffocate!" And the Madame wheezed and panted and wiped the perspiration from her face, while her huge frame trembled like a jelly, so great was her agitation.

"I will tell you, Aunt Nannette," said Ethel, dropping on her knees and taking the shaking hands in hers, while she lifted to the Madame's troubled, distressed face her own—sparkling, animated, fairly radiant with hope and gladness. "I have already planned it all, and Dr. Bland approves. There are furnished houses to let. We will write and engage one for the whole season—six or eight months—and we will take our servants with us and go directly there, leaving this house in the care of a trusty middle-aged couple I know. We will have our own carriage and horses, and drive about the beautiful park to our hearts' content. We will go now, while there is no crowd, and, having plenty of time, can see everything we care to look at without fatiguing ourselves by attempting too much at once."

"How rapid you are! Really, child, you almost take my breath away!" panted the Madame, shaking her head dubiously, though evidently attracted by the bright picture Ethel had drawn.

"But you will go? I may make the arrangements? Oh, think what it would be to find your long-lost sister!" said Ethel, pressing the hands she held, and gazing with pleading eyes into the Madame's face.

"Yes, yes! but ah, the journey! how am I to accomplish that?"

Ethel reassured her on that point, overruled one or two other objections which she raised, and, not giving her time to retract her permission, hastened to her writing-desk and wrote a note to Mr. Tredick, asking him to call that day or the next, and an answer to an advertisement of a furnished house to let in West Philadelphia, which, from the description, she felt nearly certain would suit them, engaging the first refusal, promising to be on the spot within a week, and to take immediate possession should everything prove to be as represented.

Both notes were despatched as soon as written, a message sent to the persons in whose care Ethel proposed to leave their present residence, and then she returned to her aunt.

"And now Mary and I will overhaul the trunks and decide, with your help, auntie, what is to be taken with us and what left behind."

"Child, child," cried the Madame breathlessly, "how precipitate you are! Engaged to be in Philadelphia in a week! How are we to prepare in that short space of time?"

"No great amount of preparation needed, auntie dear," laughed Ethel, throwing her arms about the Madame's neck.

"Shopping, Pansy, dressmaking—"

"Ah, we have loads of dresses already!" interrupted the girl in her most persuasive tones. "And think of the hundreds of stores and dressmakers and milliners in Philadelphia! Can't we get everything we want there? Don't let us carry too many coals to Newcastle," she ended, with a silvery laugh that brought a smile to her aunt's face in spite of herself.

Madame Le Conte's inertia was compelled to give way before Ethel's energetic persistence, and the girl carried her point. In a week they were cosily established in a very pleasant residence within easy walking distance of the great Centennial grounds.

CHAPTER XXXVI.

REUNITED.

> "After long storms and tempests overblown,
> The sun at length his joyous face doth clear."—SPENSER.

MADAME LE CONTE had found the journey very fatiguing. For a few days she utterly refused to stir out of the house, indeed kept her room almost constantly, and would scarcely allow Ethel to go out of her sight.

This was hard on the young girl, for she was burning with impatience to be looking, not upon the rare and beautiful things brought together in the Exposition from all quarters of the earth, but for the loved one of whom she had been in quest for years. Was she there? should she see her? would they recognize each other? Ah, it seemed to her that until that dear one was found she should have no eyes for anything but the multitude of faces presented to her gaze. How could she wait? how endure the slow torture of passing hour after hour, and day after day, shut up with her invalid aunt, listening to her endless fretting and complaining, her reproaches for having brought her away from the home where she was so comfortable, the physician who so thoroughly understood her constitution, wearing her out with the long journey with really no object but a wild-goose chase after the unattainable; for now she was quite convinced that her sister would have been found long since had she been in the land of the living.

Ethel's patience was sorely tried; her courage also, for it was difficult to keep hope alive in her own breast while compelled to hear an incessant repetition of these doleful prognostications.

But at last there was a rift in the cloud. Madame Le Conte woke one morning feeling rested and refreshed by her night's sleep, and consequently in tolerable spirits, and Ethel succeeded in coaxing her into her carriage. They drove to and about the park, visited the Main Building, and the Madame spent a couple of hours in a rolling chair, and returned home delighted with her day's experience.

She had no more reproaches for her niece on the score of having brought her to the great Exhibition almost against her will, but still maintained that there was no reasonable hope of finding her lost sister there.

Yet Ethel was not to be discouraged, but began every day with renewed hope that ere its close her long quest should be ended.

"Mother, mother! and Espy, my own Espy!" her heart kept whispering in the solitude of her own room, and as her eye moved from face to face in the streets, the cars, the buildings and grounds of the Exposition.

She wanted to be there every day, and all day, because there, as it seemed to her, she must find them; but her aunt could not bear the fatigue of constant attendance, and was not willing to be left at home till, to Ethel's great joy, she came upon a lap-dog the exact counterpart of the lost Frisky in appearance, and with fully as great an aptitude for learning amusing little tricks ; and the entertainment Madame Le Conte found in teaching and caressing him was sufficient to induce her to allow her niece occasionally to go out without her.

And those days when she was free from the care imposed by her aunt's companionship, and at liberty to roam about at her own sweet will, were by far the most enjoyable to Ethel. She liked to lengthen them out, and had often eaten her breakfast and gone long before the Madame awoke from her morning nap, and sometimes the sun was near his setting when she returned.

She was interested in the exhibits, yet few faces of men or women that came within her range of vision escaped her observation. The main object of her coming was never absent from her mind ; she pursued her search diligently, but at times physical weariness compelled her to pause and rest awhile.

On a lovely day early in June, after four or five hours spent in the usual manner, she turned aside from the vicinity of the hurrying crowds, and seeking out a cool, quiet retreat in a little dell by the side of a limpid stream of water, sat down on a bench in the shade of some weeping willows.

With her hands folded in her lap, her eyes upon the rivulet that went singing and dancing almost at her feet, she was thinking of her lost loved ones, and weighing the chances of meeting them, when some one sprang down the bank and pushed aside the drooping branches which half concealed her from view. Lifting her eyes, there was a simultaneous, joyous exclamation—

"Floy!"

"Espy!"

She hardly knew what followed—so sudden, so great was the glad surprise—but in another moment he was sitting by her side, her hand in his, one arm about her waist, while in an ecstasy of delight he gazed into her blushing, radiant face.

For a time their joy was beyond words ; but what need of them ? Was it not enough that they were together?

At last Espy spoke. His tones were low and pleading.

"Floy, darling, you will not send me from you again ? It is true I have not gained my father's consent (I have not even seen him or so much as heard from him for over two years), but I am no longer a child ; am pushing my own way in the world, and since this thing will affect my happiness so much more nearly than his, and probably long after he has gone from earth, I cannot think it is required of us to wait for that."

He paused, but the girl did not speak. Her eyes were on the ground, a soft blush suffused her cheek, and a slight smile trembled about her full red lips.

She perceived that Espy had heard nothing of her changed circumstances and the consequent alteration in his father's feelings ; and, for reasons of her own, she preferred that he should for the present remain in ignorance of these things ; yet she could not drive him from her again, could not deny to him or herself the happiness that now might be lawfully theirs.

Besides, she felt that his reasoning was sound ; that he was of age to choose for himself, and to disregard his father's refusal to give consent.

"Floy, Floy, you will not, cannot be so cruel as to bid me begone?"

Espy's voice was full of passionate entreaty, and his grasp tightened upon her hand.

"No, no, I cannot," she faltered ; "I cannot so reward such love and constancy as yours. When we last met you refused to accept your freedom, and— you—shall not have it now," she concluded playfully, lifting a smiling, blushing face to his for an instant, then half averting it as she caught the look of ecstasy in his.

"Your willing slave for life, I hug my chain!" he cried in transport.

"Which means me, I suppose," she laughed, for he drew his arm more closely about her as he spoke.

"A golden chain," he whispered low and rapturously ; "such fetters and warder as Fitz-James appointed for the Graeme."

Another arch smile, and another swift, bewitching glance from the lustrous eyes, were the only reply vouchsafed him ; but he seemed satisfied.

"Floy, my own little wife!" he whispered, bending over her to look into the blushing, happy face, "this moment repays me for all the loneliness, all the struggles of the past two years."

Then he went on to tell of a long, weary, fruitless search for her.

He had returned to Chicago shortly after his mother's death, hoping to learn her address from the Leas, but found their house closed and a bill of sale upon it. The newspapers told him of Mr. Lea's defalcation and subsequent suicide, but he could not discover the whereabouts of the family, nor in any other way obtain a clue to the residence of her whom he was so anxiously seeking.

At length, abandoning its personal prosecution for the time, but engaging a friend to continue it for him, he went to Italy to pursue the study of his art, determined to make fame and money as a worthy offering to his "little love" when she should be found.

"It has been my dream by day and by night, dearest," he said, "and has been partially realized. I have sold some pictures at very good prices, and am hoping much from some I have on exhibition here. If they do for me what I hope, I shall soon be able to make a home for you, where, God helping me," he added low and reverently, "I will shield you from every evil and make your life as bright and joyous and free from care as that of any bird."

How her heart went out to him in proud, fond appreciation as he said these words, his face, as he bent over her and looked into hers with his soulful eyes, all aglow with love and delight.

"But tell me," he exclaimed as with sudden recollection, "how has it fared with you during all these long, weary months that we have been so far apart? Well, I trust, for you are looking in far better health than when I saw you last. But how came you here in Philadelphia? I hoped, yet called myself a fool for hoping, that I might find you here, for I could not suppose you had means to come, much as you might desire to do so."

"Yes," she said softly, "I did greatly desire to come, and a good Providence opened the way, Espy," and she looked earnestly at him. "I have found the deed of gift, learned my true name, and discovered—no, not my mother," as she saw the question in his eyes, "but her sister, who is now helping me in my search."

"Oh, Floy, how glad I am! And I, too, will help!" he exclaimed. "Helping you to find your lost mother has always been a part of my dream, and I have been working to that end. I have thought that she, if living and prosperous, would come to this great Exhibition, this Centennial of our country, and the subjects for my pictures were chosen accordingly; I have painted for her eye more than for any other. But I shall not describe them," he continued in response to her eager, inquiring look. "They were hung only this morning, and I will take you to see them."

She rose hastily, but he drew her back.

"Not yet, Floy, darling! let us stay here a little longer. I think the crowd may lessen in the next hour, and there is so much I want to say to you—to ask you. What of this new-found relative—this aunt? Are you happy with her? is she kind to you?"

"She is very fond of me, and I have a good home with her," Ethel answered, smiling brightly as she turned her face to him. "And she will be glad, very glad, to see you, Espy. I have told her the whole story of our acquaintance and engagement, and she is deeply interested for us both."

He flushed with pleasure.

"Ah, Floy, my little love! our skies are brightening; the course of true love begins to run smooth. How glad I am for you!"

"Do you know," she said gayly, "that you have not asked me my true name? though I told you I had found it."

"Ah, yes; I want to hear it, and how and where you found the paper; but I think you must let me call you always by the name I have loved so dearly since we were mere babies. I think no other can ever sound so sweet to my ear."

"I shall allow my willing slave to have his own way in this one thing," she returned sportively. "I do not object to being Floy to you, though all others call me Ethel."

"Ethel!" he said, "that is a sweet name too."

"Yes; allow me to introduce myself. Mr. Alden, I am Ethel Farnese, sometimes called Pansy by my aunt—a pet name she had formerly bestowed upon my mother, the first Ethel Farnese."

"I like that also," he said, gazing with all a lover's admiration into the sparkling, animated face. "You are rich in sweet names, as who has a better right?"

"Where is your curiosity?" she queried. "You have not even asked if I found the will."

"No, to be sure! And you did?"

She shook her head. "I am quite convinced that it never existed."

"I presume you are right there. But I have found my curiosity, and am burning with desire to hear how you came to discover the other paper, to find your aunt, and—and all the rest of it. You remember that I know absolutely nothing of your history from the time of your leaving Cranley to this, except the few moments that we were together in Mr. Lea's library."

"And I," she returned, "am burning with desire to see those pictures, and to learn how they are to assist me in my quest. The story is too long to be told in an hour, Espy, with all the minute detail that I know you would require. So you shall have it at another time."

"Will you let me see you home, and spend the evening with you?"

"Yes, if my aunt will spare me. She's an invalid, and seems to value my society far beyond its real worth."

"Then her estimate must be high indeed," he responded in the same playful tone. "But since it is your wish, fair lady, I will now conduct you to the Art Gallery and show you the pictures."

He led her out of the little dell up a flight of steps in the grassy bank, and together they traversed the winding paths and broad avenues that led to the Art Building, walking along side by side silently, yet only dimly conscious of the delicious summer air, the brilliant sunlight, the gay parterres, the crowds of people in the walks and passing up and down the broad, white marble steps of Memorial Hall as they ascended them.

For once Ethel had utterly forgotten her quest, and did not look into a single one of the hundreds of faces she passed. But a bright little girl, standing at the foot of those same marble steps, and holding fast to the hand of a young man, was more observant.

"What a pretty lady, Ellis!" she said, gazing

after Ethel's lithe, graceful figure as it flitted by. "And she looks like Dora. I thought it was at first, but she has another sort of dress on."

"Yes, Nan, it was a pretty face, and something like Dora's, I thought too," returned the lad. "You are tired, little sister, and yonder is an empty seat. Shall we go to it?"

"Yes—no; see, they're coming now."

Then letting go his hand, and running to meet a lady and gentleman who were sauntering toward them from the direction of the Main Building, "Papa and mamma," she cried, "Ellis and I have been waiting a long time. Shall we go in now to see the pictures?"

"It is growing late, Nan, and tea will be ready by the time we can get home if we start at once," said the father. "Your mother is much fatigued, too—very tired indeed; so we will leave the pictures for another time."

"Well, I don't care, if mamma's tired," said the child, putting her hand into his.

Both parents smiled approval, and the little party walked away together toward the place of exit from the grounds.

In the mean time Espy was making way for himself and Ethel through the crowds that filled the corridors of Memorial Hall.

Reaching that portion of the building appropriated to the works of American artists, he paused for a moment or two before several paintings in succession, calling her attention to the good points of each, and giving the artist's name; but when they came to his own he waited silently for her to speak.

One glance, and she turned to him, her eyes full, her features working with emotion.

"Mother!" was the one word that came low and gaspingly from the quivering lips.

His face was a study, the gratified pride of the artist mingling with the tender sympathy of the lover.

He drew her arm within his, for she was trembling like an aspen leaf.

She allowed him to support her while she turned again to the picture and studied it with mournful pleasure.

Mrs. Kemper's face was a peculiar one, and had changed but little during the fifteen quiet, uneventful years of her life in Cranley. This picture of Espy's—painted from memory—represented her as he had first seen her, with the little Ethel by her side dressed as she was then, and holding her doll in her arms. The pretty baby-face was as perfect a likeness as the other. Memory had done him good service here also, and, in addition, he had had the assistance of a photograph taken about that time.

A second painting hung by the side of the first—a full-length portrait of our heroine standing on the threshold of her Cranley home, as Espy had seen her on looking back after bidding her good-by when leaving for college the last time before the accident that wrought such woe to the young, light-hearted girl whose pathway had been hitherto so bright and sunny.

It was a speaking likeness of a very lovely face, fair and winning, with the freshness of early youth and the sweetness and vivacity lent it by a keen intellect and a happy, loving heart. The figure and attitude were the perfection of symmetry and grace.

It received many a lingering look of admiration from strangers, but a single glance was all that Ethel bestowed upon it.

But Mrs. Kemper's face chained her. For many minutes her eyes were riveted upon it.

"Do not sell this; I must have it," she said to Espy as at last she turned sighing away.

"It is yours from this moment," he said, flashing upon her a look of ecstatic love.

"It must be late; see how long the shadows are!" she remarked as they came down the marble steps. "Ah, my aunt has sent for us! how fortunate!" as she espied a carriage at some little distance, Rory upon the box, driving slowly along and looking this way and that as if in search of some one.

She signalled him, and in another minute they were bowling rapidly homeward.

Arrived, Espy was requested to take a seat in the parlor while Ethel ran up to her aunt's room.

The Madame was at first disposed to be cross, but on hearing the wonderful news her mood changed.

"Was ever anything so fortunate!" she cried, hugging her niece enthusiastically. "My darling Pansy, I congratulate you with all my heart. He shall be quite at home here and the course of true love run smooth from this on, if I can make it do so."

Then Mary was directed to go down and show the young gentleman to a room where he could attend to the duties of the toilet, the Madame remarking:

"One always feels like washing and brushing after tramping round all day in the heat and dust. And, Pansy, you must make him understand that we consider him just one of ourselves. The tea-table is already set in my boudoir; another plate shall be added, and we will all sup there together. Now run away and make yourself fine."

"Neat and ladylike, but not too fine, auntie," Ethel responded, bending down to her with a smiling face, her cheeks glowing, her eyes dancing with health and happiness. "For a reason I have, I want him not to know or suspect how rich we are, so please help on my innocent deception."

"Very well, it is all one to me what he thinks about that," the Madame answered good-naturedly, and Ethel tripped away to make the necessary changes in her attire.

In common with other sensible people, she dressed very simply and inexpensively for a day at the Centennial. Her toilet for the evening was charmingly becoming, and suited to Espy's artist taste, yet but little more elaborate or costly than the other.

Espy was much struck by the Madame's appearance, so different from that of her fair niece—her unwieldy figure, enormous size, swarthy features, ungainly movements, and asthmatic breathing; but she was very gracious to him, an excellent foil to Ethel's beauty, and so kindly considerate as to leave them to themselves for the evening directly tea was over.

CHAPTER XXXVII.

LOVE'S POSY.

"Such is the posy love composes—
A stinging nettle mix'd with roses."—BROWN.

Two or three as blissful weeks as perhaps mortals ever know passed over the heads of our lovers. They were almost constantly together, alone in the crowd, for they haunted the Centennial daily, and Madame Le Conte, showing herself as considerate as at first, either remained at home or quickly dismissed them from attendance upon her, declaring that she wanted Mary, and Mary only, to walk beside her rolling chair, and help her to see the sights.

Espy's pictures were much admired, spoken of with marked favor by the critics, and he had several good offers for them, but would not sell.

In this happy state of affairs, and with his Floy by his side, he was in the seventh heaven.

But all things earthly must have an end, and so it was with this season of almost unalloyed felicity to Ethel and Espy.

One evening the latter, hurrying out of his hotel, bound, as usual, for Madame Le Conte's, nearly ran over an elderly gentleman who was just coming in. Scarcely looking at the stranger, he was brushing past with a hasty apology, when he felt a hand laid on his shoulder, while a familiar voice exclaimed, in loud tones of unfeigned, exultant delight, "Why, Espy! is it you? and don't you know your own father, boy?"

"Father!" he cried, stopping short and wheeling about, half glad, half sorry at the meeting, the gladness uppermost as his parent grasped his hand in warm, fatherly greeting and gazed in his face with the proud, affectionate look often in other days, ere pride and greed of gold had come between them, bent upon the bright, promising boy.

"I did not know you were in the city, sir! When did you arrive?"

"Yesterday, or rather last night; slept late; spent the rest of the day at the Exposition; just got back. Come with me to my room. I want to talk with you; have no end of things to say. Had your supper?"

"Yes, sir."

"I too; got it out there. I'm dreadfully tired, but there's an easy chair in the room; so can rest and talk at the same time. Here, let's go up in the elevator. Capital thing, isn't it?"

"Very," Espy answered absently, taking a seat by his father's side, and thinking of Floy waiting and watching for his coming.

"Well, where have you been all this time?" Mr. Alden asked as he took possession of the chair he had spoken of, and signed to Espy to be seated upon another close at hand.

The young man answered briefly that the greater part of the past two years had been spent by him in Italy perfecting himself in his art; that he was now doing well pecuniarily, and hoped soon to be doing much better.

"Very good! very good indeed!" commented his father, rubbing his hands and smiling broadly. "Glad you're doing so well, my boy; have always had your welfare very much at heart. Now about Floy Kemper—"

Espy flushed hotly, and half rose from his chair.

"Tut, tut! wait till you hear what I have to say!" exclaimed his father, breaking off in the middle of his sentence. "I withdrew my opposition to the match long ago, as you should have been informed if I'd known where to find you."

"Thank you, sir," Espy said, his countenance clearing. "Everything seems to be coming round right at last. I hope that in another year I shall be in circumstances to marry."

"He evidently hasn't seen Floy yet," thought Mr. Alden to himself. "Wonder if he even knows where she is? You do, eh?" he said aloud, rubbing his hands again. "If it was my case—I shouldn't wait half that time."

Espy's countenance expressed surprise and inquiry.

"I did not expect such counsel from you, sir," he remarked, "and I cannot think it would be prudent in me, or kind to Floy, to rush into matrimony before I have proved my ability to support a wife."

"Very wise and sensible if you were marrying a poor girl," returned his father, with an unpleasant laugh; "but the income from a hundred thousand might suffice, I should think, to begin upon in a modest way."

"What—what can you mean, sir?" exclaimed Espy, springing to his feet, his face flushing and paling by turns.

"That's the exact sum, as I've been credibly informed, that Floy's aunt has already settled upon her, and she's altogether likely to prove the only heir to the half million the old lady still has in her possession." And Mr. Alden laughed gleefully, rubbing his hands rapidly over each other; then stroking his beard and glancing at his son, he perceived with astonishment that his countenance was pale and distressed—that he looked stunned as if by a heavy blow.

"Why, Espy, what's the matter?" he exclaimed in extreme surprise; "thought you'd be delighted with such good news. But perhaps you've lost sight of the girl? Well, never mind; I can give you her address and—"

"Father, what do you take me for?" asked the young man hoarsely, rising to his feet as he spoke. "A fortune-hunter? I hope I may never deserve the name! I do not call this good news. It seems to put Floy farther away from a poor fellow like me, and it has been the sweetest dream of my life that my toil should supply her wants."

"Crack-brained fool!" muttered his father angrily.

But Espy did not seem to hear.

"I see now," he went on in a tone of bitter sarcasm, "just why you have ceased to oppose my wishes and become anxious to receive Floy into the family. She will understand it too, and I am bitterly ashamed. Thanks for your offer to furnish me with her address, but I do not care to avail myself of it."

"Humph! I perceive that it is not without reason that poets and painters are popularly supposed to lack common-sense in regard to the affairs of everyday life," sneered the older gentleman. "But come, come, I don't want to renew the old quarrel. Sit down and let me tell you about your brothers and sisters. They'll be glad to hear that you have turned up once more."

Upon that the young man resumed his seat, and for the next hour the talk was all of relatives and friends in and about Cranley.

"Well, father," Espy said at length, taking out his watch, "I have an engagement, and you look as though you needed rest; I'd better bid you good-night. Will see you again in the morning. You'll be staying some time in the city, I suppose?"

"Yes—no; that is, I'm going for a trip into New York and Canada; leave by the early train to-morrow morning, expect to be gone two or three weeks, maybe more, and then return here to do the Exposition. It's the first real vacation I've given myself since—well, before you were born, my boy, and I mean to do the thing up brown while I'm about it."

"I hope you will, sir. I hope you won't go back to work till thoroughly tired of play," Espy said laughingly. "I may not wake in time to see you off in the morning, but you'll find me here, I think, on your return to Philadelphia."

"Yes, I trust so; but if I shouldn't—"

"You shall hear from me; probably see me in Cranley in the fall. Good-night, father."

"Good-night, my son. Don't fail to keep your promises." And shaking hands cordially, they separated.

It was late for a call at Madame Le Conte's. Espy said so to himself as he left the hotel, yet set off upon that very errand, and not at all as if in haste to accomplish it. Truth to tell, he was half reluctant to meet Ethel, yet at the same time irresistibly drawn toward her.

"And she's rich!" he mused, sauntering slowly along; "rich, and a great heiress, while I—ah me!—am poor as a church-mouse. How can I urge her to marry me? Wouldn't it be like saying, 'Be my provider,' instead of, 'Let me provide for you'? I am too proud for that. But why has she left me in ignorance of her circumstances? Did she fear that I would want to marry her for her money? She might have known me better. Did *I* find fault with her for resigning Mr. Kemper's property? Did *I* want to give her up when she was poor and friendless?"

He grew angry and indignant as he put these queries to himself.

"Yes; she might have known me better," he repeated. "How could she suspect me of motives so base and sordid? But no, no, it could not be that! She *does* know me better, is too noble herself to think that I could be capable of such meanness. No, she saw that it was a delight to me to feel that my work was to provide a home for her some day, and would not deprive me sooner than necessary of that pleasure. And yet why not tell me all? She ought to have no secrets from me, her affianced husband. And why let our marriage be delayed when there is no need? If I had sufficient means, would I not tell her of it at once, and beg that there might not be another week of delay? But she, I suppose, likes to be her own mistress, and keep her newly-acquired property in her own hands. I, perhaps, am not deemed fit to be trusted with the care of it."

And losing sight of the fact that womanly delicacy would forbid the course he was prescribing as proper for Ethel, he grew angry again.

And so alternating between admiration and disgust at her reticence, he arrived at Madame Le Conte's door and rang the bell.

No one answered it. He stood waiting for several minutes, so busy with his own thoughts that this did not strike him as strange. Then, suddenly growing impatient, he was about to repeat his ring, when, glancing up, he perceived that the windows were all dark except those of the Madame's bedroom, where a faint light seemed to be burning.

"Gone to bed without waiting to see if I were coming as usual," he muttered, descending the steps.

Then he noticed that very few lights were visible in the neighboring houses, and consulting his watch by the light of a street-lamp, found to his surprise that it was near midnight.

He recollected, too, that Floy (she was still Floy to him) had looked very weary when they left the Centennial grounds together some hours before.

"Poor darling!" he said, "I'm a brute to blame her!" and went on his way, impatient for the morrow that he might seek the desired interview.

Ethel had sat up expecting him, till the lateness of

the hour convinced her that he was not coming; then she had retired, weary in body and a little heavy at heart lest some evil had befallen him, yet ridiculing and scolding herself for the folly of such fears.

> "Oh, love! how hard a fate is thine!
> Obtained with trouble, and with pain preserv'd,
> Never at rest."

When they met the next day, something seemed to have come between them.

"What was it?" Ethel vainly asked herself. Something light as air; something so intangible that she could not give it a name.

A change had come upon Espy, but when questioned he insisted that nothing was wrong, sometimes asking, almost testily, why she should think there was; then, in sudden penitence for his ill-humor, he would be more devoted than ever for a time, but presently fall back into moody silence.

He was still dwelling upon the information his father had given him, still querying as to his affianced's motives in concealing the facts from him, and alternating between anger and admiration as the one or the other seemed to him the more likely to have influenced her.

"Why will she not be open with me?" he asked himself a hundred times; "then there would be no trouble."

And she was thinking the same in regard to him.

I am inclined to think that they were both in the right there, and that perfect openness between married people and lovers would save a great deal of trouble, heartache, and estrangement.

As it was, these two began to reap a bountiful harvest of each.

Espy slackened his attentions, absented himself frequently, and when he returned to her side, Ethel's manner was constrained and cold.

The girl poured her griefs, anxieties, and perplexities into no mortal ear. She would as soon have thought of telling them to a child as to Madame Le Conte; and so, feeling the need of a sympathizing friend and counsellor, she took to longing and looking for her mother more earnestly and constantly than she had since the return of her betrothed.

"Other girls have their mothers to go to," she would sigh to herself. "Ah, that I had mine!"

Espy was not now always by her side, and on those days when she found herself alone at the Exposition she would go to Memorial Hall, and if able to make her way through the crowd to the place where his paintings hung, would stand and gaze, through gathering tears, upon Mrs. Kemper's portrait.

Espy came upon her there one day, approaching her unperceived, and as he noted the sadness of her countenance, the pallor of her cheek, and saw her hastily brush away a tear, his heart smote him.

He pushed his way to her side, and putting his lips to her ear,

"Floy, darling!" he whispered, "come with me; take my arm, and let me help you out of this suffocating atmosphere."

She made no reply, but suffered him to draw her hand within his arm and lead her away.

Neither spoke until they were clear of the crowd

and had reached a shaded walk, where they might converse without fear of being overheard.

Then turning resolutely to him,

"Espy," she said, "I cannot bear this any longer. What is wrong? what is it that has come between us?"

"Why," he said, coloring and looking down with a mortified air, "what have I done that you should ask me that, Floy? I have found no fault with you, as indeed," he added quickly, "I have had no reason to do."

"No, you have not found fault, but a change has come over you," she answered sadly, "and it would be kinder, far kinder to be frank with me. Why should you not be?"

"Because you have not been so with me," he retorted half angrily.

"I have not? Espy, you must explain; I insist upon it." And she looked so pained that his heart smote him.

"Forgive me, Floy, darling!" he exclaimed. "I am a brute to hurt you so! But why did you leave me to learn of your changed circumstances from others? Did you fear that I would covet your wealth? that I would love it instead of you?"

"Oh, Espy! as if I could have so base a thought in connection with you!" she cried reproachfully.

"But why not tell me?" he said, coloring deeply.

"Because I saw what delight you took in the thought that you were winning the means to make a home for me, and I would not deprive you of that till I must; and because I was determined that no one should say you sought me for my money."

He was deeply ashamed of his suspicions, and said so frankly, begging her pardon.

"We will exchange forgiveness," she whispered, flashing a look upon him that thrilled him to his heart's core. "I was wrong too. Henceforth let us have not the slightest concealment from each other."

"Agreed!" he said, tenderly pressing the hand he held, and gazing with all a lover's ardent admiration into the dear face at his side, while his heart bounded with hope and happiness.

And she?—ah, in the fulness of her content and joy even her long-lost, long-sought mother was for the moment forgotten.

CHAPTER XXXVIII.

"FOUND! FOUND! FOUND!"

"YES, they're splendid! they're gorgeous! superior to the best: they must be! But what is it Shakespeare says?

> "'How vain the ardour of the crowd,
> How low, how little are—'"

"Oh, that's Grey, mother! But never mind! Come—Floy!" as a lady in front of them turned suddenly round.

"Hetty! you here? and your mother too?" cried Ethel, who had been made aware of their unexpected vicinity by the sound of the words and voices so familiar to her ear two years ago.

"Yes," said Mrs. Goodenough, "we were just looking at those splendid jewels from New York."

"We have just come to the city," said Hetty; "arrived last night; and oh, I am so glad to have met you! for I have something to tell you."

The eager, animated look and tone said that it was something of importance, and Ethel's heart gave a wild bound. Was it news that would aid her in her quest?

She drew out her watch. "One o'clock: a good hour for lunch. Come with me to Public Comfort. You must be my guests."

"Thank you!" and they went with her.

"Are you here alone?" asked Mrs. Goodenough as they crossed the avenue.

"I have often come alone," returned Ethel, smiling. "A friend was with me this morning; left me half an hour ago, and will meet me half an hour hence at Public Comfort."

"A very particular friend," thought Hetty to herself, noticing the light in Ethel's eye, the deepening of the color on her cheek, as she mentioned him.

She had heard of Espy, knew something of what had been the state of affairs between the lovers.

"My dear, has he come back?" she asked in a delighted whisper.

Ethel's blush and smile were sufficient to assure her that such was the case, and her kindly, affectionate heart was overjoyed.

They were so fortunate as to find an unoccupied corner in the ladies' parlor at Public Comfort, seated themselves about a table, ordered their lunch, and while waiting for and eating it did a good deal of talking.

Hetty was the chief speaker. She began the instant they were seated:

"We've been to the sea-shore, mother and I, and it's about some people we saw on the train, as we came up to the city, that I want to tell you, Floy. Such a nice-looking family—father, mother, one son, and two daughters. And the strangest thing is that the mother and the oldest girl look very much like you."

At these words Ethel's heart beat so fast and loud it seemed to her they all must hear it, and her hand trembled so that she was obliged to set down the cup she was in the act of lifting to her lips.

Hetty saw her agitation, and made haste with her story.

"The girl looked about fifteen. The mother, I should say, might be anywhere between thirty and forty, and very handsome; has the sweetest face! Her husband, a noble-looking man, watched over and waited on her as if it were the greatest pleasure in life to do so—with a sort of pitying tenderness, so it seemed to me. And I saw her give him such a look once, as if she thought he was—well, as mother says, 'superior to the best.' But when she was not speaking or listening to him there would come a far-off look into her eyes, an expression as if she had known some great sorrow, some life-long trial that she had schooled herself to bear with patient resignation."

"Dear me, Hetty, how much you see that common folks like me would never think of!" put in her mother admiringly as the girl paused for breath.

Ethel, contrary to her usual good manners, made an impatient movement, and Hetty hastily resumed her narrative.

"You see my attention was drawn to her as they came in, for they were a little late, and had some difficulty in finding seats—couldn't all get together at first; then the resemblance to you, which even mother noticed when I spoke of it to her, and the quick, searching glance she sent round the car—for all the world as you would have done, because you are always looking for your lost mother. She seemed to scan every face, then sat down with, so at least I thought, a weary, disappointed little sigh ; and it was then I noticed the pitying tenderness of her husband's manner. Then the older girl spoke to her, calling her mamma, and I noticed that in her there was a still more striking likeness to you—though only, I think, because she is so much nearer your age."

Ethel had forgotten to eat or drink ; she was trembling with agitation.

"Oh, is that all?" she asked in tones scarcely audible, as Hetty again paused a moment.

"Not quite, dear. The little girl at first sat on her brother's knee ; then a seat was vacated just in front of me, and she took it. I smiled at her, and she smiled back. I was eager to make acquaintance, that I might find out something about them ; so presently I leaned over to her and asked if she had been at the sea-shore. She said, 'Yes, and now we're going back to the Centennial. We were there a while, but mamma got very tired one day—so tired she and papa couldn't go in to look at the pictures with Ellis and me, and we went home instead ; and we were to go to the picture place the next morning, but mamma was taken very sick in the night, and the doctor said she must go to the sea-shore for a while ; so of course we all went.'

"Then she took to questioning me, and telling me about the shells she had picked and the fun she had had in bathing, and what she had seen and expected to see at the Exposition.

"I asked her her name, and she said it was 'Nan' something ; I couldn't quite catch the last name, but it was a word of two syllables.

"Then I sat silent a while, racking my brains to think what I could do to find out whether they really were related to you, and had just decided to tell the child that I knew a young lady who strongly resembled her mother and sister, when some persons left the car, and she changed her seat again for one nearer the rest of the family."

"And that is all?" Ethel said, drawing a long, sighing breath as Hetty ceased.

"Yes, dear, all," Hetty answered regretfully, laying her hand tenderly on her friend's arm. "I wish for your sake there was something more—something certain."

For a moment Ethel hid her face in her hands; then taking them away, turned toward Hetty, pale, tearful, but with the light of hope shining in her eyes.

"It was my mother," she whispered. "Something tells me so, and that I shall find her—we shall find each other at last."

A young man had stepped upon the thresnold of the outer door, and was sending a hurried glance about the now crowded room. His eye lighted up as it fell upon Ethel's graceful figure and fair face, of which he could get but a partial view from where he stood.

In another instant she rose and turned toward him. Their eyes met, she nodded and smiled, said a few words to her companions, then made her way through the throng to his side as he stepped back upon the porch, the other two following.

Arrived in his vicinity, she introduced Mr. Alden to Mrs. and Miss Goodenough. A shaking of hands and exchange of a few commonplace sentences followed, and the four separated, Hetty and her mother returning to the Main Building, while Ethel and Espy sauntered side by side along the avenue in the direction of Memorial Hall, passing it and going some distance beyond.

Although thousands of people were wandering about the houses and grounds, this spacious thoroughfare was not so crowded that they could not with ease keep to themselves and carry on a private conversation without danger of being overheard.

In a few moments Espy had learned from Ethel all that Hetty had had to tell of her fellow-passengers of the previous day.

His interest and excitement were only second to Ethel's, and he shared both her conviction and her presentiment.

"Yes," he said eagerly, "it is your mother! I seem somehow to feel that it must be so; and now the question is how to bring you together."

"Yes," sighed Ethel, "we might all be here every day while the Exhibition lasts, yet never meet. But no, I will not fear it! I will trust in God, who hath helped me hitherto," she added, smiling brightly through gathering tears.

Espy regarded her with admiring, loving eyes.

"That is right!" he said cheerfully, "and I feel sure your faith will be rewarded. You are looking tired; let us sit down here and rest while we talk it over."

He had led her into a side path, and to a bench that stood in the shade of a wide-spreading tree.

"It may sound conceited," he said, "but I do believe that my pictures are now to play a conspicuous part in the drama and do you good service—as truly they ought, being mine, and I your humble slave," he added sportively, seeking to win her from anxiety and care.

She smiled, but sadly still, as she made answer: "I hope they may; but how is it to be managed? It is with them as with the rest of the Exposition—we and those we seek may visit them again and again, yet never at the same time."

He mused a moment.

"They would perhaps think of inquiring for the artist in case your mother recognizes the likenesses, as I do feel pretty confident she will, at least if she has a good memory for faces; for surely Mrs. Kemper's, and yours as a baby, would be likely to be strongly impressed upon it. And we must go there very often, singly or together."

"And trust to Providence to bring us there at the right moment," she added thoughtfully.

A moment of silent musing on the part of both, and Ethel suddenly sprang to her feet.

"I will go there now—this moment!"

"And may I go with you?"

"Yes, yes; come!" and she started almost on a run.

"Floy, Floy, not quite so fast!" he said, exerting himself to keep pace with her. "You will be all out of breath, and have no strength to push through the crowd."

She slackened her speed and took his offered arm.

"Yes, you are right; I shall have need of all my

strength. But oh, if I should be a moment too late!"

"Try to be calm, dear Floy," he said low and tenderly, gazing down upon the agitated face in loving solicitude. "You have been very brave and hopeful thus far, and are, I trust, soon to be rewarded for it all. But try to be calm and collected. You will need to have full command of yourself."

"I will try," she answered with a deep-drawn sigh; "and oh, I am glad and thankful that I have you with me, Espy!"

"Bless you, darling, for the words!" he said, flushing with pleasure. "To be a comfort and support to you has long been the dearest wish of my heart."

He led her on in the direction from which they had come at a rapid but steady pace, watching anxiously the while the changes in her speaking countenance. He was relieved to see a calm, peaceful, quiet look presently take the place of the painful agitation visible there a moment before.

He knew not the cause, but she had fled to the Rock that was higher than she. Whatever might befall, this Refuge could not fail, this Friend would never forsake.

While Ethel had sat listening with absorbing interest to Hetty's story the persons of whom they spoke were in Horticultural Hall, which they left at nearly the same time that the first party separated and went their several ways.

"Memorial Hall comes next on our programme, does it not, wife?" said the older gentleman as they descended the steps of the main entrance.

"Yes," she said, "but let us walk about here a little first; the sun is under a cloud at this moment, and these parterres and rustic seats are worth looking at."

"They are lovely, mamma," said the older girl; "but I've seen them several times, and I want to buy some little things at the Japanese Bazaar. So may I go on? and I'll meet you in the avenue near the Art Building."

Permission was given, and she tripped away. The others soon followed. Presently she came running breathlessly to meet them.

"Papa, mamma, I've had an adventure! An elderly gentleman rushed up to me, holding out his hand in the most cordial manner and looking as pleased as if he had just come upon his best friend after a long separation. 'Why, Floy, my dear child, I am delighted to see you!' he said, but I of course drew back and told him as politely as I could that he had made a mistake; that was not my name, and I was quite sure we had never met before. Then he grew very red in the face, and stammered out an apology He had taken me for a young lady he used to know very well indeed, but hadn't seen for two or three years; hoped I would excuse him, but really the resemblance was wonderful."

"A mere pretence, you may depend!" cried her brother angrily. "And, Dora, you are not to go alone into a crowd again; you are quite too young and pretty."

But the mother appeared strangely agitated. "Oh, my child, where is he?" she cried, trembling and turning pale. "Oh, if I had but seen him!

Which way did he go? could you point him out to your father or me?"

"I think I should recognize him if I met him again," the girl answered in surprise, "but I do not at all know where he went. But why, mamma, why should you wish to see him?"

The mother did not answer, did not seem to have heard the question. She was leaning heavily upon her husband's arm for support, while he bent over her with low-breathed words of comfort and hope.

"Dear wife, bear up! What is this but another gleam of light for you?"

"Hush, Dora," whispered the lad, drawing his sister aside. "Can you not guess? have you forgotten our mother's quest—her life-long sorrow?"

"Oh, Ellis! to be sure! How could I be so stupid! Oh, why didn't I think to detain and question the man? But, Ellis, it wasn't the right name."

"No; but what is easier than to change a name?"

"Yes, yes, that is true! Poor mamma! poor dear mamma! She will never rest; she cannot, till she finds her or knows that she is no more."

"She has such a loving mother-heart," said Ellis, "and she *will* blame herself, though I'm sure she has no reason."

"What are you talking about?" asked little Nan, coming skipping back from an erratic excursion into one of the side paths. "Oh, Dora! did you get me that necklace?"

"Yes, little puss, I have it safe here in my bag."

"Let me carry that; I did not notice that you had it," Ellis said, taking the satchel.

He was invariably as politely attentive to his mother and sisters as to any other ladies.

The parents were moving slowly forward, the mother having recovered her accustomed calm, quiet manner, and the young people had fallen slightly into the rear. Another moment, and they were all passing up the broad marble steps leading into Memorial Hall.

They had hardly disappeared within the portal, when Espy and Ethel might have been seen traversing the avenue in the same direction.

Indifferent as to which part of the building received their first attention, the foremost party turned, as it were by a mere chance, into that appropriated to the exhibition of native talent. They moved slowly along, the parents still in advance, pausing as others were doing, now here, now there, as one painting or another drew their attention.

Suddenly the lady grasped her husband's arm, a low, half-stifled cry escaping her lips. Was it joy? Was it anguish? It seemed a mingling of both.

"What is it, wife?" he asked in a startled tone, and throwing the other arm around her, for she seemed about to faint.

"Look, look!" she said, pointing to Espy's picture of the child, beneath which they were standing. "It is—it is my baby! my little Ethel! my lost darling!" she sobbed half inarticulately, gazing at it with streaming eyes.

"Ha!" cried her husband, "is it possible! My darling, are you sure?"

"Yes, yes, it is she! Could a mother's eyes be deceived? Can a mother's heart forget? And the woman—the one who took her from me! That is her face. I remember perfectly every lineament. Oh, Rolfe, Rolfe, it is my lost baby! And there," pointing to the companion picture, "there she is, grown to womanhood! Is not this a clue?"

"Yes, yes; the artist—we must find him."

Their tones had not been loud, yet, in connection with the lady's evident agitation, had attracted some notice, and a younger pair had hurriedly pushed their way toward them, coming up so close in their rear as to catch the last two or three sentences.

"I am the artist," said Espy, "and this," glancing at Ethel as the others turned quickly at the sound of his voice, "is the original of those two—"

"Your name? your name?" gasped the lady, gazing eagerly, longingly, into the pale, excited face of the girl.

"Is Ethel Farnese. My mother's was the same; and she, a widow, poor, dying as she believed, gave me to that woman—Mrs. Kemper."

"I knew it! I knew it! My child! my long-lost child!" and instantly they were locked in each other's arms, Ethel sobbing:

"Mother, mother! my own darling mother!"

CHAPTER XXXIX.

THE MADAME'S QUEST IS ENDED

"I cannot speak; tears so obstruct my words
And choke me with unutterable joy."—OTWAY.

"Were my whole life to come one heap of troubles,
The pleasure of this moment would suffice,
And sweeten all my griefs with its remembrance."—LEE.

MADAME LE CONTE had remained at home that day, had slept all the morning, and now, in the latter part of the afternoon, was occupying a lounging chair in her boudoir and amusing herself with a novel.

"Hark! wasn't that a carriage stopping at our door?" she said, looking up from her book and addressing her maid. "Yes, there's a ring."

"Katty'll go. It's Miss Ethel come home early, I presume, Madame," answered Mary, not troubling herself to rise from her chair.

There was the sound of Kathleen's step in the hall, the opening of the door, a man's voice speaking, then the girl came quickly up the stairs and appeared before her mistress.

"Mr. Alden, Madame, and he wants to know may he come up here and spake till ye? Oh, don't go for to be scared! Miss Ethel's all right," as the Madame turned pale and half rose from her chair.

"Bring him up then," she gasped, falling back again and panting for breath.

She put no faith in Kathleen's assurance, and was terribly alarmed. To lose Ethel would be almost like losing her own life.

But one glance at Espy's face reassured her.

"Ah, Madame," he said cheerily, declining by a wave of the hand the seat she pointed to, "I met a gentleman out at the Centennial who says he is a very old friend of yours, and would like much to see and speak with you. I have brought him to the house, feeling pretty sure you would be pleased to see him, but thought best to give you a little warning and an opportunity to decline doing so if you wished."

"Who is he?"

"He requested me not to give his name, as he is anxious to see if you will recognize him."

The lady's curiosity was aroused.

"Very well, I will see him," she said. "You may bring him up here at once; I am quite ready for the interview."

The stranger, apparently troubled with no doubt that he would be received, had crept noiselessly up the stairs and was already almost at the door of the boudoir. Espy had only to turn and give him a nod, and instantly he stepped forward and stood before Madame Le Conte—a tall, handsome, middle-aged man.

But he started with amazement as his eye fell upon her face and figure.

"Do I—do I see before me my old acquaintance, Nannette Gramont?"

"That was my maiden name," she said, gazing earnestly into his face as she half rose and held out her left hand, "but I am greatly altered, as I think you must be also, for your looks are utterly strange to me."

"Rolfe Heywood," he said, taking the offered hand while still keenly scanning her face.

"Rolfe Heywood! is it possible? can it be? Ah, yes, I know you now; I remember your smile. But —oh, can you tell me anything of my sister—my lost Ethel—my darling Pansy?"

The words came pantingly, sobbingly, while great tears chased each other down the bloated, swarthy cheeks.

"Yes, Nannette, she has been my wife—my beloved wife—for many years," he said with emotion, thinking of the shock her sister's changed appearance would give to the gentle, loving heart.

"Oh, thank God! thank God! Then she has not perished with want! I have not the darling's blood on my hands!" cried the Madame, sinking back into her chair and weeping as if in bitterest grief.

"No, Nannette, though she was once very near it," he said, bending over her and speaking in a very low tone.

"Do not reproach me!" she cried. I too have suffered! God only knows how much!"

He signed to the wondering Mary to leave the room. His look, his gesture, were imperative, and the girl reluctantly obeyed.

"Poor creature!" he said, turning to the Madame again, "I do not reproach you, nor does she. No, her gentle heart is—has ever been—filled with sisterly affection toward you, and she now waits impatiently to be summoned to your presence."

"Waits, do you say? Is she here?—my sister—my darling! Where? where? Oh, I beseech you not to keep us another moment apart!"

And she started up, wringing her hands and looking imploringly into his face.

"Calm yourself, Nannette; this agitation will hurt you," he said in a kindly tone, gently forcing her back into her chair. "Your niece—my Ethel's dear child—has told us of your invalid state, and I see that this excitement has almost deprived you of the power to breathe."

"Don't stop to talk now!" she panted, pushing him from her. "I shall go wild! Go, go and bring her! Bring her, or I shall die before your eyes!" And she struggled frantically for breath.

He was frightened lest she should indeed fail to recover it. He glanced hurriedly about the room, sprang to the bell-pull, but as he laid his hand on it, Mary, listening at an inner door, threw it open and rushed in.

"You'd better have let me stay, you see, sir," she said a little sarcastically. "But don't be scared. It's more hysterics than anything else, and they're not dangerous. I'll bring her round presently."

"Oh, will you go?" gasped the Madame, looking at her visitor and drawing a long breath that ended in almost a shriek.

"As soon as you are calm, Nannette," he answered pityingly; "but till then I dare not bring her."

"You'd better go out, sir, and I'll call you the moment she's fit," said Mary. And he went.

Espy, standing in the open door of an opposite room, beckoned Mr. Heywood in there.

Downstairs mother and daughter waited, in no haste to be called; for what greater joy than to be as they were now for the first time in so many, many years—alone together, and clasped in each other's arms, cheek to cheek and heart to heart.

They sat in silence, broken only now and then by a sob (for the deepest joy is strangely akin to grief in its outward manifestations) or a whispered word of endearment.

"My precious, precious child! my long-lost darling!"

"Mother, mother! sweetest, dearest, darling mother!"

It was Mr. Heywood who at length broke in upon the glad interview.

"Ethel, love, my dear wife," and his hand touched her hair gently, caressingly, "she will see you now."

Mrs. Heywood started, strained her new-found daughter once more to her bosom with a long, silent, most tender caress, and, releasing her, left the room, leaning on her husband's arm. She needed its strong support, for she was trembling very much.

"Be calm, love," he whispered, bending over her and just touching his lips to her fair, open brow, as he paused with her at the foot of the stairs. "One moment. I must prepare you to find your sister much changed—greatly broken in health, yet not, I think, with any dangerous disease," he hastened to add as he saw a look of anguish come into her eyes, the color suddenly fade out of her cheek, leaving it of an almost death-like pallor.

"Thank God for that!" she whispered faintly, "but how?—what?—"

"She seems to be somewhat asthmatic and very nervous; has grown immensely fat, lost her clear complexion, vivacity of look and manner, and, I think, partially the use of her right hand also. She gave me the left in greeting."

"Oh, Rolfe! is it so?—all that? My poor, poor dear sister!" she murmured, tears trickling down the pale cheeks.

He soothed her grief as tenderly as she would that of her little Nannette—the namesake of this beloved only sister—and at length, when she had grown calm again, half carried her up the stairs.

The Madame, listening to their approach, was threatened with a renewal of her hysterics, but Mary was equal to the emergency.

"Madame, Madame," she said hastily, "calm yourself, or I shall have to call to them not to come in."

"No, no, you shall do no such thing!" cried her mistress, controlling her nerves by a mighty effort; then, as at that instant the slender, graceful figure of Mrs. Heywood appeared in the doorway, she sprang up with a cry, extending both arms, while her huge frame trembled from head to foot.

Mrs. Heywood flew to meet the offered embrace. "Nannette, Nannette!" and tears fell fast as lip met lip in a long, clinging kiss.

"Pansy, Pansy! oh, my little Pansy! my darling! my wronged, long-suffering, abused little sister!" sobbed the Madame, holding her close, "can you, will you, forgive me, dear?"

"With all my heart, my own Nannette," returned Ethel, weeping on her neck. Then, lifting her head and gazing tenderly into the agitated face so painfully changed to her, and noting the tumultuous heaving of the broad chest, "Oh, my poor, poor dear sister, how changed you are! how ill! You seem hardly able to breathe!"

"Yes, I have suffered," panted the Madame. "I have mourned and wept over your loss, Pansy, and for many years have been constantly searching for you. Heaven be praised, darling, that I have found you at last!"

The last words were spoken gaspingly, and Ethel felt the stout arms relaxing their hold on her. Mr. Heywood sprang forward just in time to save his sister-in-law from falling, and with Mary's assistance got her into her chair again, where she lay back on her cushions wheezing and panting in a way that greatly alarmed her sister.

Mary reassured her:

"It is nothing, ma'am. You'd know that if you'd been with her as long as I have. She'll get over it in a few minutes. You see she gets kind of upset with anything that excites her."

Mrs. Heywood knelt by the side of the chair, and, with tears streaming over her cheeks, took the Madame's hand in hers, stroked it, and talked to her in soothing tones with loving, tender, pitying words, while Mr. Heywood stood by plying a fan and the maid administered remedies.

CHAPTER XL.

THE CUP OVERFLOWS.

"Swell, swell my joys ; and faint not to declare
Yourselves as ample as your causes are."—JONSON.

OUR heroine, left alone in the parlor below, paced excitedly to and fro for several minutes ; then dropping into a chair, rested her elbows on a table and covered her face with her hands.

Her heart was swelling with joy unutterable and thankfulness to that heavenly Friend who had been her ever-present help in time of trouble, her comfort and support in the dark days of adversity, and had at length brought her quest to this happy ending, and she was sending up to Him her silent but most fervent thanksgivings.

In an adjoining room three young people had been sitting for the last half-hour or more, very quiet and still, yet full of an eager expectancy that made the waiting time seem very long and tedious. They exchanged glances, and drew nearer together as Mr. and Mrs. Heywood mounted the stairway.

"What shall we do, Ellis?" whispered one. "She's in there all alone, and must we wait till some one comes to take us in and introduce us in due form?"

"No, Dora, I should say not. Why should we? Come, both of you. I'll be spokesman."

Ethel heard the approaching footsteps, quiet, almost stealthy as they were, and taking her hands from her face, turned it toward them.

A lad with a noble face and gentlemanly manner, a fair young girl whom to look upon was like seeing her own reflection in the glass, except that this face was somewhat more youthful, lacking the maturity, sorrow, and care far more than years had brought to hers, and a little girl with a sweet, winsome face, blue eyes, and soft, flaxen curls, stood before her.

"Excuse us if we seem intruders," said the lad, with a courtly bow and offering his hand, "but we don't know how to wait till some older person shall find time to introduce us, for we know we have a right in you, if you will pardon me for saying it ; but these are your sisters and mine, and I am your brother. Their names are Dora and Nannette Heywood, and mine is Ellis."

"Oh, I am glad, glad!" cried Ethel, her face sparkling with pleasure as she embraced each in turn, then made them sit down, and called Katty to bring refreshments. "I am so happy, so happy!" she said, glancing from one to another with tears of joy trembling in her eyes. "To have found my dear, dear mother, for whom I've been searching for years, seems to fill my cup of bliss to overflowing ; and now I have a dear brother and sisters in addition —oh, it seems too much delight for one heart to hold!"

The tears fairly rolled down in a shower as she concluded, and Dora, springing up, threw her arms about her neck.

"Oh, I love you already!" she cried. "Dear Ethel, dear sister!"

"Sister!" Ethel exclaimed. "Ah, I never thought to find any one who had the right to call me that! I had dear, adopted parents, who, until the day of their death, I supposed were indeed my own, but I never had a brother or sister, and I have often envied those who had. But how is it that I did not see you before, and that you know all about me?" she asked, looking from sister to brother.

"We were not far in the rear of our parents when they came upon the picture, and we heard and saw all that passed," said Ellis.

"And understood it," added Dora with eager animation, "for all our lives long mamma has talked to us of her dear, first-born baby, her darling little Ethel, lost in so sad a manner, and we have known that she was always looking for you and hoping to find you. Poor dear mamma!"

"Dear, happy mamma now!" corrected Ellis, with a smile and an affectionate, admiring glance at his newly-discovered sister.

For a short space overpowering emotion kept Ethel silent. How sweet it was to know that there had never been a time since her birth when she had not had a warm place in that loving mother-heart!

"Yes," said Dora, "you are right there, Ellis. What joy there was in her face—although she was weeping, too—as I caught sight of it as papa helped her into the carriage that brought them here, and placed sister Ethel by her side."

"That reminds me," said Ethel, with sudden recollection, "that you did not come with us—you three. How did you get here?"

"The artist gave us the address while father was putting you ladies into the hack," replied Ellis. "He told us, too, that it was our aunt's house; and knowing that you were our sister we felt pretty secure of a welcome, so followed on. The distance, you know, is not great, and the street-cars brought us part of the way."

"Now, Ellis, let our new sister talk awhile; I think it's her turn," said Nannette; and coming to Ethel's side, and looking coaxingly into her face, "Won't you please tell us where you've been all this time, and what you've been doing?" she asked. "How could you ever do without mamma, 'specially when you had no papa either?"

"I have wanted her very, very much since—since my dear adopted mother died," Ethel answered, tears trembling in her eyes, while she put her arms about the child and kissed her tenderly. "Yes, little sister, I will tell you what you have asked," and she went on to give a rapid sketch of her life, dwelling more at length upon her early childhood than on the events of after-years.

All three listened with intense interest, one or another putting an occasional question when there was a pause in her narrative.

Then she asked for a return of her confidence, and her request was granted with evident pleasure. Ellis was the chief speaker, the girls now and then assisting his memory till they had given Ethel quite a clear idea of their home life.

A very charming picture it seemed to her, and her

heart swelled with increasing joy and gratitude at the thought that she would now have a place in that happy family—the place of one who possessed an equal right there with the others, and joyfully acknowledged by them, for Mr. Heywood had already embraced and called her "daughter" in such tender, fatherly fashion that she could not doubt her welcome from him.

CHAPTER XLI.

AFTER THE RAIN, SUNLIGHT; AFTER THE STORM, A
CALM.

> "Oh, love! how are thy precious, sweetest moments
> Thus ever cross'd, thus vex'd with disappointments!
> Now pride, now fickleness, fantastic quarrels,
> And sullen coldness, give us pain by turns;
> Malicious meddling chance is ever busy
> To bring us fears, disquiet and delays."

Espy, having seen the door of Madame Le Conte's boudoir close upon Mr. and Mrs. Heywood, stole softly down the stairs, thinking to join his Floy in the parlor. But as he neared the half-open door he caught a glimpse of Ellis and his sisters, and heard the voice of the latter, who was at that moment making his little introductory speech.

Espy turned away and quietly left the house, unable to reason down a jealous feeling, which he was only dimly conscious was such, that he was no longer necessary to Floy's happiness.

"I will not go back again to-night," he said to himself. "She will not miss me."

He had fully sympathized in her joy over the discovery of her long-sought parent, and he was very glad for her even now; but physically weary, and suffering from the exhaustion consequent upon the reaction from great excitement, he began to be oppressed with gloomy thoughts and forebodings.

"These people are rich," he soliloquized. "They will despise me for my poverty, will want Floy to give me up for some wealthier suitor; and if they fail in that, will make the poor darling wretched by their opposition. Yes, that's just how it will be; it's always the way; the more people have the more they want." And at that moment he almost hated the gentle, sweet-faced woman and noble-looking man whom an hour ago he had most heartily admired.

Arrived at his hotel, he was hurrying to his room, intending to shut himself up there to the undisturbed indulgence of his dismal prognostications, when his steps were arrested by a waiter, who handed him a card, saying:

"The gentleman's in his room, sir—No. 58, second floor—and wishes you to call on him there, sir. Told me to deliver card and message right away when you came in."

"Very well," Espy answered shortly, and obeyed the summons at once. The card was his father's.

Mr. Alden was in excellent spirits, and greeted his son with effusion. He was glad to see him looking so well; hoped his affairs were prospering as regarded both the paintings and his relations to Floy.

Then, hardly waiting for a reply, he went on:

"I've had a delightful time; got back this morning; landed from the train at the Centennial; spent the day there; and, by the way, I met a young thing out there this afternoon who is wonderfully like Floy. Took her for her at first sight, and made a fool of myself by rushing up and offering to shake hands. Have been cogitating on the subject, and come to the conclusion that it may be a younger sister—half-sister, you know—supposing the mother lived and married again. What do you think?"

" Floy *has* a sister—two of them, in fact," returned the son dryly, "and I think it altogether probable that the girl you speak of was one of them."

"You don't say!" cried Mr. Alden in astonishment. "And she's found her mother, has she?"

"She has."

"And sisters too?"

"And brother and step-father; there's a whole family."

"Whew! So many more to inherit the old Madame's estate! Bad thing for Floy that!"

"She doesn't think so," retorted Espy indignantly. "I never saw her look so unutterably happy, and I honor her for it."

"Humph! you do, eh? And what effect will all this have on *your* prospects? Will the new-found parents approve the choice of the lovely heiress?"

"That remains to be seen, sir," Espy answered, coloring deeply and half averting his face. "It is not many hours since the first meeting of mother and daughter after their long separation, and, of course, they have not yet been able to think beyond the present moment."

"Well, well, my boy, I hope no objection will be raised; but if there should be, don't you be too ready to give her up. And it's my belief that she'll stick to you through thick and thin."

"I don't know, sir; she might deem it her duty to wait for her mother's consent," Espy answered despondingly.

"Well, yes, maybe so. I remember she has a troublesome conscience, or streak of stubbornness, whichever you please to call it. But don't borrow trouble. Many a one would think a rising young artist of good disposition, respectable family, and fine appearance not a very bad match even for an heiress," remarked the elder gentleman, regarding his son with a proudly affectionate smile.

"If they could see him through his father's eyes," Espy said, returning the smile, more reassured and comforted by the fatherly flattery than he cared to own even to himself. But when he had retired to the solitude of his own room he presently returned to his bitter and desponding mood. How could he feel sure even that Floy might not in time be weaned from him by these new-found relatives in case they did not fancy the match, seeing that already she was so taken up with them that he was quite forgotten? The greater part of the night was spent in gratuitous self-torture, but toward morning he fell into a sound sleep, from which he did not wake till the sun was several hours high.

He started up with a confused feeling that something was wrong. Then it all came back to him in a flash—yesterday's happy ending of Floy's quest, with its attendant scenes.

His first emotion was, as before, one of keen sympathy in her abounding joy, but this was speedily replaced by the jealous pangs, the doubts and fears, from which sleep had brought him temporary relief. Upon inquiry he learned that his father, with whom the keeping of early hours was a life-long habit, had already breakfasted and gone out. Then the question suggested itself whether he himself should go, as usual, to Madame Le Conte's to learn Floy's plans for the day, and become her escort to the Exposition or elsewhere, if such were her pleasure.

He held the point in debate for a time, but finally decided to stay away for the morning at least, saying gloomily to himself:

"She will not need me, very likely will not so much as miss me; and the others will most assuredly not desire my presence."

The morning and most of the afternoon were passed in tedious lounging in the gentlemen's reading-room of the hotel and aimless wanderings about the city streets. Then the longing to see Floy, and learn what effect these changes really were likely to have upon his future relations with her, became so overpowering that he turned his steps perforce toward the Madame's dwelling. It was Ethel herself who admitted him.

"I knew it was your ring," she said, hastily closing the door and lifting to his a face perfectly radiant with joy and gladness.

He had been reproaching himself only a moment before for the anxiety and sadness his absence had probably caused her, but it seemed she had felt nothing of the kind.

"Ah," thought he, "it is plain to be seen that I am no longer necessary to her happiness."

"But what is the matter?" she asked, the brightness suddenly dying out of her face as she caught the dismal expression of his. "Are you ill, dear Espy? Have the pictures been abused by those cruel critics? I feared something was wrong when I found you were staying away so long."

"Did you, indeed? I'm sorry, but hope it has not troubled you greatly," he returned in a slightly sarcastic tone. "No, there is nothing wrong with *me*," putting a meaning emphasis on the personal pronoun.

She gave him a surprised, hurt look, but merely said in a quiet tone :

"Come into the parlor, Espy. There is no one there."

He followed her in, feeling ashamed of himself, but, too proud to show it, put on an indifferent air, and leaning against the mantel, toyed idly with its ornaments, leaving it to her to break the silence that succeeded their entrance.

"Espy, is this kind? is it generous?" she said at length.

"Is what? I'm doing no mischief here," he said, willfuly misunderstanding her ; but turning, and seeing the pained expression of her face, his better nature conquered. "No, Floy, darling, it is neither ! it is shameful!" he cried, hurrying to her and taking both hands in his. "But the demon of jealousy has taken possession of me. I see now that it is that."

"Jealousy ! of whom ?" she asked in surprise, but not repulsing him.

"Of—of your mother, brother, sisters," he said, coloring with shame. "There ! it is out ; and what do you think of your lover now ?"

"That he is—what shall I say ? more fond than wise ?" and she looked up brightly, the red lips smiling, the large, lustrous eyes a trifle misty.

"Let's kiss and make up, as the children say," he whispered, bending over her till his mustache came in suspiciously close proximity to her face.

"*I* haven't been quarrelling," she returned, with an arch smile.

They sat down side by side on a sofa.

"I have missed you, naughty boy," she said, still playfully, "because I wanted somebody to tell my gladness to, if for no other reason. Oh, Espy!" and her tone changed to one of deep feeling, "I am so blest! I seem to have nothing more to ask for! I, who have been such a lonely waif, have now found not only the mother I have been so long almost hopelessly seeking (and such a dear, darling mother, too), but father, brother, sisters, and even grandparents. Old Mr. and Mrs. Heywood were here this morning—they are the loveliest old couple!—and took me right to their hearts, bidding me call them grandpa and grandma, as my brother and sisters do."

"Very strange, *very!*" remarked Espy, with a smile that belied his words. "Ah, Floy," he added with a sigh, "I only wish I had some assurance that *I* shall find equal favor with them, or at least with your mother."

"You need have no fears, Espy," she said. "My mother and I passed the night together in each other's arms—she sharing my bed—but not sleeping much, you may be sure. We talked till daybreak, each giving the other an account of her life during the years of our separation. I told her all about you—yes, everything—and she fully approves my choice, is ready to give you a son's place in her dear, warm heart, only she says we must not ask to marry for a year or more (which you know we did not expect to do anyhow), because she must have me for a little while."

His face was radiant.

"Bless her!" he cried. "I was afraid she would object to my poverty, particularly as I imagine them to be very wealthy."

"Mother says they are not that; only comfortably well-to-do. Their home is in that land of fruit and flowers, Santa Barbara, and Aunt Nannette has already promised to go with them on their return and make her home there, and—ah, don't look so dismal, for though I, of course, cannot consent to be left behind, all want you to go also and settle there."

"I've not the least objection; in fact, am delighted with the idea!" he said with animation. "And so it's all arranged! Everything has come out right in spite of the doubts and fears with which I've been tormenting myself."

"Ah, there was no need," she said gayly; "but

"'Human bodies are sic fools,
For a' their colleges and schools,
That when nae real ills perplex them
They mak' enow themsels to vex 'em.'"

"Burns was a sage," he remarked, laughing, "but I can't say that I find the application particularly complimentary. And you are not disappointed in your mother?"

"Disappointed! I would not have her different in any respect. I find, to my unspeakable joy, that, besides possessing the sweetest natural disposition, she is an earnest, devoted Christian."

"I am glad for your sake. Where is she now? I should like to see her again."

"Stay and spend the evening with us, and you shall. Just now she is lying down. I persuaded her to try to take a nap while Aunt Nannette was doing so."

"Thank you. Then I will come back," he said, rising, "but I must leave now for a while. I had forgotten a business letter that must go by the next mail."

He went, and Ethel stole softly upstairs to her own room and sat down there to think over her great happiness—so great that hardly yet could she fully believe in its reality. Presently she started up, and going to a bureau-drawer, took from it the old, worn, faded pocket-book that, because of her love for the departed, in whose service its brightness had grown dim, was so precious a relic. A moment she stood gazing upon it, a tender dewiness in her soft, bright eyes, then opening, drew forth a tiny folded paper. A light, quick step coming from an adjoining room caused her to turn her head.

"Mother!" she cried in low, musical tones, rapturous with love and gladness.

"Darling daughter!" Mrs. Heywood responded, putting her arms about the slender, girlish figure, and folding it to her heart with a tender caress.

Their joy, though no longer expressed in tears, was still almost too deep for words.

For several moments they stood holding each other in a silent embrace; then Ethel, putting the folded paper into her mother's hand, said:

"Here, dear mamma, is a proof of my identity that till now I had forgotten to produce."

"It is altogether unnecessary, my precious child," Mrs. Heywood answered, opening the paper as she spoke. But as her eye glanced down the written page her cheek suddenly paled, and she uttered a low cry.

"This!" she said, with a shudder, "my contract with Mr. Kemper! Child, child, put it into the fire! Never let me see it again! Oh, what the signing of it has cost me!"

THE END.

www.ingramcontent.com/pod-product-compliance
Lightning Source LLC
Chambersburg PA
CBHW021153230426
43667CB00006B/379